The Rise of Brands

LIZ MOOR

Oxford • New York

First published in 2007 by
Berg
Editorial offices:
1st Floor, Angel Court, 81 St Clements Street, Oxford, OX4 1AW, UK
175 Fifth Avenue, New York, NY 10010, USA

Berg is the imprint of Oxford International Publishers Ltd.

Library of Congress Cataloguing-in-Publication Data
Moor, Liz.
    The rise of brands / Liz Moor.
        p. cm.
    Includes bibliographical references and index.
    ISBN-13: 978-1-84520-383-2 (cloth)
    ISBN-10: 1-84520-383-6 (cloth)
    ISBN-13: 978-1-84520-384-9 (pbk.)
    ISBN-10: 1-84520-384-4 (pbk.)
  1. Branding (Marketing) 2. Brand name products—History.
3. Branding consultants. 4. Intellectual property—
Management. 5. Marketing—Social aspects. I. Title.

    HF5415.1255.M66 2007
    658.8'27—dc22   2007031786

British Library Cataloguing-in-Publication Data
A catalogue record for this book is available from the British Library.

ISBN 978 1 84520 383 2 (Cloth)
ISBN 978 1 84520 384 9 (Paper)

Typeset by Avocet Typeset, Chilton, Aylesbury, Bucks
Printed in the United Kingdom by Biddles Ltd, King's Lynn

www.bergpublishers.com

The Rise of Brands

WITHDRAWN

for my parents

Contents

List of Illustrations

Acknowledgements

A number of people have helped in the preparation of this book; I would particularly like to thank Celia Lury and Scott Lash for their support during the early stages of the project, and Jo Littler, Steve Cross, Andy Pike and Guy Julier for reading parts of the manuscript. Don Slater, Angela McRobbie, Gary Hall and Paul Frosh were supportive and encouraging at key points, and Tristan Palmer has been a patient and sympathetic editor throughout. All mistakes and omissions are, of course, my own.

I would also like to thank the people that agreed to be interviewed as part of my research for the book, as well as Daniel Markham at Imagination, Nikl Westling at Samsung, Roxanne Peters at the Victoria and Albert museum, Belinda Lawley for permission to use her pictures of the We Are Londoners campaign and Roger Felton of Felton Communication for permission to use one of Felton's images in Chapter Four.

Friends and colleagues at Middlesex University supported me in the preparation of the manuscript with a period of sabbatical leave, and a further period of research leave funded by the AHRC helped a great deal towards the end of the project.

I am also grateful to Rachel Abrams, Jenny Carpenter, Steve Cross, Martin Edwards, Lynda Dyson, Anna Egan, Ruwan Fernando, Jo Harvey, Jo Littler, Daire Moffat, Jenny Reindorp and Mike Silk.

CHAPTER 1

The Rise of Brands

Brands and logos are all around us, from the clothes we wear and the objects we put in our homes, to the hoardings that line our streets and the adverts that cover buses, taxis and trains. Branding is also increasingly used as a marketing strategy for non-commercial organizations like political parties and charities, and as a means of enhancing the profitability, productivity and efficiency of a range of actors, including sports organizations, celebrities and cities. As an industry, branding is a key mechanism in ensuring the smooth functioning of a global capitalist economy, and in public discourse it frequently serves as an index of both the increasing commodification or 'marketization' of everyday life, and of a particularly ruthless, Western-dominated form of globalization. The ubiquitous application of branding strategies raises fears of cultural homogenization, but the logos, symbols and imagery produced by these techniques have nonetheless already become an important resource for individuals in fashioning a workable identity, and in carving out a sense of place and self within a complex global system. How, then, are we to make sense of branding?

In what follows, I attempt to answer this question by presenting an empirical and historical account of the rise of the brand and its associated industry, and by exploring the ways in which brands operate across a range of contemporary contexts. These include the use of branding in the design, promotion and circulation of consumer goods, but also in urban regeneration projects, charity fundraising, governmental activities and the state's attempts to communicate with its citizens. In this way the book seeks to delineate both the scope and the nature of branding, to specify where and how it intervenes in social life, and with what kinds of aims and outcomes. In addition, the book seeks to situate branding within a social, economic and political framework characterized by informationalization, globalization and the dominance of neo-liberal forms of governance, and to show how the practice and regulation of branding therefore intersects with a number of other important trends in contemporary life, such as the increasing significance of intellectual property rights, the expansion of promotional activity into a broader social realm and the formation of both individual and collective identities.

A further task of the book, although one that remains largely implicit in much of what follows, is to question the centrality of advertising within sociological studies of cultural intermediaries, and in cultural studies of the economy and of consumption. These disciplines, when they have looked at the ways in which economic structures and practices become socially embedded and reproduced over time, have overwhelmingly focused their attention on advertising as the paradigmatic mechanism through which citizens become sutured into a capitalist system and through which the consumption of goods provided by the market is presented as the only means to achieve various social and personal ends. This fascination with advertising remains powerful even as studies of advertising have themselves shifted focus from the semiotic structure of advertising 'texts' (e.g. Williamson 1978; Leiss et al. 1986) to the institutional organization and everyday practices of advertising as an industry (Miller 1997; Nixon 2003; McFall 2004; Slater 2002b), a shift which has revealed advertising to be much less powerful and much more constrained than previously imagined. At the same time, 'real-world' changes within the advertising industry, including the migration of audiences for advertising to non-traditional media (particularly the internet), declining audiences for film and television advertising, associated decreases in advertising revenue from traditional media, and the rise of technologies that allow consumers to bypass conventional advertising altogether, have in general failed to be reflected in the sociological literature on the subject.

This continued focus on advertising has, then, been at the expense of other forms of marketing and promotional activity that have recently become more significant to the form and functioning of an increasingly 'cultural' economy (Du Gay and Pryke 2002). These include direct mail, retail and point-of-purchase design, 'viral' marketing, sponsorship deals, 'experiential' marketing and a range of other more ambient promotional forms (including a renewed emphasis on industrial or product design), many of which are designed and produced by branding consultancies, or which are produced elsewhere but based on assumptions and rationales derived from the worlds of design and branding rather than advertising.[1] The lack of attention to these practices is all the more peculiar given that branding – as, among other things, a process by which commodities are given an explicitly self-promotional form (Lury 1993) – would seem to exemplify the blurring of the distinction between object and image, and between 'culture' and 'economy', upon which many of the more recent studies of advertising are in fact premised. The omission has a further consequence, however, which is that very little attention has been paid to the specific ways in which daily life has been opened up to more intense scrutiny and activity by a range of marketing-related industries, and on an increasingly global scale. This can be seen in the rise of non-traditional or 'ambient' media (such as bus tickets, milk cartons and even golf holes) but this in turn is part of a broader trajectory in which the spaces and surfaces of everyday life are used as points of communication and as technologies for the governance of human conduct across a range of spheres of activity. To expand our conception of economic and cultural intermediation to include branding as well as advertising is therefore to direct our attention to the role of *design*, a discipline which, unlike advertising, does not simply provide models or representations with which consumers are invited to identify, but also operates in a more immediate way to frame everyday life and provide pathways for certain types of action rather than others.

The Rise of Branding

Although brands themselves are not new, and indeed have operated as a force in the organization of production since the mid to late nineteenth century (Lury 2004), the term *branding* has only come to prominence in the last ten to fifteen years. It was during the 1990s, in particular, that a previously diffuse set of practices – product design, retail design, point-of-purchase marketing, among others – became consolidated into an integrated approach to marketing and business strategy known as branding. This in turn was linked to the institutionalization of branding, in the form of specific agencies known as branding consultancies and in the establishment of 'brand management' positions in an increasing range of organizations. Branding consultancies, as we will see in Chapter Two, emerged out of the confluence of a range of factors, including changes in the nature of media and technologies available to consumers, scepticism about the cost and effectiveness of conventional advertising, national economic policies that produced privately owned utilities companies and mergers between other major corporations, new understandings of the role of product design and innovation in expanding markets, and a growing demand for the service of design agencies operating in areas such as retail design, events and exhibition design, annual report design, packaging and so on.

In many places the term branding came to *public* attention with the publication of Naomi Klein's (2000) *No Logo*, a book which, in essence, provided a revised account of commodity fetishism and outlined the role played by marketing professionals and multinational corporations in disguising the global and highly asymmetrical relations of production through which many types of commodities – especially fast-moving consumer goods – were produced. Klein drew particular attention to the role of branding in this, and specifically to the expanded *spatial* scope of this form of marketing as it moved away from the simple application of a name and logo in the packaging and advertising of products, and into a wider array of public spaces in the form of sponsorship, 'viral' marketing and more elaborate retail sites. Although this was hardly the first time that the promotional activities of commercial organizations had been subject to public criticism and activism, Klein's intervention was important and timely in identifying new directions in the nature and scope of marketing activity, and in connecting these to the globalization of labour markets and its effects. As we shall see at various points throughout the book, the association between branding and broader issues in international trade continues to be a matter of public debate, and has given rise to new developments in both consumer activism and corporate strategy.

In Britain, however, the emergence of the term branding predates Klein by a few years because of its association with the 're-branding' of the British Labour party from the mid-1990s onwards, and the party's subsequent political rehabilitation under the name 'New Labour'. This re-branding exercise involved updating the party's logo and visual identity, and also an attempt to change the party's 'style', by focusing not only on what was to be said to the public and the media, but also on how it was going to be said (its 'tone') and who was going to say it (Heffernan 1999). There was, in other words, an explicit attempt to develop a unified political message and 'corporate image', to be promoted through the elaboration of a series of common themes, and to be embodied not only in policy statements, party manifestos and press releases but also in specific people and modes of behaviour. Although this public relations-style campaign model was not fundamentally new, it took a more systematic and strategic approach than previously, and incorporated many more insights from the worlds of marketing and public relations. It made use of focus groups, for example, to research, test and package policy ideas, and developed a series of key themes (akin to the 'brand values' of commercial operations), such as 'new', 'dynamic', 'moderate', 'trustworthy', to counter existing perceptions of the party as 'old-fashioned', 'extremist', 'out of date' and so on (Heffernan 1999). In one, perhaps slightly mythologized, account of the party's 'brand management' techniques during the late 1990s, party strategists are reported to have instructed senior politicians to avoid being photographed or videotaped in front of 'anything old', in order to cultivate and protect the association between 'New Labour' and a 'New Britain', or 'Cool Britannia' (Molotch 2003: 230).

In fact, contrary to claims from opposition parties that this 're-branding' was simply a cosmetic exercise and did not involve any change in the party's more general orientation, 'New Labour' also reviewed many areas of policy at this time, culminating most notably in the reformation of Clause Four of its constitution, which had previously contained the party's commitment to common ownership (Taylor 1999). It was not, in other words, simply the party's visual and behavioural 'communicators' that had been re-branded, but many more substantive areas too. Core values, once seen as non-negotiable and self-evident, had become expedient in the context of a policy review organized around the strategic goal of getting elected rather than the substantive project of redistributing wealth. The shift prompted many important, and ongoing, questions for the party, most notably in relation to its efforts to deny or stifle internal conflict, and to turn strategic shifts of emphasis into policy fixtures via their incorporation into a 'permanent election campaign' (Heffernan 1999: 52). In marketing terms, however, the increasingly strategic organization and presentation of social, political and cultural values once deemed non-negotiable – indeed their transmutation from strategic elements to defining qualities – has much to tell us about how branding now operates. New Labour's adoption of strategies and techniques more commonly associated with commercial re-branding exercises may have been novel (and controversial), but it is by no means unique. Such techniques are now at the heart of business development plans, but perhaps more importantly are also evident in less ostensibly commercial spheres, from charity fundraising and 'human resource' management to the design of tax forms and the coordination of Olympic bids.

Defining Branding

The ability of commentators in the 1990s to construe the Labour party's activities as a 're-branding' initiative itself depended in part upon the more widespread dissemination of the language and principles of branding in the form of various business and marketing texts (e.g. Murphy 1990; Aaker 1991; Kapferer 1992; Upshaw 1995; Hart and Murphy 1998). These texts emerged in some cases from the marketing departments of business schools, but also very often from the corporate identity agencies and branding consultancies, in Europe and North America in particular, for whom these texts often served as a type of promotional material.[2] These agencies did not only bring a new set of techniques and new ways of acting upon the social and economic realms, but also a new conceptual vocabulary to describe the evolution of their own ideas and practices. The rise of branding in this sense can be described in terms of a more reflexive capitalism (Thrift 1997; 1998), in which a range of actors are encouraged to reflect upon the organization and practices of firms, and to construct generic models to embody the latest ideas about the best way to run a business. Branding is also, therefore, a conceptual abstraction, that in some instances may border on what James Carrier and Daniel Miller describe as 'virtualism', that is, 'a practical effort to make the world conform to the structures of the conceptual' (Carrier 1998: 2).

Despite their tendency to generalize and make abstractions from processes which, in reality, are very often formed out of the highly specific contextual factors in which they are embedded, the definitions of branding that emerged from these new sites of marketing agency remain an interesting resource for those seeking to trace the emergence of branding *as a discourse* (which, as we shall see in Chapter Three, may have a rather uneven bearing upon practice). Many accounts produced in the early 1990s describe branding in terms of its more traditional roles – developed in the latter part of the nineteenth century and early years of the twentieth century – in reassuring consumers of quality and origin and differentiating otherwise similar products (Murphy 1990; Kapferer 1992). Thus Murphy (1990: 2) argues that the brand can be defined as 'the unique property of a specific owner [that] has been developed over time so as to embrace a set of values and attributes (both tangible and intangible) which meaningfully and appropriately differentiate products which are otherwise very similar', but also notes that the brand has the ability to 'reassure consumers as to the quality and origin and ... provide them with a simple route map through what may otherwise be a bewildering choice' (40).

At the same time, many commentators and practitioners were also recognizing new potential roles for branding in reorganizing marketing activity and even shaping business strategy itself. Kapferer (1992: 15–18) argues that branding is a means to segment markets (rather than differentiate products *within* a market), and that it can be used by corporations to harness the positive feelings or memories that consumers have about a particular product in order to build 'goodwill' for future products or services launched under the same name. For the same reason, Batchelor (1998: 97) describes brands as embodiments of an 'ongoing relationship between consumers and businesses' and therefore as 'wealth generating financial assets', while Upshaw describes brand identity as:

> the whole *fabric* of how a product or service is seen by its constituencies, the *integrated composite* of how it's perceived to perform. That includes the strategy that dictates how it will be sold, the *strategic personality* that humanizes it, the way in which these two elements are blended, and all those tangible and intangible executional elements that ideally flow from their joining, such as the brand name, logo, graphic system, and so on. (1995: 13, my emphasis)

By the 1990s, then, branding was seen by many commentators and practitioners as embodying a range of additional functions and possibilities above and beyond those developed at the beginning of the twentieth century to differentiate products and reassure consumers. The status of brands as assets was emphasized, and this in turn was understood in terms of the brand's ability to organize both marketing activity and actual markets. Partly for this reason, the status of brands as forms of private property also received renewed attention, with many accounts of branding including discussions of intellectual property law and of the ways in which both branding and trademark law could be used to capture or 'fix' the promotional investments that had been made by the parent company (see e.g. Murphy 1990). Finally, almost all accounts produced at this time saw brands as incorporating far more than simply a name, trademark and associated badge or logo, and assumed instead that brands should embody 'relationships', 'values' and 'feelings', to be expressed through an expanded range of 'executional elements' and 'visual indicators'. The extension of these elements into a wider environment has underpinned many of the more high-profile critiques of branding, which see branding as encroaching upon more and more of public space (e.g. Klein 2000).

Academic accounts of branding have been slower to emerge, although the centrality of intellectual property rights in general, and branding in particular, to contemporary forms of economic organization has been noted in some of the major analyses of post-Fordism (e.g. Lash and Urry 1994). The role of intellectual property rights in shaping cultural production and politics has also been recognized in a number of works (Gaines 1991; Coombe 1998; Buskirk 1992; Lury

2002a), while studies in the area of design and design history have considered the impact of corporate identity (Baker 1989) and branding concerns (Julier 2000; Woodham 1997) on those fields. More recently, two major sociological accounts of branding have been produced, both of which engage with the new centrality of brands as assets, and with the role of branding in organizing economic production and attempting to guide the activities of consumers. Celia Lury (2004) sees the brand as a complex 'new media object' that increasingly drives production and guides programmes of innovation.[3] This new *productive* role for brands is related directly by Lury to the new centrality of marketing as a discipline, which, she argues, 'not only provides the rationale for increasing the rate of product differentiation (as markets are conceived to be dynamic), but also provides the framework in which product differentiation occurs (as markets are reconfigured in terms provided by marketing knowledge about the consumer)' (Lury 2004: 28). Adam Arvidsson (2006) focuses more closely on practices of brand management and its efforts, firstly, to guide consumers' social and affective investments in brands in ways that 'reproduce a distinctive brand image and strengthen brand equity' (74) and, secondly, to devise standardized measurement techniques by which this concept of brand equity can be translated into 'a quality that is compatible with other qualities' (130). In both accounts, branding is understood as taking place within a context in which consumers' activities have become increasingly valuable for capital, and in which marketing therefore has an expanded role in profiling this activity and feeding it back into the production process.

Defining branding remains difficult, however, because branding proceeds in different ways in different institutional contexts, and because new accounts of, and prescriptions for, branding are being produced all the time by various marketing gurus and branding consultancies. Branding is assembled or 'put together' differently in these different contexts,[4] where it makes use of different forms of representation, different techniques and technologies and different kinds of relationships for different kinds of strategic purpose. What gets accomplished in the name of branding varies, for example, according to whether it is conducted internally by an organization's brand manager and marketing team, or externally by a branding consultancy or freelance designer. There may also be considerable variations in the services offered by agencies, and the extent to which these are tailored to the needs of a particular sector or organization. Smaller agencies and freelancers, which constitute the majority of those branding consultancies currently operating in Britain (British Design Innovation 2005), may specialize in providing services for particular sectors (e.g. the non-profit sector) but they usually lack the resources available to larger consultancies and are often unable to offer the same range of services (such as market research, design auditing and strategic management) as larger institutions. Finally, branding exercises, whether conducted internally or externally, may be more or less closely integrated with overall business strategy and with innovations in product and service design; in some cases they may be applied to only a limited range of visual materials, whereas in others they may involve more wide-ranging changes, not only to promotional materials, the design and location of buildings, websites and uniforms, but also to internal structures and hierarchies, staff training procedures, the design of technologies and databases, and many other aspects of the design and production of specific goods and services.

Although branding is similar to other forms of marketing activity in working on the visual and material culture of organizations, it tends to have a much more expansive notion of the appropriate *media* for communications than either advertising or other aspects of marketing, and it tends to take a much more strategic, programmatic and totalizing approach to such communications. Similarly, because branding is so often entwined with efforts to reorganize an institution's productive activity (something that is almost unheard of within conventional advertising agencies), it tends to imagine itself as having a longer-term perspective than other forms of marketing intervention, and in some cases to be more akin to management consultancy. Finally, because branding entails a much closer relationship between the marketing and managerial functions of an organization, and because it intervenes in an organization's behaviour as well as its promotional strategies, it is also more heavily implicated in the various regulatory and policy issues that surround contemporary institutions. Some of the issues arising from this are explored in later chapters.

Structure of the Book

In many ways this is an empirical book. My understanding of what branding is and what kinds of things it does has been formulated in large part in response to the interviews I conducted with branding consultants, designers and advertisers in London from 1999 to 2002 (material from these interviews is included in Chapters Three and Six), and from an ongoing engagement with the considerable marketing and business literature on branding. Although the book does not provide an ethnographic account of brands (either in terms of their production or consumption), it does attempt to use concrete examples and case studies of the application of branding techniques to illustrate its arguments. The book does not attempt to formulate precise theories and definitions of branding, and I hope that the reader will retain a sense of the diversity of ways in which branding is currently applied, even when the narrative takes a more generalizing tone.

Despite this largely empirical orientation, the analysis of branding put forward here is still grounded in certain presumptions about both branding itself and the broader social context within which branding exercises (and the consumption of branded goods and services) tend to take place. First and foremost, the book views the rise of branding as inextricably linked to the changing role of design in social and economic life. Rather than seeing it as merely the latest stage in the history of advertising (cf. Paterson 2006), the emergence of branding is traced instead to the development of industrial design, and specifically to the mutation of many design agencies into corporate identity consultancies from the 1980s onwards. This historical link between branding and design is already well established among those in the field of design history (Woodham 1997; Julier 2000; Molotch 2003), with Harvey Molotch (2003: 210) arguing that branding is, in effect, 'design made corporate'. Although many parts of the book are in broad agreement with this analysis, they are also careful to note that this 'corporate' use of branding is not synonymous with commerce, since branding is often recruited by public or non-profit institutions for a range of other strategic ends.

At various points in the book the work of branding is also connected, more or less explicitly, to the context of an information society in which symbolic power is increasingly informational rather than ideological (Lash 2002), and in which branding operates to meaningfully pattern units of information and link them across spaces. As I have suggested above, branding is much more immersive and immediate than advertising, and concerns the design of objects (products, stationery, uniforms, furniture) and spaces (shops, showrooms, events, trade stands) rather than – or in addition to – visual images on billboards and other types of screens. Its informational qualities are therefore tactile and sensory rather than predominantly visual. This meaningful patterning of information is also understood in much of what follows as a form of governance, since branding also entails the effort to pattern information – and to embed informational qualities in material goods – in order to organize experiences and perception in line with particular strategic ends. This involves 'marking out a territory in thought and inscribing it in the real' (Rose 1999: 34), through the composition of different forces, technologies, artefacts and forms of knowledge (Rose 1989: 6–8). Branding is a conceptual enterprise, in the sense that it involves the formation of generalizations and abstractions, but it is also a performative and a material one (see Miller 2005) because it is constituted in large part through its own practical enactment and because it involves the use of very 'physical' forms of knowledge and has tangible effects upon the design of spaces and objects.

The latter parts of the book also link branding directly to the broader framework of a neo-liberal society, in which, at a global level, deregulation and free trade are prioritized above other concerns (with historically dominant nations exerting a disproportionate control over the terms of their implementation) and, at a national level, many areas of activity that used to be considered the province of the state have been either left to market mechanisms or farmed out to non-state organizations of various kinds (Harvey 2005). Needless to say, such a society is also one in which there are huge disparities in wealth and income, and in which the ownership of property takes on a correspondingly large weight in defining the self and presenting that self to others. My understanding of the significance of the consumption of brands, although limited to some brief comments in Chapters Five and Six, is shaped by this insight. Finally, the book's geographical scope is restricted because its accounts of the activities of branding consultancies involve only British and North American examples. Some references are made in Chapter Six to the attempts by large marketing agencies to put together multinational teams for global campaigns, and to the rules relating to the protection of national or regional brands, but I have not been able to explore the commercial uses of branding techniques in countries such as India and China, despite the fact that branding is likely to be a growth area in these and other emerging economies in the very near future. Although many of the branding strategies and techniques described in this book have originated in European and North American institutions, and are disseminated across the world through business schools, management seminars and the movement of both students and teachers, the form that branding will take as it spreads internationally, and the uses to which it will be put in its new contexts, is by no means clear. Tracking the patterns of dissemination, innovation, indigenization and international exchange in the uses of branding will be an important task for the future.

The chapters are loosely structured into two parts. In the first part (Chapters Two and Three), I outline the history of branding and explain why it has become such a powerful force in recent years, and then consider how the work of branding differs from advertising and how particular goods and services get branded or 're-branded'. In the second part (Chapters Four, Five and Six), I look at some of the major functions of branding in different institutional contexts, explore the political and legal frameworks that protect the creation and circulation of exclusive brand identities, and consider the interplay between local, national and international dynamics in the production and consumption of branded goods and services.

Chapter Two traces the history of brands and brand-like marks from the Roman Empire onwards, noting in particular the importance of printing, paper-making and packaging technologies in facilitating the production of mass commercial branded goods. The chapter also traces the processes through which the surfaces of branded commodities became sites for the communication of meaning and values, and the early importance of national and imperial themes in this project of endowing relatively similar products with distinct identities. The chapter then considers the move 'inwards' from the surface packaging of the product to the product itself through the emergence of the discipline of industrial design. The emergence of industrial design is particularly important to the history of branding, and specifically to that aspect of branding concerned with the organization of product innovation (Lury 2004). Early industrial designers' experiments with the possible relationships between the form and function of goods, their use of design to convey emotional or associational qualities and their understanding of product design as a form of 'consumer engineering' (Sheldon and Arens 1932) all anticipate contemporary branding preoccupations in ways that are easy to overlook if branding is approached as simply an outgrowth of advertising and marketing.

The chapter goes on to explain how these understandings of the role of design in industry and commerce led, by the end of the 1960s and through to the end of the 1970s, to the emergence within design consultancies of an interest in corporate identity, and in the coordination of packaging and product design with a wider range of designed materials produced by corporations to communicate with internal, as well as external, audiences. Finally, the chapter shows how the economic policies put in place by rightwing governments in Britain and North America during the 1980s created new opportunities in these countries for design consultancies specializing in branding and corporate identity work. The privatization of previously state-run industries, the high number of mergers and acquisitions and the rise of the service sector all led to a new interest in developing and consolidating brand identities, not only through more careful attention to brand-based product design but also through the creation of 'brand environments' and brand-based customer relations management techniques.

Chapter Three begins by outlining the impact of the rise of branding on the wider field of marketing-related industries. It shows how and why advertising agencies began to face increasing competition from other 'symbolic intermediaries', particularly from the early 1990s onwards, and outlines some of the ways in which advertising agencies responded to this challenge. The chapter then goes on to consider what is distinctive about the work of branding, drawing attention to its particular conceptualization of what counts as a medium or communicative site, and to the use of design to divide up space and to translate abstract brand 'values' into material form. This work of design translation involves decisions and judgements which depend in turn upon the mobilization of various kinds of knowledge and expertise, and the latter parts of the chapter assess the different uses made by branding consultants of academic theories and research, business publications, market research and ideas about their own personal 'creativity'. The chapter concludes with a critical assessment of the relationship between branding consultants as 'proxy consumers' and their various audiences, and the impact of this relationship upon the potential effectiveness of branding campaigns.

This theme is continued in a slightly different form in Chapter Four, which considers the ways in which branding is used in contexts that are not predominantly commercial. The chapter begins by considering the role of branding in organizing production and argues that rather than considering branding under the general theme of 'commodification', it is more appropriate to see it as a means to divide up already-established markets and to create opportunities for organizations to compete across a range of sectors. The chapter then turns to consider the uses of branding in either non-commercial or non-profit-making spheres of action, arguing that branding is increasingly used in such contexts to organize human and technical productivity in line with various strategic ends. The social significance of branding becomes particularly clear here, as various aesthetic and cultural themes and signifiers are mobilized to support projects that are essentially about governance.

Chapter Five begins to consider the social and political issues surrounding branding in more depth. The chapter focuses on the relationship between branding and the growing significance of intellectual property regimes in

organizing production and trade, and specifically on the ways in which intellectual property rights are used to protect some forms of cultural and economic activity while excluding or even criminalizing others. The chapter traces
the historical emergence of the definitions of, and justifications for, the institution of private property, and assesses the implications of applying these in an
unmodified form to 'intellectual' and often intangible goods. The chapter then
turns to consider the contemporary dominance of trade-related concerns in
the institutions that regulate intellectual property on an international level,
and looks at how these have shaped debates about bio-prospecting, the protection of indigenous knowledge and the availability of basic resources in
poorer nations. The latter parts of the chapter are concerned with copyright
piracy and trademark counterfeiting, conceived largely in terms of a response
on the part of poorer nations to the unequal organization of the global trading
system, and specifically of the rent-seeking and monopolistic activities of
Western corporations protected by strong intellectual property laws. The
chapter concludes with a consideration of the relationship between intellectual
property's legal ability to exclude or prohibit certain types of practice and its
economic purpose for the accumulation of value to a sole owner.

Chapter Six continues to explore the intersection between the marketing and
business strategies of corporations and broader issues in global trade, this time
looking at the ways in which globalization and the social and political issues surrounding it have shaped marketing activity. The early parts of the chapter look
at attempts to harmonize and in some cases homogenize the content and promotion of specific brands, but these practices are contrasted with other contexts
and examples where local or national specificity remains important, and indeed
is used as a point of distinction and source of added value. The chapter draws
particular attention to the rise of proprietary (i.e. branded) forms of 'ethical'
consumption and looks at how the diffusion of a neo-liberal approach towards
national and international economic governance has created new market opportunities for producers, who can place new products and services in relation to
the ethical gaps and anxieties created by the retreat of states and international
institutions from legislating on behalf of poorer countries. The chapter contrasts
this absence of legislation on workers' rights with the growing (although contested) significance of legislation designed to protect nationally based marketing
activities that derive much of their power from historically unequal trading relationships.

The latter parts of Chapter Six look at the consumption of both branded and
non-branded goods, as these relate to intra- as well as international concerns. It
approaches consumption as a set of practices embedded within local and personal contexts, but shows that these are also connected, in many instances, to
trans-local concerns even while they are more immediately framed within
national or local horizons. Consumption is also shown here to be involved in the
marking and maintenance of various sub-national distinctions, including most
notably those organized around class and status, with branded goods operating

as a form of objectified cultural capital and part of the way in which the social-ization of taste takes place. Finally, the chapter considers the extent to which nation-states are able to use the realm of consumption for their own ends, and argues that even in the face of growing constraints on its ability to act in this way, the nation-state often attempts to imbue mundane consumption activities with a political resonance.

The conclusion summarizes the book's main arguments and returns, briefly, to some of the main questions these raise: What can the rise of brands tell us about business, consumption and culture in a global era? How far is branding likely to remain central to corporate strategy in the future? How has a growing interest in the ethics of commodity production and international trade impacted upon the uses of brands? And how might we respond to the strengthening of intellectual property laws in favour of the marketing activities of large corpora-tions and powerful regional economies?

CHAPTER 2

The Brand in History

Branding has taken on a new significance in the last fifteen to twenty years, but its history is much longer, stretching back to the nineteenth century for mass-produced goods, and much further for hand-marked goods. Branding has developed from initially marking property and ownership, and identifying the origin and content of goods, to connoting different types of values, meanings and reputations. More recently, branding has also come to act as the basis for the launch of new products and as a focus for consumer identification and aspiration, and has been extended outwards from the product into a wider range of materials and environments. This history is in many ways a history of the changing industrial and commercial uses of design over the course of the twentieth century, and specifically of the closer integration of the functional properties of objects with their capacity to signify and accrue meanings. This chapter aims to track these shifts, and to show how and why the strategic and commercial value of different types of design work has come to be recognized by a broad range of institutions.

The chapter also aims to place such shifts in the function of branding in a wider social and economic context. The mass production of brand-name commodities from the mid-nineteenth century onwards was made possible by a series of developments in packaging and printing technology, which themselves were part of the development of modern industrial nationhood. Similarly, the differential development of the discipline of industrial design in Britain as compared to America is linked to the different social, political and economic contexts of those two countries, and specifically to British efforts to hold onto its Empire and to use imperial trading connections, rather than industrial design, as a major part of its economic strategy. The form and content of branded goods in these countries also reflects these different social and political preoccupations. Finally, the consolidation of branding into an industry from the late 1970s and early 1980s onwards is linked to the economic policies of the rightwing governments elected in Britain and the United States during this time. These policies led to the privatization of many state industries, the decline of many manufacturing sectors, the rise of the service sector and the deregulation of media industries. All of these changes created new opportunities for those working in corporate identity and branding, and laid out a new social context for the strategic use of design.

Early Functions of Branding

The first brand-like marks, existing long before industrialization and the emergence of distinct commercial brands, included monograms, earmarks, ceramic marks, hallmarks, watermarks and furniture marks (see Mollerup 1997). Some of these marks have been traced to Ancient Greece and Rome, while others, such as hallmarks and stonemasons' marks, date from the fourteenth century. The earliest function of these marks appears to have been to indicate ownership, with people marking their weapons, or early craftsmen marking their products. Early brand-like marks were also used to indicate the origin of goods. Sometimes this meant the person who made a given product, and who might identify themselves with a signature, but it could also refer to a region of origin, or to an imperial power under whose jurisdiction an object was made. Indeed imperial conquest provided an early impetus for marking both the ownership and the origin of goods, as both objects and people travelled over increasingly large distances.

Early brand-like marks were also used to *describe* in various ways the content of an object or container. Just as buildings might have been marked to indicate the trade or craft of their inhabitants, jugs and containers would have been marked with symbols and pictures to indicate their contents, for example with a bunch of grapes indicating wine (Davis 1967). Such descriptive marks have been subject to detailed elaboration over time, with rules developing to specify how and where marks should be used (as in heraldry and cattle branding) and how particular qualities, such as composition or date of manufacture, should be indicated. In some cases, marks may indicate several distinct types of qualities. Watermarks, for example, typically describe the size and weight of the paper, as well as its manufacturer or place of origin, and in Britain hallmarks for gold, silver and platinum comprise four smaller marks indicating the composition of the metal, the regional office in which it was tested or approved, the date of issue and the name of the 'sponsor' or manufacturer (Mollerup 1997: 35). The attempt to develop typologies of different markings, and to tie the use of such marks to exclusive meanings, is analogous to contemporary procedures for the registration and protection of trademarks, which will be explored in more depth in Chapter Five.

Marks such as these, intended to guarantee the 'quality' or properties of goods and to distinguish them from goods produced by others, are in many ways early forerunners of twentieth-century brands, whose aims were also – at least for the first half of that century – to guarantee quality through a mark of origin, and to imply superiority in relation to one's competitors. Yet in most cases these early marks indicated a fairly straightforward relationship of ownership between a person and a thing, and only later came to include more intricate qualities that would have been of interest to a trading community. In fact, a more important incentive for early brand-like marks appears to have been the extension of goods in time and space, which itself derived from war and conquest as well as trade. The historical emergence of the brand-like marking of goods was therefore fundamentally related to the expansion of empires, which provides both the precondition for, and the first example of, the separation of production from consumption, on which branding depends.

Imperial conquest also appears to have been responsible for another important function of branding, namely its use to indicate status or reputation. Following the European conquest of the Americas and the setting up of the transatlantic slave trade, people, as well as things, were to be branded. Although slavery had existed in ancient and medieval societies, relatively few societies in the premodern world branded their slaves (Patterson 1982). During the period of the transatlantic slave trade, by contrast, branding was routinely used not only to identify slaves and indicate their status as property, but also as a form of punishment and humiliation. As Patterson notes, all ceremonies and rituals of enslavement, of which branding often was a part, were 'deeply humiliating, sometimes even traumatic, for the slave' (1982: 52) since they were designed to mark the 'natal alienation' of the slave and to both establish and 'advertise' his or her new status as a 'permanent marginal' within a new kinship network. Branding was used in this way in the Americas and the Caribbean until the late eighteenth century, and in some cases continued after this point as a way of punishing runaways and insubordinates. In parts of South Asia under the control of the East India Company, branding and tattooing were used as ways of marking convicts and preventing them escaping or passing themselves off as indentured labourers (Anderson 2000), and in both cases there was a functional fit between public identification, punishment through shaming and humiliation and the broader control of populations. At the same time, however, the marks made by slave-owners were sometimes treated as 'badges of honour' by slaves, particularly when they had been used to mark or punish runaways who had formed Maroon communities (Patterson 1982: 59). In these cases, the meaning of the brand was partially reversed and used as a focal point for resistance and solidarity; indeed, in some slave systems there was resistance to enforcing any visible indicator of slave status, since this might allow slaves to immediately recognise their numerical strength (59).

Brands and the Communication of Values

The tendency of descriptive signs and symbols to accrue alternative or unintentional meanings and values, as well as the efforts of various actors to shape and control these meanings, will be explored in more depth in later chapters, but efforts to use brands and brand-like marks to inscribe meanings, rather than simply describe or indicate origin, gained extra force from the nineteenth century onwards due to a series of technological developments. Although examples of commercial packaging can be found from the 1550s onwards, prior to the eighteenth and nineteenth centuries, goods (and people) were marked by hand, and this made it difficult to attach meanings or values to goods in any systematic way. It was not until the rapid economic and industrial expansion of the nineteenth century that innovations in production, printing and packaging made the mass branding of goods possible. The 1890s have been described by some as 'the first golden era for the modern brand mark' (Ellwood 2000: 13) because it was only at this point that individual packages of branded goods became available for consumers to buy. Previously, most goods available to consumers would have been ordered by retailers from wholesalers in large quantities, and then weighed, blended and packaged for consumers in their stores.

Industrialization and Packaging

As capitalism developed, however, manufacturers were able to use packaging techniques to regulate production and to design attractive containers that created demand for their products, rather than those of their competitors. Such techniques allowed the contents of packages to be automatically weighed, measured and filled, and by the 1880s Cadbury's in Birmingham, for example, had a machine that could measure out 12,000 packets of cocoa a day (Davis 1967). Many of the brands established during this 'golden era' (including Levi's and Coca-Cola) have become a significant part of twentieth-century mythology (Pavitt 2000), connoting both national identity and industrial modernity itself. Part of what made this possible was the fact that such innovations were occurring alongside the development of railways and steamships, which meant that manufacturers could trade nationally and internationally with much greater ease than before. The development of packaging was itself a major force in the shift from local agriculture to corporate food production at the turn of the century (Lupton and Miller 1992), because it made it easier for companies to exploit national railway networks to transport and distribute pre-packaged goods from a central manufacturing base.

From the point of view of manufacturers, innovations that allowed them to package their own goods rather than rely on retailers also represented a considerable advance because they made it possible to standardise the size and therefore price of their products, and thus to more effectively regulate and predict their profit margins. They also helped them to mark out their products as distinct from those their competitors, both in terms of content and consistency (which they could now control without interference from the retailer) and also, because of developments in printing, in terms of image and presentation. This development is central to the history of branding, since it allowed the surface of a product to be used as a communicative site in a consistent and systematic way. Brands and brand-like marks had appeared on goods prior to this point, but the development of commercial packaging techniques made it possible to intentionally communicate a greater array of images and meanings, combining information about the name of the manufacturer, the content of the product and the place of origin with other graphic symbols and text to create a distinct identity for the product.

The creation of 'values' around mass-produced brand-name products that began at this time was intimately connected, certainly during the first half of the twentieth century, to the forging of associations between brand names and national or imperial projects, but the design of early packaging was also influenced by broader aesthetic trends. At the beginning of the twentieth century, European artistic movements such as Dada and Surrealism were a major influence on graphic design on both sides of the Atlantic (both Dali and Magritte had designed perfume bottles). Many European designers, particularly those associated with the Bauhaus, moved to America during the Second World War and were employed by major corporations (Jankowski 1998), and despite initial hostility to European modernist design in America, the 'new international style' was eventually embraced by American corporations as well suited to their need to market their goods to an international consumer base. Packaging design was also influenced by wider social changes such as the growth of cities and, later, the increasing numbers of women in the labour force. The impacts of such changes could eventually be fed back to corporations through the emerging disciplines of market research, which attempted to discover what a changing population wanted, and consumer psychology, which tried to delineate what motivated different types of consumers to purchase particular goods, and how such knowledge could be exploited by packaging designers. The growing number of supermarkets and chain stores, particularly after the Second World War, would provide a further stimulus to growth in the packaging design industry, with manufacturers keen to make their products stand out, and retailers keen to provide attractive surroundings to entice consumers to spend longer in their stores (Pilditch 1961). By 1963 packaging had become the sixth largest industry in America (Jankowski 1998: 18).

Packaged Goods and Nationhood

Ideas about the nation were also an important source of inspiration for packaging designers, and these designs came, in turn, to influence how the nation itself was viewed, both by its own population and by those abroad. Indeed the development of packaging was, along with the emergence of national railway systems noted above, heavily implicated in the consolidation of ideas about nationhood, since forms of production and consumption that had previously been conducted at the local or regional level were now increasingly organised by national corporations, whose names, logos and imagery were circulated across the country and sold in general stores as *mass* products designed for consumption by what was increasingly construed as a *national* market. This development might be compared with Benedict Anderson's (1991) analysis of the role of other print-based forms, such as the novel and the newspaper, in providing a new technical means for presenting and imagining the nation as a particular type of 'imagined community'. Like the early mass-produced novel – and unlike commodities that had previously been measured out locally by retailers – brand-name consumer goods were reproduced on a large scale and yet addressed their audience 'intimately' and as part of a common, known group. And like the readers of newspapers, the consumer of the brand-name commodity would have been aware that his or her consumption practices would be replicated elsewhere by 'thousands (or millions) of others of whose existence he is confident, yet of whose identity he has not the slightest notion' (35). Finally, brand-name commodities would have contributed to national consciousness through their creation of 'unified fields of exchange and communication' (44), and through an awareness among consumers that they shared a particular and bounded language-field with others, even if those 'others' numbered thousands or millions.

It was not only the form of brand-name goods (thousands or millions of exact replicas of particular combinations of language and image) that contributed to national consciousness, but also their content, and this in turn reflects a concern to make branded commodities meaningful (and therefore valuable) by imbuing them with various cultural connotations. As I have suggested above, one of the ways in which this took place was through the incorporation of iconic national imagery into the design of packaged commodities. During the interwar years, for example, the iconography of the city came to be a dominant feature in American design, as part of an organized effort to arrive at an 'indigenous' US style after the end of mass immigration (Woodham 1997). Similarly, the 'space race' that developed in response to the Soviet Union's launch of the first artificial satellite in 1957 became a theme for many prominent graphic designers, and middle-class Americans fell in love with the 'space modern' look, with images of rockets, jets, planets and stars appearing on the packaging of products ranging from sewing kits to beer cans (Jankowski 1998). As we shall see below, these particular types of national content in branded goods varied across time and place, and projects of 'Americanization' through consumption varied in content, if not necessarily in form, from the versions of national identity and connectedness being promoted in Britain. The broader point, however, is that although merchants had long recognised the necessity of cultural value for economic value (see Mukerji 1983), developments in packaging design and technology made it possible for such values to be distributed on a much larger scale, with a higher degree of standardization, and with the profits that derived from such cultural associations accruing to specific brand owners rather than being dispersed more evenly across the commercial field.

Early in the twentieth century, the very existence of neatly designed packages for standardized consumer goods sent a message to those both within and beyond the borders of the United States about the emerging capitalist nation and their potential role within it. As Stuart and Elizabeth Ewen (1982) show, in their account of the role of commercial imagery in the emergence of capitalist individualism in America, brand names and trademarks on packaged goods became central to the 'Americanization' of both newly arrived immigrants and existing inhabitants living in rural America. At a time when large numbers of people were leaving behind their stable existence in Europe or rural America and moving to the city, these trademarks and brand names were often the most familiar and stable features of a strange new environment and, in some cases, the only bond between people who were otherwise culturally heterogeneous. People were encouraged to buy these brand-name products as a sign of their own loyalty to this new version of America, but the success of such injunctions appears to have depended in large part upon the fact that brand-name commodities would have fulfilled a pressing social need for common bonds, and for a common vernacular language, among socially disparate groups during a time of immense upheaval.[1]

The British Context: Advertising and Empire

Similar advances in industrial production and packaging were occurring in Britain during the same period, and here too packaged commodities were part of an ideology of the modern industrial nation. In Britain, however, the Empire loomed large as both a project and a source of anxiety, and the values inscribed on the packaging of brand-name commodities reflected a persistent concern on the part of government to inculcate in British consumers an 'imperial patriotism' that could counter both domestic worker militancy and foreign perceptions of the declining potency of the British Empire. The superiority of British manufacturing had already begun to be called into question by the end of the nineteenth century (Woodham 1983), and by the early twentieth century competition from the United States, Germany, France and Japan had become a significant worry for the government, in part because of the worker unrest that accompanied it. Yet despite efforts by some government departments in the early years of the twentieth century to promote industrial design as the solution to Britain's waning international competitiveness in manufacturing, many in government continued to resist such solutions, and turned instead to a greater emphasis on trading within the protected markets of the Empire (see Hall and Jacques 1989: 29). This, it was argued, could open up a new route to future economic prosperity, whilst also restoring 'national pride' to a working-class population increasingly drawn to socialism.

One element of government policy in this area was the creation of the Empire Marketing Board, which was set up in 1926 as part of a broader 'Empire Free Trade Crusade', and which spent huge amounts of money – mostly through its publicity sub-committee – on posters and other promotions aimed at encouraging British consumers to buy Empire produce (Ramamurthy 2003). Its strategies were subsequently adopted by commercial producers too, who began to produce their own forms of imperial propaganda through their advertising and other marketing techniques. An example of this was the widespread production and distribution of cigarette cards (used not only in cigarette packets, but also in tea, magazines and confectionery), a type of free gift offering a 'panorama of the world at large' (Roberts, cited in MacKenzie 1984: 24) and frequently depicting the armed forces, pictures of Empire flags and colonial troops, as well as the products and industries of Empire.

Figure 2.1 Poster for the Empire typewriter, 1897, by Lucien Faure (© V&A Images/Victoria and Albert Museum, London).

Yet although the Empire Marketing Board gave a renewed impetus to the commercial exploitation of imperial imagery, advertising had in fact drawn upon Empire since its emergence as a significant force in British culture at the end of the nineteenth century (Figure 2.1). References to Empire were used on a variety of forms of packaging and promotion from the 1890s onwards to convey the romantic and adventurous connotations of a company's products (MacKenzie 1984: 26), while a famous Bovril advert during the Boer War purported to demonstrate that Lord Roberts' route had spelled out the word Bovril across the Orange Free State (MacKenzie 1984; McClintock 1995). Tea, biscuit and tobacco companies displayed various images of national and imperial identity on their packaging, while companies such as Fry's and Cadbury's sought to demonstrate both their imperial connections and their ostensible social concern for the domestic labour force and their colonial suppliers (MacKenzie 1984: 26). As Anne McClintock notes in her history of soap advertising, commerce was seen as a way of holding Empire together, while the exploitation of images of Empire in advertising worked to strengthen the boundaries of a social order 'felt to be threatened by the fetid effluvia of the slums, the belching smoke of industry, social agitation, economic upheaval, imperial competition and anti-colonial resistance' (1995: 211).

While we cannot be certain how such imperial propaganda was received by British workers and consumers,[2] it is clear that the period from the end of the nineteenth century to the beginning of the Second World War saw a steady flow of 'imperial bric-a-brac' (McClintock 1995: 219) into British homes, and a concerted effort on the part of government, enthusiastically followed by commerce, to promote a version of British identity inseparable from the fact of Empire. The emergence of individually packaged brand-name products in Britain was thus accompanied by a series of efforts to make British consumers conscious of the Empire in their most mundane consumption activities, and British imperial power was effectively 'domesticated' as it entered homes in miniaturized and sentimentalized forms where it could either be stored in kitchens and living rooms or, as was sometimes the case with cigarette cards, swapped with friends. In this way, the emergence of a system that could link brand names to broader values and meanings was itself fundamentally linked, at least in its foundational years, to a system of national and imperial power, in ways which marked out a distinct trajectory for advertising in the years that followed.

From Packaging to Product Design: Heritage and Futurity in the Interwar Years

The 1930s saw renewed efforts to build the discipline of industrial design in Britain, through the creation of two government-funded design bodies and a series of exhibitions in which British design was displayed and promoted. Yet the goods displayed at these exhibitions continued the imperial themes of early advertising and packaging, with the wider context of threats to Britain's industrial leadership and imperial power leading not only to a greater emphasis on trade within the Empire, but also to an urge to demonstrate that British imperial power itself significantly predated the industrialization process, and lay rather in an 'essentially British' cultural heritage (Woodham 1997). The exhibitions placed great emphasis on design that appeared to locate the essence of Britishness in the pre-industrial past, producing a combination of 'retrospection and ruralism' that would come to typify British design style and preference for many years into the future (see also Conekin 1999; Sparke 1986). The British sections of the Monza and Paris exhibitions, for example, included displays of sporting goods, which, according to a design journal at the time of the Monza exhibition, showed that 'the Englishman invented modern sport and stands supreme in the design and execution of its appliances' (cited in Woodham 1997: 92). The prominence of 'country sports' in these exhibitions, Woodham suggests, reinforced the idea that the countryside was the essence and origin of British identity, whilst simultaneously alluding to notions of 'sporting behaviour' and 'fair play' that had themselves formed a central ideological plank of Britain's imperial policy.

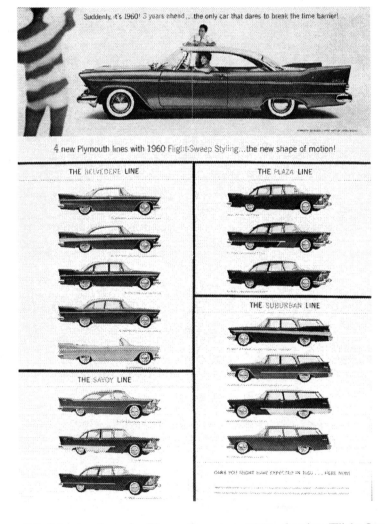

Figure 2.2 Sales brochure for Plymouth cars, c. 1957, showing 'Flight-Sweep Styling' (© V&A Images/Victoria and Albert Museum, London).

In contrast to this continuing emphasis on imperial themes in British product design, industrial design in America was developing rapidly during the interwar years, and taking on increasingly futuristic forms. The combination of an indigenized version of modernism and the iconography of transport, urbanism and science fiction led, by the 1930s, to an emphasis on the 'streamlining' of products (Figure 2.2), in which the intricate decorative surfaces of earlier goods were replaced with non-porous materials and smooth, rounded shapes borrowed from the field of aerodynamics (Lupton and Miller 1992). While the clean lines and smooth surfaces of these new objects seemed to be consistent with a general modernist aesthetic of futurity and progress, the application of aerodynamic styling to products like refrigerators and waffle irons that were so far removed from the aviation industry clashed violently with the most fundamental modernist design principle, that form should follow function. As Dick Hebdige notes, streamlined objects were seen by the European design establishment as bordering on blasphemy, since they represented 'the intrusion of an expressive design vocabulary which bore no *intrinsic* relation to the commodities it shaped' and 'introduced the possibility of an *intertextuality* of industrial design – of the unrestricted passage of signifiers across the surfaces of a whole range of unrelated products without any reference whatsoever to "essential" qualities such as "function"' (Hebdige 1988: 60, emphasis in original).

These changes were important to the development of branding in two key ways. Firstly, they represented a shift in which not only packaging and advertising, but also the surface of the product itself, became a communicative site, and thus a space that could be manipulated by manufacturers to gain competitive advantage. Packaging design was a major influence on the early industrial design profession (Lupton and Miller 1992), and a series of technological and engineering advances during the twentieth century, from the development of plastics to the miniaturization of internal mechanisms, would make it increasingly easy to use the surface of objects in this way (Manzini 1989; Julier 2000). Equally, there were (and continue to be) many cases in which there was little obvious distinction between the outer edge of an object and its packaging,[3] suggesting a growing functional basis for the blurring of object and image that characterizes contemporary branding. Secondly, as Hebdige suggests, experiments with streamlining from the 1930s to the late 1950s made it clear that there was very often *no* necessary connection between the function of a commodity and the form it took, and that modernist rhetoric itself sometimes rested on arbitrary architectural analogies. In this context, an 'expressive design vocabulary' could draw upon signifiers from a virtually unlimited range of sources to endow brand-name products with new meanings and associations. Such insights were seized upon by designers for the rest of the century, perhaps finding their ultimate expression in the emphasis on 'product semantics' and 'design by association' in the 1980s and 1990s, when product design itself was increasingly subordinated to an overall brand strategy or ethos (Julier 2000). The move 'inwards' from package to product design that occurred during the era of streamlining remains a crucial moment in this story.

Branding and Product Design: the Post-war Period

The period from the end of the nineteenth century to the middle of the twentieth century was characterised by increased competition between relatively similar products, and a more systematic use of advertising as well as packaging to make products more attractive and to attach various kinds of 'values' and associations to their goods in order to distinguish them from those of their competitors (Nevett 1987). However, notwithstanding the participation of British manufacturers in some of the design exhibitions held during the interwar years, this period of intensified economic competition both within and between nations did not lead to a substantial increase in the degree of attention paid to product design by them, and there was certainly little integration of product design with packaging and advertising. Indeed during the interwar years and for quite some time afterwards, simply producing products in large enough quantities to meet consumer demand presented a challenge for British manufacturing, and advertising and packaging were used largely as 'gloss' added at the end of the production process, just prior to goods being presented to the public for purchase.

Figure 2.3 The Emerson Patriot radio, c. 1940, designed by Norman Bel Geddes, incorporated a 'Stars and Stripes' design and was available in red, white and blue (© V&A Images/Victoria and Albert Museum, London).

This began to change after a period of post-war economic recovery (which was slower in Britain than in many other nations), and many companies found themselves able to produce a greater quantity of goods than ever before. In some cases this led to a renewed emphasis on the role of industrial design in product differentiation and corporate strategy. Such attention to product design was not without pre-war precedent in the United States, where the first generation of industrial designers (including figures like Norman Bel Geddes, Harold Van Doren and Raymond Loewy) had emerged during the 1930s. Many of these designers had worked for major corporations and their work had already been distributed on a wide scale (Figure 2.3). Moreover, these designers had also begun to systematise their approach and explain it in written form. In 1932 Roy Sheldon and Egmont Arens's *Consumer Engineering: A New Technique for Prosperity*, had emphasized the ways in which greater attention to the design of everyday goods could function as a 'potent means of shortening the cycle of consumption' (Woodham 1997: 66), and such ideas were increasingly accepted by manufacturers. This emphasis on designing goods with an eye to fashion and 'planned obsolescence' was considered by many to have been a significant factor in the relatively quick recovery of the United States economy after the war, and in the post-war period American industrial power was such that it was able to export vast numbers of its new products to countries across the world.

One of the early proponents of industrial design was Harold Van Doren, whose 1940 textbook *Industrial Design* traced the emergence of the profession and its gradual acceptance by large corporations. For Van Doren, the economic motivation of industrial design was clear; he argued that the job of the industrial designer was 'to interpret the function of useful things in terms of appeal to the eye; to endow them with beauty of form and color; *above all to create in the consumer the desire to possess*' (Van Doren 1940: xvii, my emphasis). This was to be achieved through 'increased convenience and better adaptability of form to function; through a shrewd knowledge of consumer psychology; and through the aesthetic appeal of form, color, and texture' (3). However, he was quick to point out that industrial design was *not* simply about attractive packaging. It was not, he said, 'an eleventh-hour costume for a fancy-dress ball, to be put on just before the product goes to meet the public. On the contrary good looks must be built in, not draped on. The designer worthy of the name is blood brother to the engineer' (xviii).

Like other early industrial designers, Van Doren was well aware that heightened competition between manufacturers provided the major stimulus for greater attention to design, and moreover that such competition was increasingly taking place in the context of an 'economy of abundance', in which potential supply could consistently outstrip demand. In a situation like this, he argued, the lack of obvious differences between products made good appearance a 'necessity' (13). He also pointed out that the emergence of industrial design was proving something of a challenge to 'old-line manufacturers', since its ascent was evidence of the increasing primacy of merchandising and marketing

concerns over manufacturing ones. 'Today', he said, 'the shape, color, and
appointments of a product are more important from a merchandising point of
view than its mechanical features' (43). Van Doren recognised that consumers
very often had no way of comparing the performance of different appliances, and
therefore frequently made purchases on the basis of 'smart and gleaming appearance', but he also knew that the emergence of organized consumer groups and
consumer protection legislation was beginning to change this situation. Research
conducted by these groups, he said, showed that 'the best selling appliances,
when put to impartial tests, turn out to be the least efficient' (44). Industrial
design, then, would have to be about more than simple styling.

American Influence in Product Design

The impact of the Second World War on national economies meant that
America was well placed to exert a considerable influence on the direction of
industrial development in a range of countries during the post-war period. Many
countries were receiving financial aid from the United States through the
Marshall plan, and some German companies were controlled by American
capital. Major Japanese industrialists – including Soichiro Honda, employees
from Matsushita, and the chairman of Hitachi – visited America to study its
industrial organization and management techniques, and many American
designers (including Raymond Loewy) were invited to spend periods of time in
Japan (Woodham 1997). The importance of design in product development was
an important feature of such exchanges, and research and design subsequently
played a central role in Japan's commercial successes, from 'capsule' hotels to
transistor radios and, in 1979, the Sony Walkman (139). Such developments
would later come to be seen as typical of the post-Fordist production paradigm,
in which a more careful integration of marketing-oriented design work into the
early stages of product development would provide a new bridge between the
production process and the marketing of goods to consumers, but these innovations were themselves outgrowths of the growing importance of industrial design
and design management in America from the 1930s onwards. In fact, in the
years following the Second World War American industrial design influenced
not only producers but also consumers, who in many nations came into contact
with American brand-name products through the presence of American troops
in their countries and through the influence of the American film industry,
which itself reinforced a general 'ambience' of American design and its broader
connotations of American capitalist democracy and the idea of most ordinary
people having a relatively high standard of living.

In Britain, the importance of good design for economic development had, as
suggested above, been debated and acknowledged on many occasions, but little
had been done to implement these ideas. After the Second World War even
major design advocates like Nikolaus Pevsner conceded that design debates were

largely meaningless without radical social change and a government commitment to slum-clearance, rehousing and improved standards of environmental
planning (Woodham 1997: 117). Nonetheless, the Council of Industrial Design
(later renamed the Design Council) was established in 1944, and in 1946 it put
on the 'Britain Can Make It' exhibition, to show manufacturers, retailers, the
public and foreign buyers that Britain was intending to take design seriously in
the post-war period (Sparke 1986; Maguire and Woodham 1997). However,
design consultancies following the American model were not really established
in Britain until the early 1960s (Julier 2000). One of the earliest of these was
Allied International Designers, set up in 1959 and led by James Pilditch.
Pilditch's book *The Business of Product Design* (Pilditch and Scott 1965) inadver-
tently testifies to the slow development of industrial design in Britain, since
many of its ideas about the value of good design had been set out by Harold Van
Doren nearly twenty-five years earlier. Like Van Doren, Pilditch emphasizes the
general context of supply outstripping, or potentially outstripping, demand, and
the new role for marketing in disposing of this excess of goods in a profitable
fashion, and also like Van Doren he argues that designers should be involved in
the production process at a much earlier stage, not 'at the end merely [to] make
things look pretty' (1965: 19). Where he is perhaps more explicit than Van
Doren is in arguing that designers should be less constrained by the needs of the
production department, and more closely allied with both the marketing department and, ultimately, with consumers themselves. Very early on in the book he
makes what looks in hindsight like a classic statement of the post-Fordist reorganization of the production process: 'For years manufacturers have made what
they could, then pushed the results out to the public to buy. They looked
inward, at their productive capacity. Only recently has industry begun looking
out. Now it finds itself having to look out. It must discover what the public
wants, *then* learn to make it' (1965: 4, emphasis in original).

   This was not the first time that such an observation had been made in Britain;
in 1944 an internal report from the Board of Trade had noted that British manufacturers had historically 'tried to sell *against the fashion* by producing 'what
their machines would make' rather than what the public required' (cited in
Maguire 1997: 40, emphasis in original). However, Pilditch's claim was important because it made the case for a considerable expansion of the scope of the
designer's role, bringing it far closer to the general public than previously:

> Not only must he understand production techniques, he should also be familiar
> with new developments in fields outside his own. He must recognize the needs of
> sales and promotion. At best, he should intuitively feel the public pulse but, at
> the same time, be capable of using and interpreting market research. He needs
> imagination and logic and a number of special skills. Above all, his bias should
> have swung from production in a narrow sense to marketing in the widest. (1965:
> 65–6)

Here, the designer has become a fully-fledged symbolic intermediary, no longer simply responsible for designing or styling attractive and efficient objects, but now expected to identify him or herself with consumer taste and to both interpret and shape it.

Corporate Identity and a New Social Context for Brands

These ideas about a new and expanded role for design in industry and commerce were a crucial stage in the formation of the modern brand consultancy, and took further shape in the decade between the end of the 1960s and the end of the 1970s in work from both America and Britain devoted to the issue of 'corporate identity'. In 1967 Henrion and Parkin published *Design Coordination and Public Image*, and in 1970 James Pilditch published *Communication by Design: A Study in Corporate Identity*. Both texts were a major influence on Wally Olins, who published *The Corporate Personality* in 1978. Olins was a co-founder of Wolff Olins, initially a design consultancy specialising in corporate identity, but now one of the world's largest brand consultancies. In many ways these texts were ahead of their time, for the corporate identity industry did not start to grow significantly until the sharp rise in corporate mergers in the 1980s. Yet even in the 1960s there were good reasons for corporations to be concerned about communications management; the increasing globalization of trade, the growing number and power of multinational corporations, the broader social and economic context of post-war trade and, in many European countries, the decline of Empire all had a significant impact upon the context in which trade took place. National corporations could no longer rely to the same extent on their own markets or those provided by colonial territories, and almost all corporations were operating in an international market dominated by American exports. For this reason there was a renewed emphasis on industrial design as the key to economic competitiveness, and a greater degree of attention paid to ways of making corporations 'intelligible' in foreign, and often unfamiliar, markets.

Brands and Media: the Idea of 'Design Coordination'

The new emphasis on corporate identity and 'design coordination' was in many ways an obvious adjunct to this greater attention to product design, but its specific contribution lay in its appreciation of the different *audiences* for corporate output and, by implication, the different *media* through which people approached the corporation itself. As Henrion and Parkin note:

A corporation has many points of contact with various groups of people. It has premises, works, products, packaging, stationery, forms, vehicles, publications and uniforms, as well as the usual kind of promotional activities. These things are seen by customers, agents, suppliers, financiers, shareholders, competitors, the press, and the general public, as well as its own staff. The people in these groups build up their idea of the corporation from what they see and experience of it. An image is therefore an intangible and essentially complicated thing, involving the effect of many and varied factors on many and varied people with many and varied interests. (Henrion and Parkin 1967: 7)

The problem, they argued, was that most corporations' visual identities were currently created by several different actors, from industrial designers and advertising agencies to freelance graphic designers. The result of this was often 'images in conflict' (8), leading to a lack of overall control over public perceptions of the corporation. The solution, they suggested, was for modern corporations to incorporate a new function of 'design coordination', a role that could 'coordinate the many separate items all belonging to the one corporation, to achieve coherent and controlled results over a long period' (6).

Henrion and Parkin provide little explanation of how, exactly, a greater coordination of design output could lead to 'controlled results over a long period', relying instead upon apparently self-evident examples of 'good' design coordination from companies like IBM, Olivetti, Sainsbury's, London Transport and Braun. What they do introduce, however, is the idea that the *timescale* of design coordination is different from that of other marketing-based activities such as advertising and public relations. Where the timescale for advertising and PR departments is 'immediate, short-term and fashion-oriented', based on annual or seasonal renewal, the timescale for design coordination is 'decades' (8). Moreover, where advertising and PR functions would very often have been conducted 'in-house', Henrion and Parkin suggest that responsibility for design coordination should be outsourced to an independent consultant, who could approach the matter with a 'fresh eye' and 'put himself in the place of the customer or the man in the street' (8). As with Pilditch's account of the role of designers in *The Business of Product Design*, what Henrion and Parkin do here is make the case for corporate identity consultants as uniquely placed symbolic or cultural intermediaries; that is, as people concerned not only with producing or presenting symbolic goods and services, but also with *mediating* between the activities of producers and those of consumers.[4]

During the 1970s the case for independent design and corporate identity consultancies was made again by both James Pilditch (1970), in *Communication by Design*, and Wally Olins (1978) in *The Corporate Personality*, but in contrast to Henrion and Parkin's design-led manifesto, Pilditch and Olins paid much greater attention to the social, political and economic rationale for this proposed shift of focus. Pilditch, writing at the very beginning of the decade, devotes the first two chapters of his book to an analysis of the impact of the social changes of the 1960s on the relationship between business and the public, noting that rising standards of education, the decline of traditional sources of authority, the emergence of youth culture, the growth of urban living and an apparent 'collapse of boundaries of all kinds' (1970: 5) may lead to businesses and professions becoming the 'new focal point for self-identification'. Furthermore, he proposes a new understanding of media derived from the work of Marshall McLuhan in which, he says, corporations must 'turn from the content of messages to study their total effect' (McLuhan, cited in Pilditch 1970: 9). He argues that it is this 'total situation ... of information movement' that should be the focus of corporate concern, and that 'far from being an adjunct of advertising, corporate communications have become the new total ... Advertising, like public relations, architecture, merchandising materials, and any part of a company's outpourings, must be coordinated with the rest so that each contributes to one appropriate whole' (9).

Olins, like Pilditch, makes a similar case for the need for a consultancy role that can coordinate different areas of design output, but his main focus in making this case is the shifting international economic context in which corporations operate, and the impact of these shifts upon organizations. Like Pilditch, he sees recent social changes as posing significant challenges and opportunities for businesses, but writing at the end, rather than the beginning, of the 1970s he is more attuned to their potential to combine with a shifting economic situation to produce levels of worker unrest that might well threaten corporate profitability. Olins notes that in a global economic arena in which the old protected markets have more or less come to an end, and new trading communities are still being formed, corporations that want to compete must shed, or at least manage more carefully, their 'national' identities. However, he is also aware that this drive for international competitiveness leads to economic changes (mergers, takeovers, redundancies) that are likely to test worker morale and loyalty, and lead to negative perceptions of business on the part of the public as a whole. It is in this context that Olins calls for a more 'total' approach to corporate communications, in the form of the corporate identity consultancy, but one that is not only concerned with 'external' perceptions of the corporation, but that can also shape internal perceptions and bring about behavioural change. Writing about the impacts of mergers on a company's employees, he argues that bringing previously separate companies together 'demands the creation of a *common culture*. It means that when employees visit one another's factories and offices they find familiar things, familiar names, familiar signs, familiar systems, even familiar furniture – things that make them feel at home' (1978: 61, my emphasis).

What Olins had in mind, then, was not simply the projection of identity, the *image* of coherence, to an external audience, but the actual *creation* of a group ('corporate') identity for workers through any and every possible means. This was seen as necessary for all modern corporations which, in this new economic and political environment, must make themselves more appealing to potential workers at the same time as they attempt to make themselves more intelligible and appealing to foreign markets. Such a project, he asserted, was far beyond the capability of graphic design alone, and demanded a dedicated and multidisciplinary consultancy. Indeed Olins' vision of the modern corporation was one in which teams of product designers, environmental designers, architects, management consultants and public relations experts would work alongside experts from 'anthropology, sociology, economics, marketing and other "non-design" subjects' (163) in the service of corporations that they would not only promote but also, to a significant degree, *assemble*. This vision is very much of its time, and from his vantage point at the end of the 1970s Olins could clearly see not only how the social and economic changes of the 1960s and 1970s had impacted upon people's relationship to business (and to each other), but also how the general trajectory of the economy would bring about further upheavals for corporations.

Pilditch's more sociological and media-based insights seem to resonate more strongly with the consumer-oriented brand consultancy work of the 1990s, but in fact both writers were keen to distinguish their own emphasis on 'corporate identity' from the matter of product branding, which they saw as aimed only at the consumer rather than at a broader range of audiences. This meant focusing on the parent company rather than its brand-name assets which, they implied, could be taken care of through a careful blend of product design and good advertising. And yet the frequent oscillation, in both of these works, between conceptions of workers as employees on the one hand and consumers on the other, suggests a growing awareness of the shifting relationship between production and consumption, in which people's identities as consumers were becoming nearly as important as their identities as workers. This in turn was related to a series of broader changes, including the rise of the cultural – or symbolic – intermediary as a major profession within post-Fordist economies (see above), and the move towards economic models emphasizing the role of design in value creation; both of these were linked, in turn, to a reorganization of production such that it could both interpret and flexibly respond to or incorporate information about changing consumer trends (see Harvey 1989; Lash and Urry 1994; Castells 1996). At the same time, the trend towards mergers and multinational corporations identified by both Pilditch and Olins would take on a pace in the years to come that put the matter of branding in a much more central role than either of these early texts could have anticipated.

Mergers and Acquisitions: the Brand as Asset

The election of rightwing governments in both Britain and America at the end of the 1970s and beginning of the 1980s was to have significant implications for the development of branding, since both governments pursued policies of privatization and deregulation, facilitating a higher degree of competition in the provision of services and a marked growth in the number of company mergers and takeovers. Indeed the number of annual mergers and acquisitions during four years of the 1980s exceeded the total for the whole of the 1970s (Napier, cited in Julier 2000: 17). This in turn led to substantial changes in the structure, size and nature of corporations, which frequently turned to design and corporate-identity consultants for help in shaping new identities and communicating these to consumers and other audiences. The privatization of many public services meant that these too were repositioned as players in a competitive market, and had to find ways of defining themselves and addressing their new audiences of shareholders, 'consumers' and indeed their own workers, whose roles shifted as they became employees of commercial and corporate organizations rather than state industries (Julier 2000). Both sets of developments provided a growth in the amount of work available for corporate identity consultancies, and corporate identity became one of the major growth areas for design practice in the 1980s.

An additional consequence of the rising number of mergers and takeovers during the 1980s was that brand names began to become much more visible as corporate assets, with the acquisition of particular brands seen in many cases as the driving force behind takeover bids (Hart and Murphy 1998). Despite the lack of an agreed mechanism during this period for measuring and quantifying the value of brands, the perception that brands were valuable was clear, perhaps most obviously in the 'huge gap between the tangible assets and the market cap-italization of many brand-based companies' (Batchelor 1998: 98). At the begin-ning of the 1980s, tangible assets (such a company's equipment or factories) represented by far the greatest proportion of the amount bid for companies, but by the end of the 1980s they only represented 30 per cent of this amount, with intangible assets – usually in the form of brand names – representing the larger share (Batchelor 1998). There were a number of reasons for this shift, but one of the most important was the perception that brands were 'wealth generators', and a type of asset whose value, unlike that of tangible assets, increased, or at least did not decrease, with use. Strong brands were also seen as a form of insur-ance against the risks of shareholder investment in new product lines, because they were believed to represent customer 'goodwill' and an ongoing relationship between consumers and businesses. They could, in other words, 'ensure both a level of demand and a security of demand that the business would not otherwise enjoy' (Batchelor 1998: 97). Brands were assumed to provide the strongest basis from which to launch new products, and it was estimated that 95 per cent of the new products launched each year in America were brand extensions (Murphy 1998). In fact, the success of some brand extensions during this period sug-gested an enormous potential for growth in this area. Virgin, for example, managed to successfully diversify from its original market (music) into quite unrelated product and service areas, and appeared to have done so entirely through the manipulation of intangible qualities and perceptions. At the same time, there were also examples of brands that had attempted to diversify into new areas and failed; Cadbury's failed attempts to launch a range of soups, bev-erages and dried milk products was widely attributed to the brand's very tangible product-based associations with chocolate (Murphy 1998). Clearly brands had to be carefully managed if they were to act as wealth-creating assets for the cor-poration in the future; if not, they might become the cause of expensive failures.

The potential of brands to endure over time, to guarantee certain levels of income and to generate growth in new areas was one of the major 'discoveries' of the increasingly brand-driven takeovers of the 1980s, and it led, ultimately, to a much greater emphasis on the cultivation of brands, and to their protection and management. It was during this time that the 'second wave' of British advertising was taking place (Lash and Urry 1994), involving the production of increasingly creative representations of brands and their growing association with abstract rather than product-related values and ideas. Conventional advertising techniques were now being used, in other words, to create quite unconventional sets of values and associations for brands. These strategies were not without success, and the advertising industry went through a boom period, but in hindsight this high point for film and television advertising must be seen within the context of a broader environment in which audiences for mainstream media were beginning to decline, and in which renewed attention was being paid to brand identities and their cultivation over time. These developments would ultimately lead branding to become less reliant on television advertising for the creation of meanings, and to embrace many of the more material and 'environmental' ideas and principles that had underpinned corporate identity work.

Design, Branding and the Service Sector

A further significant development at this time, related to the wider economic context set up by the Conservative government in Britain and the Republican government in the United States, was the now well-documented decline in the manufacturing sector, and growth of the service sector. The implications of this in design terms were that although design for manufacturing did not actually decrease, there was considerable growth in design for the service sector, including retail design, packaging, events and exhibition design, and annual report design (Julier 2000: 17). In some cases, these growth areas could be traced directly to the economic policies that allowed conglomeration and mergers; the expansion of retail design, for example, was facilitated in large part by the growth of retail chains that increasingly came to replace independently owned shops, while the growth in packaging design work was fuelled by what Julier calls the 'massification of shopping', in which supermarkets moved to own fewer but larger stores (often far away from town centres) and in which individual products faced a greater degree of competition over 'shelf space'. The disappearance of manufacturing industry from entire regions led to the reinvention of those areas through forms of service delivery; the growth of the 'heritage industry' was one area that provided much of the basis for the growth in events and exhibition design, and for various kinds of architectural and retail design work (Julier 2000: 17.). Elsewhere, the more stringent enforcement of laws against retail price fixing, and the rise of competitive discount pricing, meant that many retailers could only remain profitable by manufacturing their own brands. The intensified battles over price created by these shifts led retailers of all kinds to place greater emphasis on brand image, store design and the 'shopping experience' as a source of added value (Williams 2006). In some countries (e.g. India) foreign direct investment in the retail sector was only allowed by single-brand stores or through franchise agreements, and this too has led to an ongoing effort to cultivate brand image and brand reputation through design and the cultivation of distinctive 'customer experiences'.

The growth of the service sector also provided a further rationale for the adoption of corporate identity strategies such as those proposed by Olins, most notably in the attempt to create a 'corporate culture' among workers and, in particular, to make more active use of these workers as a resource for the projection of corporate image. Efforts to shape workers' behaviour in order to present a particular image or to generate particular effects were not new (Hochschild 1983), and are often directed at other producers or commercial clients as much as consumers or end users (Ross 2003a). However, the fact that employees of both private and public corporations were increasingly involved directly in the presentation or delivery of *branded* goods and services to the public (whether essential utilities or fast food) made it all the more important to plan and control those moments of contact between consumer and corporation. Celia Lury (2004: 29), for example, notes that the growth of the Starbucks chain of coffee shops was accompanied by an extension of the length of the employee training programme, which by the mid-1990s took three days and included the inculcation of strict rules and procedures governing the style and timing of specific parts of the job, as well as lessons in how to 'weigh, measure and grind beans, fill one-pound bags, and fix the sticker with the name of the particular coffee exactly half an inch over the Starbucks logo'. The intersection of this growing service economy with the rise of branding also made it possible to use workers as extensions of the brand, and as additional resources for animating the brand 'personality', which entailed not only careful training but also more brand-oriented forms of recruitment. Lynne Pettinger's (2004) study of retail fashion chains, for example, shows how variations in the nature and quality of personal service offered in different fashion stores reflects managers' interpretation of a brand's values, but also how failing to conform to types of *embodiment* consistent with the brand's image could lead to exclusion from certain types of work or to being sent home (see also Williams 2006: 39).

This attention to employee conduct and its use in communicating brand values is arguably especially important in those types of service organization (such as utilities companies or mobile phone service providers) in which there are few material or tangible points of contact with the company or brand, and it is perhaps unsurprising that the organization of staffing in areas such as customer call centres and telephone helplines has become subject to such intense managerial discipline and intervention.[5] Nonetheless, even in areas with tangible products and elaborate retail spaces, employee training has become subject to increasing levels of design intervention in an attempt to ensure that 'positive' employee qualities, whether behavioural (e.g. politeness) or relatively fixed (e.g. age, beauty), feed back to the corporation as perceptions of the brand rather than simply being attributed to the individual. The wider point, though, is that these intensified managerial interventions into employee presentation and behaviour were themselves only one component of a more general effort to use *all* aspects of customer or client contact with a brand as potential communicative opportunities and sites at which brand equity can be enhanced. The same dynamic can be seen in the area of retail design which, by the 1990s, was being used not only to persuade consumers to buy goods or to spend more time in stores, but also to 'reinforce the brand message' and to 'create an emotional bond with customers' (Lamacraft 1998). Such efforts, as we shall see in the next chapter, are partly motivated by attempts to control the context of consumption, but they also emerge from the design-minded assumption that it is possible to translate relatively abstract brand values into material forms that will resonate with consumers in a commercially useful way.

From Products to Brands?

By the late 1990s, brands and branding had taken on a significant number of new functions. Arguably their status as indicators of 'origin' and guarantors of quality had more or less disappeared (see Lury 2004), facilitated in part by highly standardized production practices and, in many countries, by forms of regulation that guaranteed fixed levels of consumer protection for all types of goods.[6] Perhaps the most important new role for branding was in organizing production. As we have seen above, as brands became recognized as assets, they began to be used more frequently as the basis for the launch of new products, offering familiarity to consumers and an associated decrease in risk for corporations and investors. For this reason, innovations in product design, and the strategic management of corporate expansion and growth more generally, became increasingly organized around the brand. This led to a greater emphasis on the cultivation of brand values that were more abstract, and less tied to specific product categories or product-based associations. This can be seen in examples such as Virgin, outlined above, but it can also be traced in other brands, which tried to cultivate and use more abstract sets of values to provide leverage for line extensions into new areas. The brand, as Celia Lury puts it, had facilitated a conception of markets as more dynamic, and had itself become 'a mechanism – or medium – for the co-construction of supply and demand ... an abstract machine for the reconfiguration of production' (2004: 27–8).

This cultivation of more or less abstract values around brands relates to a second new function of branding, which concerns its growing efforts to use consumer affect, and socialized forms of exchange more generally, as sources of value. Brands now rely more heavily on consumers to provide feedback, in the form of information, that can be put back into the production process and used in the development of new commodities and in the anticipation of future demand. The capacity to flexibly respond to consumer trends has been a part of post-Fordist economic organization since the 1970s, but it requires constant updating, and increasingly makes use of automated forms of consumer profiling. Consumer profiling techniques use information from a range of sources, including loyalty cards, purchase data, surveys, focus groups, financial records, property records, credit card data, product warranty cards and so on, and in ways that increase consumer surveillance and make consumer input less and less a matter of choice (Lury 2004: 133; Elmer 2004). In addition, brands now try to make use of consumers' emotional or affective associations with goods as ways of building brand equity (Moor 2003), a type of 'value' which, as we have seen, can be included on company balance sheets and can contribute to stock market value. This in turn entails the development of techniques for the measurement of consumer perceptions, and a greater role for brand management as a discipline that attempts to shape and control consumers' associations with brands (see Aaker 1991; Arvidsson 2006). Taken together, such developments have been argued to institute the brand as the embodiment of a new form of *informational capital* (Arvidsson 2006), in which consumers' general social productivity – their production of themselves and of their social relationships – are appropriated by brands as sources of private wealth. This argument will be explored in more depth in Chapter Four.

While brands have undoubtedly become a motor force in the contemporary production of exchange-value (and use-value too, if one believes more orthodox economic accounts),[7] the past decade has also seen branding expand beyond the commercial sector and get taken up as a production and management technique in areas of social life that are not usually considered commercial, or which are not primarily conducted for profit-making purposes. Some examples of this are outlined in Chapter Four. These point, in many cases, to a further role for branding as a form of *governance*, a way of managing populations and reshaping existing perceptions and practices among citizens as well as workers and consumers. What unites these more recent functions of branding is a renewed emphasis on the tactility and materiality of communication, and its capacity to affect people at the level of perception and affect rather than only through the more obviously cognitive work of 'persuasion'. Such an emphasis, as we have already seen, also entails a diffusion of promotional content and form *outwards* from the conventional media of advertising (film, television, radio, print) and into a more environmental setting that includes retail spaces, furniture, staff uniforms, stationery, 'ambient advertising', commercial vehicles and corporate events, as well as a move back 'inwards' to the product, or product experience, as a locus of communicative possibility. It is this shift in the media and materiality of communication that most signals the rise of branding, and it is to the role of the design profession in this shift that I want to turn in the next chapter.

CHAPTER 3

Brands, Culture and Economy

The growing interest in cultivating brands as assets through material and 'experiential' means has combined, in recent years, with declining audiences for mainstream advertising media, and has led to a situation in which advertising increasingly functions as just one among a number of possible strategic efforts on behalf of the brand. Although television advertising often remains a privileged instrument for imbuing brands with particular meanings and associations, it now competes with other forms of symbolic intervention for the marketing budgets of major corporations. Commercial organizations have a wider range of marketing options at their disposal, and are often as likely to spend their marketing budgets on the redesign of retail environments and on event-based marketing and sponsorship activities as they are to spend them on high-profile advertising campaigns. This in turn means that various types of design work have become important aspects of the strategic marketing practices of a range of institutions. The size and shape of the design industry testifies to this: in Britain the work of design consultancies is overwhelmingly concentrated in communications design, digital and multimedia design, and interior and exhibition design (Design Council 2005). Design consultancies currently employ 60,900 people and have an annual turnover of £5.1 billion, although total national employment and revenue from design is much higher because of the large numbers of people working as freelance designers or in in-house design teams (British Design Innovation 2005).

The literature on post-Fordism has provided useful accounts of *why* design has come to be so economically important (see especially Murray 1989; Lash and Urry 1994), yet there is relatively little work explaining what those working in brand-oriented design consultancies actually do, how design relates to other forms of symbolic work, or how it contributes to the creation of value (although see Shove et al. 2005). This is partly due to the fact that design is a notoriously insular profession (Soar 2002), but it is also because advertising has historically been the most visible, spectacular and eye-catching of marketing functions. Yet as design becomes more closely implicated in the growth of the economy across different sectors there is an urgent need for a greater understanding of its inner workings. This question is taken up in this chapter through an analysis of interviews conducted with both branding consultants and advertising practitioners based in London between 1999 and 2002, and is organized into four main sections. Firstly, the chapter sketches out some of the general changes that have taken place in the marketing landscape in recent years, and the role of branding and design consultancies within this. It then considers the different conceptions of media and space that underpin the work of branding consultancies, before going on to explore the materiality of branding work and its efforts to translate abstract values into material form. Finally, the chapter outlines the different forms of knowledge and expertise employed by those working in this sector in making decisions about appropriate solutions for clients. The chapter concludes with an assessment of the significance and impact of contemporary branding and its relationship to the forms of knowledge and activity generated inside the branding consultancy.

Changes in the Marketing Landscape

Chapter Two argued that branding initially emerged from the discipline of industrial design, and more recently from the growth of corporate identity work – and the rise of independent corporate identity consultancies – during the 1990s. These latter developments were facilitated in part by the sharp rise in mergers and acquisitions during this period, and specifically by the fact that newly merged corporations often sought help from design consultancies in devising identities that could more appropriately reflect their new position to employees, clients and consumers, as well as to other audiences in government, business and the media. These developments were followed by a greater emphasis on the cultivation and protection of *brand* identities, as it became clear that brands themselves could be valued and used as assets, and could provide the basis for future expansion and growth.

The initial impact of the 'design boom' of the 1980s was an enormous expansion in the amount of work available for designers, especially in areas such as corporate identity, retail and events design, and packaging design. By the late 1980s and early 1990s, however, the internal structure of design agencies had also changed to incorporate more strategic and planning roles. The rise of the account planner, in particular, was 'predicated on the assumption that the client was too close to the brand being advertised to have an objective view of the consumer's experience' (Julier 2000: 19–20). Planners were responsible for commissioning market research and for coming up with a 'creative brief' for designers, but they were also involved in the development of a longer-term strategic view of the direction of the product or brand (19–20). As such, they were responsible for drawing the 'creative' and business sides of design work together. The adoption of planning roles within design agencies at this time was therefore an important stage in the development of British design consultancies, who were able to position themselves as 'strategic design', 'corporate identity' or

indeed 'branding' consultancies, and thus as potential rivals to advertising agencies.

This was particularly useful during the 1990s, which saw a growing demand
for work in the areas of corporate identity, retail design and packaging, and led
ultimately to the consolidation of a new industry called branding. The recession
of the early 1990s meant that design agencies were forced to reduce the number
of staff they employed and the scale of their operations. At the same time, they
had to increase the range of services they offered, so that, for example, graphic
designers also began to offer '3-D' services such as exhibition-stand design, and
companies in general became more adaptive to the demands of potential clients.
This remains a relevant point today; although some design consultancies specialize in one discipline (e.g. product design), many consultancies and freelancers operate across more than one discipline (Design Council 2005). Perhaps
more importantly, however, many design agencies began to offer more strategic
services such as 'design audits' (discussed in more detail below), in which the
design output across *all* levels of a company's operations would be assessed.

At the same time as design consultancies were expanding the range of services
they offered, the recession of the early 1990s was causing problems for their
competitors in advertising agencies. Potential clients for advertising agencies had
been questioning the effectiveness of 'above-the-line'[1] advertising in particular,
and the quality of service offered by agencies in general, since the early 1980s
(Nixon 2002). Many organizations that might previously have employed advertising agencies to produce high-profile television advertising campaigns began to
reassess their media placement strategies, and in some cases to use cheaper
'below-the-line' options, such as direct marketing, or 'through-the-line' options
designed to be scalable across different media. This questioning of advertising
effectiveness intensified as the range of media outlets increased and the size of
individual audiences declined. Developments in the availability and nature of
media continue to cause problems for traditional advertising agencies, as audiences decrease further in size and new forms of marketing emerge to take advantage of the opportunities offered not only by the internet but also, for example,
by wireless telephony and portable digital music and media technologies.

It was against this context that advertising agencies began to face much
sharper competition from a range of other symbolic intermediaries, including
management consultancies and other 'media independents' (Nixon 2002).
Branding consultancies were in a particularly strong position, since what they
purported to offer was a 'total communications package', rather than simply the
making and placing of advertisements in specific media. This 'package' involved
a blend of business strategy, design expertise and marketing advice, including
advice on when and how to place adverts, and even what they should contain.
The power of such consultancies was also strengthened when a number of
smaller companies merged in the late 1990s, creating a 'big five' group of major
branding consultancies with the staff and resources to take on a much larger set
of clients. Although a very high proportion of design agencies in Britain employ

only a few staff, the 10 per cent of agencies employing over fifty staff account for nearly half of all designers working in agencies (British Design Innovation 2005). These larger companies in some ways represent the greatest competition for established advertising agencies, since they can incorporate a greater variety of expertise under one roof and offer a more 'complete' service to clients.

Strategy and Creativity

Such moves towards a more integrated approach are perhaps unsurprising in a context where aesthetic differences often add the greatest value to products, and in which brands seek not only to operate *within* markets but also to shape the very structure of those markets (see Slater 2002a). However, branding consultancies have also challenged the implicit hierarchies between different marketing functions, and have in some cases removed advertising agencies from their previous position of centrality. One of the ways in which this has occurred is through corporate identity and branding consultancies claiming to take responsibility for all aspects of an organization's communications activity, including its products, its staff presentation and behaviour, its advertising, delivery vans, trade-show stands and so on. This involves the effort to establish the continuities and discontinuities between all symbolic and material aspects of a company, with distinctions between above- and below-the-line media making less functional sense as they are subject to a strategic analysis 'from above'. What this means, in effect, is that all elements of a company's symbolic and material culture become subject to the same degree of analysis and design-intensivity as would previously have been accorded to the product and its advertising.

It is useful to contrast this more expansive notion of commercial communications with trajectories within advertising agencies during the same period. Advertising agencies have historically been characterized by a very clear distinction between 'creative' and 'marketing' personnel (Nixon 2003), and persuading members of an agency's creative team to work with those more directly involved in selling or marketing can be difficult. One former director of an advertising agency described to me the difficulties he experienced in trying to incorporate a sales-promotion and product-placement section into his advertising agency during the 1990s:

Nobody in [advertising] agencies is interested in store design, how they look and all that kind of stuff. 'Shelf wobblers' is the ultimate insult ... people used to really resist [it] ... We did a thing with BHS where we created a BHS road show ... but we had no one who really, well we had one person who did understand this, but she had no respect inside the agency, they didn't want to spend any time with her, they didn't really value it because none of their mates were going to BHS, right, they wouldn't be able to win an award for it at any time, you know, so what's the point of doing it? You know, you're twenty-six, you've got better things to do with your life than worry about middle-aged women in BHS, frankly.

'I'd like to work on the next Tango[2] ad, please,' so I can be a hero [laughs]. (A. Lury 2001)

There are a number of possible reasons for such difficulties; this informant argued that there was a general mistrust between advertising agencies and sales promotion agencies, but also that those working within advertising agencies (and particularly those working in the creative department) tended to hold those working in sales promotion, product placement and retail more generally in low esteem. This in turn reflects both a general disdain for the crassly commercial, as well as an idea specific to some working in advertising that their work is ultimately more 'creative' than commercial.

Of course, such insistence on the unique 'creativity' of advertising agencies might also be read as a rational choice about how to position oneself in an increasingly competitive market. The informant cited above had been part of an explicit attempt to reposition his own agency as a marketing and communications company (see Nixon 2003 for further details), and his comments illustrated how difficult it could be to implement this self-conception at the level of everyday work practice. Other agencies, by contrast, did not seek to extend their activities in this way, and responded to the new competition from branding consultancies and other strategic consultants by attempting to bolster and defend their existing identity and reputation as storehouses of a particular kind of creative expertise. The work of advertising does, after all, consist primarily in the making and placing of advertisements, and to focus on this is to play to one's strengths.

Among informants working outside of advertising, however, advertising agencies are often seen as reactionary, lacking in creativity and as being, in the words of the director of a small branding agency, 'the ones who hold back the whole brand experience movement in this country, because they're so eager to hold onto what they've got' (Jackson 2001). For another informant, a freelance branding consultant who had worked in various branding consultancies, the secondary role of advertising agencies when compared with the more encompassing reach of branding was clear:

> very few advertising agencies create brand identities. They may think that they create the brand because they are selling it to the consumer or the end user or whatever. But they don't start from scratch and they don't have that expertise either, because they tend to be quite blinkered in the way they look ... there is a big sort of rivalry between advertising and the sort of design consultancies that do branding, because it seems a very different role, and ad agencies do tend to think that they can do it, but when it comes down to it they don't have the sort of people that think that way. (Sutton 2002)

The same participant pointed out that in many cases advertising agencies are now having to follow guidelines laid down by branding consultants when interpreting briefs from clients, since brand consultancies often have an input into advertising by providing strategic advice on the use of photographic style, colour and types of imagery.

This is not to suggest that advertising agencies are now always and everywhere positioned in such a way that they are only reacting to a pre-ordained set of brand guidelines, but rather to indicate that some of their apparent power to mediate between producer, product and consumer should more accurately be placed with brand consultancies. As I have already argued, it is usually the case that advertising agencies simply make and place adverts. They do not, or only rarely, engage in 'experiential marketing' or the production of branded spaces, and their *strategic* input has been largely eclipsed by branding consultants. Branding and design consultancies, by contrast, claim to 'think about the brand *wherever* it is' (Sutton 2002, my emphasis) rather than simply in relation to existing advertising media. By attempting to influence an entire environment in this way, their potential sphere of influence extends well beyond that of the advertising agency. The implications of this can be grasped more fully if we compare the different ways in which branding consultants and advertising agencies think about their respective media outlets and broader spatial scope.

Media, Space and Experience

The combination of the recession of the early 1990s and the increasing variety of media channels available to the general public led to a greater scepticism on the part of potential advertising clients about the effectiveness of the conventional thirty- or sixty-second television advertisement, a more critical approach to the services provided by advertising agencies and a greater willingness to consider alternative ways of spending (sometimes significantly reduced) marketing budgets. This is one of the main reasons why the internal role of media planner, and the external role of media placement agencies (see Nixon 2003), grew significantly during this time. Since then, there has been a greater willingness on the part of advertising agencies to suggest the use of non-conventional advertising media to their clients, and to the more widespread use of 'ambient' advertising. This has led to a degree of convergence between advertising agencies' and branding consultancies' uses of different media although, as I shall suggest towards the end of this section, there are some important limits to this.

Advertising and Media Planning

One of the main shifts within advertising during the 1980s and particularly during the 1990s related to the growing recognition on the part of agencies that consumers' responses to television advertising varied in ways that were not captured by the existing ratings system for media purchasing, in which peak slots in the early evening would command higher rates than later slots with smaller audiences. As one former agency director told me:

> [it] took three or four years to get other people to realise that, especially if you talk to people about what they watch, they've told you that they watch different programmes in different ways, and in different frames of mind ... Who watches television at six at night, you know? You're putting the children to bed, you're going out ... Of course the television's *on* – no one's had time to switch it *off*. (A. Lury 2001)

Such insights, circulating within this particular informant's agency from the late 1980s and early 1990s onwards,[3] and attributable in part no doubt to the growing presence of media studies graduates in advertising agencies, contributed a great deal to the sense of disenchantment with the conventional use of thirty-second television adverts during peak time, and to the increasing emphasis placed – by this agency at least – on the use of 'niche' media. These strategies might include placing advertisements during television programmes with small but dedicated audiences (the above informant recalled placing ads during late night re-runs of cult TV programmes in order to engage 'interesting' audiences), or the strategic use of older (and cheaper) advertising media such as press adverts and billboard posters, whose deployment would now incorporate new insights about consumers based on a more ethnographic understanding of audience reception. Such experiments have had a lasting impact on media planning in advertising agencies. Another informant, also working in the advertising industry, told me about a campaign for an online travel agent, and how it was designed to correspond both temporally and spatially with a particular set of consumer experiences:

> So it would be a massive poster ad which says 'remember you're a product of your environment' as you're standing there in this horrible crowded tube station. It's all designed ... to talk to you when you're travelling to work and you're really stressed. And things like the [sponsored] tube wallet ... are just kind of, you get it out every time you're going home from work late or you're going in early in the morning. So all the stuff is literally really, really careful placement, so it's only on roads where there are traffic hot spots, not because you're slowing down but because that's where you feel the stress of being in that situation. And we did things like sandwich bags ... which were kind of when people come in and they sit at their computer eating their lunch, you've got a sandwich bag which is there, and trying to get it into the office to talk to them at that point. (Lovell 2001)

Such 'ambient advertising' was also described by one of the previous informants, who talked about how his agency, during a campaign for a new soft drink, had gone to a number of pop concerts and littered the surrounding area with empty drinks bottles. For him this involved just taking the notion of the world as a place that you can use. You know, basically I said *everything is unpaid media if you want to use it in that kind of way*. (A. Lury 2001, my emphasis)

At the time of these interviews, this kind of ambient advertising was the exception rather than the norm, and was not widely used by advertising agencies. It has, however, become more significant in recent years, in part because the advertising agency Mother won the coveted 'Golden Pencil' advertising award in 2001 for a campaign based solely on 'ambient' media.

Branding and Space: 'Everything is Media'

Yet even when such changes within advertising agencies are taken into account, their approach to what counts as communicative media is still some distance away from the approach taken by branding consultants. Those working in branding tend to take it for granted that 'everything is media'; that any site where a brand appears is a potentially communicative medium. 'Media', in this sense, are not a discrete entity or set of entities; they are simply the context in which *all* marketing takes place. Anywhere that the brand appears is a potential medium for communication with both internal and external 'audiences', and these sites are by no means limited to the paid-for slots brokered by media placement agencies. This does not mean that branding consultants have nothing to say *to their clients* about the use of different media for specific marketing campaigns, but rather that there is an underlying sense that all of the spaces in which the brand appears should be treated as a communicative medium or opportunity, and as a site for building or consolidating relationships between consumers and brands.

The clearest manifestation of this approach can be seen in the 'design audit'. These audits are a central feature of the early stages of any branding or re-branding exercise. As one freelance branding consultant, who had previously worked as designer, told me:

A lot of design consultancies, brand consultancies, when they're in the early stage of the research will do an audit questionnaire ... it is just a list of questions about where the brand appears and how it appears. And it's basically to make the client think about things ... but it's [also] so you know exactly what it appears on. So it's like 'have you got vans?', you know, and 'if you've got delivery vans do the delivery people wear uniforms?', just everything like that ... and then you get stationery and order forms and ... you've got to just think about absolutely everything. (Sutton 2002)

Figure 3.1 Delivery vans and carrier bags are considered communicative media by brand consultants and brand managers (© Tesco plc).

From this perspective, it is not only the case that design and branding consultancies see all forms of media as equally important, but also that many aspects of material culture that would not usually be considered 'media' at all are recast as communicative sites. The design audit, in fact, extends the idea of 'media planning' far beyond its usual scope, even when the more recent rise of 'ambient advertising' or 'ambient media' is taken into account. What is offered instead is the idea of an entire *environment* of visual and material culture that should be coordinated in order to render it more coherently communicative (Figure 3.1). This in turn is premised on a model of consumer perceptions that emphasizes immersion and habituation rather than stimulus-response or entertainment, and on the idea that it is possible to translate ideas and values into visual and material form.

These ideas about communication as essentially experiential and immersive were shared by many informants:

> brands need to build organically ... can you just tell people about your brand? No, you have to kind of let them *live and experience your brand over time* for it to be really kind of long-term rather than going in and trying to buy your way into a market ... (Patel 2001, my emphasis)

> The work that we were doing was about how Orange was experienced as a retail environment, how Orange was experienced as a kind of customer proposition, how Orange was experienced through its advertising ... And how Orange was experienced internally, so kind of the culture within the organization. (Blackburn 2001)

'Experience' here was seen as a product of spaces and encounters, whether these were retail spaces, promotional events, encounters with staff or company representatives, or the emotional 'space' created around the brand through the combined effect of these different interventions. Branding in this sense is a kind of spatial extension and combination, in which previously discrete spaces of the brand – the advert, the point of purchase, the product in the home – are both multiplied, so that there are simply more 'brand spaces', and made to refer back and forth to one another so that they begin to connect up or overlap. One informant used the example of Disney to explain this idea of 'experiential marketing':

> they've gone from the service they provided, which was kind of family-friendly holidays effectively, through to … an experience that's still a Disney experience, but it's on your high street because it's a shop. It's still a Disney experience but it doesn't cost half as much … it's no longer just a retail experience, it's the, you know, they have in-store characters and interactions with the kids and stuff like that, so it is a family experience … And through to now where, do you know they've got a housing estate? … And the experience is that you live in a house in a community that lives the Disney values. So you're no longer watching a cartoon, you're living the Disney experience. (Patel 2001)

Interestingly, the Disney films only feature as an afterthought in this analysis (and then only in terms of how characters from films appear in shops), which supports the notion that branding is now less about specific products and more about extendable brand experiences. Although the provision of an 'in-store experience' is partly a strategic device to persuade consumers to spend longer in the store, and therefore to increase the chances of a purchase, it is also an attempt to consolidate consumers' relationships with Disney *as a brand*, in which browsing in a Disney Store does not simply promote the Disney goods on sale there, but may also make consumers more likely to (for example) take a holiday to Euro Disney.[4] This spatial consolidation of brands is not only a multiplication of opportunities for purchase (although increasing profits is, of course, the bottom line), but also an attempt to intensify the flows between consumer, product, experience and brand, by making different spaces and experiences refer back to each other. This logic can perhaps be seen most clearly in those branded spaces in which consumers are not actually able to purchase products, but rather are invited to come and 'experience the brand'. Hence the Samsung Experience in New York (Figure 3.2), for example, encourages consumers to 'see, hear and touch Samsung's most innovative products before they're available … [and] discover how Samsung elevates your lifestyle' (www.samsungexperience.com).

Figure 3.2 The Samsung Experience in New York (© Samsung).

This attempt to extend the brand into a set of mutually reinforcing branded spaces hinges on the contributions of designers, and more specifically on their capacity to manipulate materials in order to establish a kind of 'design coherence' across different sites. This was theorized by some of my informants in terms of the need for brands to create for consumers a sense of orientation in relation to the brand. More than one informant argued that design should help consumers 'locate' themselves in relation to the brand, regardless of the presence or absence of the brand's name or logo:

> things like McDonald's, you know, they all look the same or similar. Starbucks, even more, they all look the same or similar. And it's not, you know, the brand isn't just that Starbucks logo. It's the fact that they have the same sort of lighting, the same sort of chairs ... you could probably blindfold somebody and put them in a Starbucks and not see the logos and say 'which coffee shop are you in?' and they'd know. (Sutton 2002)

While this description of branding as spatial and tactile was mostly linked to physical spaces (informants spoke variously of McDonald's, Starbucks and Niketown as exemplary brand environments), it was not restricted to them and was also evident when informants discussed online branding. Here a website producer explains the importance of applying a brand's design principles consistently online:

I went maybe four clicks down on the *Independent*[5] site and got to a page that looked completely different to all the pages I'd just been on. And it was just because it was a video shop, and they thought 'Oh it's a video shop, it's not the paper, so we'll make it look different. It doesn't matter.' And actually that's not the point ... you know you're on Amazon [because] the DVD page looks exactly the same as the books page. It's not the point that DVD and books are different. The point is ... you could block out the logo and you would go 'Oh that's Amazon.' That's the thing. (Fox 2000)

Figure 3.3 A series of leaflets positioned by the checkouts of British supermarket Tesco advertise its expansion into the area of financial services (© Tesco plc).

This comment illustrates something fundamental about the relationship between branding's communicative function and its economic function, since the informant draws attention to the difference between stand-alone product brands restricted to a particular sector and brands that act as the basis for expansion into new and different sectors. Amazon has successfully expanded from selling books to selling a range of other goods, such as DVDs, household appliances and photographic equipment, in part by remaining consistent as it moves between sectors; the point, as the informant suggests, is not that books and DVDs are different, but that Amazon is *the same*. This sameness – this consistency of the brand across different market categories – is achieved in large part through design (Figure 3.3), the principal mechanism through which consumers are able to see and feel a commonality across disparate activities, and through which the brand itself can emerge as 'the organisation of sets of relations between products or services' (Lury 2004: 26).

Branding and Materiality

So how is such consolidation and internal referral achieved? One of the distinctive outcomes of branding work is its ability to recommend and implement actual changes in the materials associated with specific brands, whether in the form of changes to the product itself or changes in the retail environments through which branded products are promoted and sold. Unlike advertising agents, branding consultancies often have considerable scope to make such changes to the actual product or service that the brand offers. This is where the design roots of branding become most important, since branding consultancies often employ product designers and architects as well as graphic designers; even staff working in strategic or planning roles may have backgrounds in design, and indeed be trained designers. This expertise in multiple aspects of the design field gives branding consultants a useful edge over advertising agencies when marketing themselves, since their ability to make 'creative' changes in the design of different aspects of a brand's identity is highly integrated with strategic and business-planning functions at every stage.

Design and Translation

One of the main roles of the designer employed in a branding consultancy is to translate ideas and 'brand values' into visual and material form. Clients who come to branding consultancies may already have an idea of the 'values' they want their brand to embody, or alternatively these may emerge during the agency's own research and planning process. In either case, the proposed changes that emerge from this process must ultimately be translated into a set of perceptible visual and material shifts in the nature of the product and its surrounding environment. To begin with an example, one of the branding consultants I interviewed had previously done some work for the luxury car manufacturer Lexus. Here she explains why the company had approached a branding consultancy in the first place and the initial changes that the consultancy had made in response:

> the brand, as it was, was very sort of nouveau-riche appeal, very glitzy, very sort of Chigwell *Birds of a Feather*[6] type stuff, a bit of a gangster car as well ... they are

positioned price-wise in with Mercedes, but *obviously Mercedes has got a much more classy feel about it,* and they wanted to move that way. So basically we took all the gold out and toned it all down ... And looked at the badgeing in the cars and everything. (Sutton 2002, my emphasis)

The same consultant also described a similar example from her work with a different car manufacturer, in which an existing model of car was to be divided into four new versions. The branding consultancy here was charged with designing both the interiors and general 'look and feel' of these new cars, and also with naming them. In the case of Lexus, and more generally in branding work, changes to the product – in this case its colour and interior styling, as well as its 'badge' or logo – were then accompanied by a series of further changes to the car showrooms and to a range of other places where the brand was encountered by consumers and other 'external' audiences:

We did look at their trade stand and changed that. But then we had to look at what the girls on the trade stand were wearing ... So I went around the Paris Motor Show taking notes about what everyone was wearing on all the different stands. The Lexus ones were looking very glitzy, little black dresses with gold, they looked, oh they looked quite cheap and tarty, it was awful ... So we recommended some more modern, modern outfits ... very stylish, very sort of, sort of Prada Sport type thing ... you know ... very clean lines and in certain colours that went with the colours that we were using as the colour palette as well. (Sutton 2002)

The significance of these taste judgements ('cheap and tarty', 'glitzy', etc.) will be discussed in more detail below, but here it is simply useful to get a sense of the sheer range of sites in which the branding consultant may intervene. Describing the more general process of translating brand values and guidelines into material form, the same informant explains how a branding consultant might change a brand's retail environment:

You've got your basic brand guidelines, you'll have a colour palette that goes with that, and when you get into doing interiors you'll take the basic colour for the corporate identity and you'll *move that into an environmental setting.* So say you've got a silver, you'll maybe use brushed steel ... *because the brand personality is set, you can translate that into certain types of material.* (Sutton 2002, my emphasis)

Similar processes are used in many organizations; in Starbucks, for example, an in-house team of designers, architects and construction managers assembles new stores in line with the brand's fixed parameters, which usually include hardwood cabinets and slate flooring (Lury 2004: 30). These activities are not simply attempts to display the product in a flattering way (cf. Wernick 1991), but reflect a general shift brought about by branding consultancies, in which retail environments, trade stands and even the clothes worn by salespeople become opportunities to 'embody' the brand and communicate brand values. This in turn is premised on the assumption that abstract values, or the brand's 'personality', can be translated into materials of all kinds (and precisely *not* simply those used in the product itself). All kinds of materials and spaces become sites in which the brand may be endowed with sensory meanings and associations, and through which consumer perceptions may be shaped and changed. Hence the growing pressure from corporations to be allowed to patent or trademark colours and colour combinations, design forms, plastic technology and even smells – for these material and sensual qualities are one of the most important tangible forms that brand 'value' takes (see Lury 2000; Manzini 1989).

These developments are also related to the greater emphasis within the design world since the 1980s on 'product semantics' (Julier 2000), which has involved a more rigorous examination of the ways in which 'emotional' or 'cultural' qualities can be designed into products from the outset, rather than added on through consumer advertising or marketing techniques. Julier draws attention to some of the ways in which designers attempt to engage with such issues; these include the creation of 'mood boards' and 'mood environments' when planning the design of new products (see Julier 2000: 95–7), attempts to correlate all the possible formal features of various products with assumed 'emotional effects' (94–5) and the use of more sophisticated consumer research techniques, such as ethnography, to plot 'lifestyle trends' and forms of product use (97–100). Such efforts are increasingly organized in relation to the brand, and indeed in many ways it is the emphasis on the creation of brands and brand values, rather than specific products, that instigates this more rigorous exploration of product semantics in the first place. These values will be decided upon via a process of consultation between client and the more strategic- and planning-oriented personnel within the branding agency, and then presented as a brief to both product designers and to a range of other designers working on packaging, retail design, promotional materials and so on. These in turn will recommend specific changes to the brand's various materials, and will also produce a 'design manual', outlining the form that any future changes should take.

Julier is understandably sceptical about the extent to which the emotional and associational qualities of various design features can be objectively measured and, by implication, about the extent to which supposed 'brand values' can be translated into material form. After all, he notes, something that appears to have a 'progressive' or 'futuristic' design for one person may well appear highly conventional to another, and inevitably such classifications tend to reveal far more about the tastes and sensibilities of the classifier than the qualities of the actual object (Julier 2000: 95). Julier's objections are highly pertinent, but they also raise a further point about the extent to which the 'success' of a branding or re-branding operation must therefore depend upon the capacity of various personnel within the branding consultancy to firstly identify various 'worldly' qualities, values and ideas that will be meaningful and recognizable to a specified target audience, and then to find or create a series of replicable design features that will reliably convey these preferred ideas and associations in visual and material form. This process of giving material form to ideas and values, which Grant McCracken terms the 'substantiation of cultural categories in goods' (1988: 75), is likely to be a contingent and unstable process, creating a situation in which 'imprecision and error ... are not only possible but legion' (78). This relates to the point made by Dick Hebdige (1988), noted in the previous chapter, about the absence of any *necessary* connection between the function of a commodity and its outward form. Thus although the work of branding consultants involves making genuine changes to many elements of material culture in an effort to render them more communicative and meaningful, the impact of these changes in terms of achieving their specified objective is rather less certain. To explore the implications of this a little further, I want to turn now to a consideration of the forms of knowledge upon which branding consultants draw in the course of their work.

Forms of Knowledge and Expertise in Branding Consultancies

The uses of market research have received considerable attention in sociological studies of advertising and marketing (see e.g. Lury and Warde 1996), and I do not want to review these in detail here. Rather, I want simply to note two distinct trends. On the one hand, there has been a proliferation in forms of knowledge and expertise from which marketers can draw in the formulation of marketing strategies, re-branding initiatives and advertising campaigns, and these have often been formalized into proprietary research techniques. Among branding consultancies, such 'scientific' approaches tend to revolve around the idea that it is possible to design both products and promotional materials to reliably convey particular and specific meanings and associations through, for example, the use of particular shapes, colours and materials. Such approaches are appealing to clients because they appear to reduce the risks of producing unpopular or ineffectual products or campaigns, and to provide greater certainty that money spent on marketing will have the desired effect in terms of changing customer perceptions or increasing sales. At the same time, however, there is also evidence of a countervailing tendency to denounce an over-reliance on market research as inhibiting innovation and creativity, and as leading to the production of bland marketing materials that actually fail to distinguish a product or service from those of its competitors. Perhaps unsurprisingly, this latter argument is most commonly made by those working in creative and planning roles, since it tends to privilege their own insights and expertise over those of market researchers or consumers. In what follows, my aim is to outline some of the different forms of knowledge and expertise that those working in branding draw upon as part of their work, but also to show how the persistence of discourses of 'creativity' leads to a situation in which branding consultants are often called upon to act as 'proxy consumers' who have the final word in matters relating to both consumer trends and the use of particular marketing materials.

Academic Knowledge and Independent Market Research

One of the main sources of information for those working in branding, and particularly for those working in strategic and planning roles, is the quasi-academic knowledge that comes from both their own educational backgrounds and, increasingly, from specialist research institutions staffed by university graduates from a range of disciplines.[7] The informants I interviewed were able to draw upon a wide range of theoretically informed knowledge, and although there are no doubt specific reasons why they would be keen to display such knowledge to an academic researcher, it was also clear that they made regular use of this knowledge in their professional lives. In particular, such displays were part of the way in which they established legitimacy in the face of both their internal superiors and external clients. One example of this is a branding consultant who referred explicitly to his degree in geography as having provided him with knowledge that he later drew upon in the creation of promotional events. His degree, he said, had helped him to understand 'the effects of the built environment on consumers' behaviour ... loads of interesting stuff about Paris and how Paris was designed ... all that work that Hausmann did' (Patel 2001). Other informants, with degrees in sociology, described the ways in which they had incorporated sociological theories into their research for particular projects, or had drawn upon sociological insights in promoting their company's work to potential clients (Lovell 2001; Blackburn 2001).

This kind of academic knowledge and research is most commonly used by those in planning and strategic roles in both branding consultancies and advertising agencies. However, research and expertise is also used, as I have suggested above, in the development of 'creative' solutions for branding projects. This can be seen in the various strategies used by designers to correlate product features with 'emotional' responses, but is also evident elsewhere. One of my informants was the director of a small 'sonic branding' company, which provided audio branding products and guidelines for blue-chip clients and for larger branding consultancies. I asked him about how his work contributed to a branding exercise and whether it was possible to provide precise meanings through sound:

DJ: Brand recognition is only a small part of it. There's also the depth of feeling, and what those feelings are towards the brand. Music can change people's whole perception of a brand, not just increase its recognition, which is the traditional role of the jingle ... music is a direct communication of feelings ... you can change how people feel very, very quickly.

LM: Can you really kind of control those feelings? Is it that scientific?

DJ: Mm, yes and no ... There are some things that are absolutely a hundred per cent, we can always predict what people will think. Like if you use a French horn, it's very English corporate. It sounds like a bank. A French horn sounds like Lloyds or Barclays, or the traditional idea of a big stone-faced bank.

LM: How do you know that?

DJ: Because that's how, *that's our creative process.* We play people mood chords, different kinds of music, and we get feedback on what different kinds of music mean to them ... with every single client we go through that workshop process ... So we may do five or six different workshops, we may expose probably fifty, sixty people to maybe ten tracks of music, and ask them about the sounds, ask them about the use of strings or that melody or that rhythm. What does it make them feel? And is it consistent with the brand that we're trying to work on? And just by getting enough of that feedback we know, you know, what it means. (Jackson 2001, my emphasis)

This proprietary research process was a major part of how the company promoted itself and developed both an external client base and alliances with other marketing agencies. Similar attempts to systematize (and in some cases patent or trademark) the creative components of marketing strategy are becoming more common, not least because of client pressure to demonstrate the likely effectiveness – and uniqueness – of one's interventions before hiring decisions are made.

Marketing Books and Industry Publications

Despite this trend, a number of other sources of knowledge and expertise are used by those working in branding, including, most notably, the use of business and marketing textbooks. Many informants, working in both advertising and branding, referred to such books during interviews in order to either explain their own approach to their work, or to explain how particular projects had been devised and rationalized. Two of the most frequently mentioned were *The Tipping Point* by Malcolm Gladwell (2000), and *The Experience Economy* by Pine and Gilmore (1999). This latter text seemed to be particularly popular among branding consultants, perhaps because of its general emphasis on environmental and experiential forms of marketing as offering a privileged form of 'connection' between brand and consumer.

Although marketing and business books are useful for gaining ideas and inspiration, they are also used in presenting pitches to both internal and external audiences. One freelance consultant told me that she kept a range of marketing books at home, and tried to read them prior to attending interviews or meetings with new clients: 'you can dip into things if you do need a bit of theory, sort of marketing theory ... to get all the sort of like, the buzzwords up in my head' (Sutton 2002). She also noted that every design consultancy she had worked for kept a range of such texts in their offices, and that these would be used periodically to check the 'correct terminology' for certain practices, or to remind employees of key ideas in different areas of branding. She also said that she read

Design Week on a regular basis in order to keep herself abreast of current trends and activities, but again suggested that this was more useful as preparation for conversations with clients and potential employers than as something that would actually affect her work. As she put it: 'the trick is to know what's going on, because really the principles behind what you're doing never really change that much'.

A similar phenomenon is reported by Anne Marie Ennis (2005) in her study of the North American graphic design industry. She found that most of the designers she interviewed made use of design books and magazines because they felt they had to 'stay on top of things', and that very often they considered the use of such texts as something of a 'necessary evil' (Ennis 2005: 73). Ennis situates the use of such materials in the wider context of designers' 'routines of production' and 'occupational formulae', suggesting that these in turn function to hasten the process of creative production and reduce the work involved in producing an acceptable solution for clients. Many of her informants found such books and magazines useful in a context in which they were perhaps juggling several projects at once and working within tight financial and time constraints. However, a large proportion of her informants also expressed dissatisfaction at their necessary dependence on such 'short-cuts', feeling that it was unchallenging and that it inhibited their own creativity.

The Discourse of 'Creativity'

The question of 'creativity' was also a preoccupation for many of my own informants. Notwithstanding the continuing growth of various forms of research and knowledge production (including, as we have seen, various attempts to produce a 'scientific' account of the meanings of different sounds and materials) as complementary activities to the general work of marketing, many of the branding consultants I spoke to were dismissive of what they saw as an over-reliance on ideas derived from marketing textbooks, and from market research more generally. One consultant (working for a major branding consultancy) told me:

> I see people that are addicted to books like that, and it's not something ... I work in a *creative business*, where what organizations really, really want is people that, I don't know ... sometimes understanding the right questions is far more important than any book that you've read or any model that you have. (Blackburn 2001, my emphasis)

Market research findings were also treated with some caution by some of the informants I spoke to. Focus groups are frequently used in the preparation of marketing campaigns for fast-moving consumer goods, both to gather information about the target market and its perception of particular brands, products or product categories, and to test specific marketing or branding 'solutions'. Here, however, someone employed as an account manager in an advertising agency explains why she was reluctant to rely too heavily on the findings of such groups:

> consumers can't tell you what you can be, they can only tell you parts of it ... most people are not experts and they don't have the knowledge. We're the ones who should be visionary ... The consumer can't give us that. They can give us useful information, they can tell us where they're at, but they can't give us the answers. (Lovell 2001)

A number of academic writers have made similar points, noting that research is often used within advertising agencies as a way to legitimate, rather than decide upon, campaign strategy (Miller 1997), and that one of its functions is therefore to act as a 'comfort mechanism for decision makers' (Schudson, quoted in Miller 1997: 181). This sentiment was echoed by the informant above, who said that when colleagues talked about getting a campaign idea 'through the research' it often indicated a lack of faith in their own creative work, or in the likelihood that it would be well-received by the target audience. Often, however, there is a very real need to get proposed solutions 'through the research', because the research process itself is increasingly used as a way of promoting the services of particular agencies to potential clients. One of the ways in which advertising agencies have responded to increased competition from other symbolic intermediaries, and to the declining faith in the traditional television advertisement, has been to market their agencies on the basis that they provide clients with a more rigorous, methodical and above all transparent creative process, so that clients can see how their money is being spent and can be reassured, as far as is possible, that there is a degree of 'science' and method in the workings of the agency.[8]

This necessity to incorporate some kind of 'self-auditing' process into the work of the advertising agency or branding consultancy clearly stands in tension with the self-perception of many of those employed in marketing and branding, who see their work as fundamentally creative and therefore not something that can be conducted according to a pre-ordained set of guidelines or 'outsourced' to the participants of focus groups. This emphasis on the creativity of individual workers reflects in part the more general 'cult of creativity' within advertising (Nixon 2003) and other marketing agencies, where positioning oneself as a 'creative' person is also a way of claiming a degree of symbolic power within the agency hierarchy. It may also represent a line of defence against what may be experienced as growing pressures and constraints imposed from outside of the agency. What is notable, however, is the specific *form* of creativity to which many of those I interviewed laid claim. For the most part, informants occupied planning roles within branding consultancies and advertising agencies, and were not involved directly in the production of specific design solutions for branding projects. Their own claim to creativity rested instead upon their supposed expertise in relation to the consumer market, and their special understanding of consumers and the visual, rhetorical and material forms through which they could be reached. Lury and Warde (1996) have noted that claiming 'expert knowledge' about consumers is one of the ways in which advertising agencies respond to their relatively weak position vis-à-vis clients, but the forms that this expertise takes, within branding consultancies and elsewhere, have interesting implications for the overall power and effectiveness of the industry.

Proxy Consumers

The capacity to imaginatively project oneself into the lives of others and to assess their values, tastes and preferences was often seen as one of the more pleasurable aspects of work for those I interviewed who occupied strategic or planning roles in branding consultancies, and it was certainly one of the areas in which they were most fluent. However, this practice, which Ennis suggests positions the designer or branding consultant as a 'proxy audience member' (Ennis 2005: 92), is common to both strategic and creative positions, and emerges in a number of ways. Firstly, designers and branding consultants may be explicitly called upon to act in this way if there is, or is perceived to be, a lack of sufficiently detailed knowledge about the target market for a particular project or product. This in turn may occur because the client has not provided the agency or freelance designer with adequate information, because there is not the time or money to conduct further research, or because research findings themselves are unhelpful. In these situations, and particularly in an agency or consultancy context, designers may therefore be selected to work on a project on the basis that their own demographic profile fits with that of the target consumer. Ennis notes one instance in which two young female designers were selected to work on a project to design branded T-shirts for young women, despite the fact that neither of them had any previous experience in this particular type of design work, because they were part of the same demographic group as the target market (Ennis 2005: 92).

The casting of designers and branding consultants as proxy consumers based on their membership of specific demographic groups was a common finding in Ennis's research, and occurred in both agency and freelance contexts because of a lack of research provided by the client. In some cases, clients appeared to have approached the agency in the first place because of the demographic profile of its employees, and Ennis reports that it was common for designers to be told that the target audience for a given project was 'just like us' (cited in Ennis 2005: 85).[9] Nonetheless, designers and branding consultants are also frequently called upon to provide strategic or creative solutions to projects aimed at consumers who do *not* resemble themselves in any meaningful way, and it is here that the capacity to draw upon a wider cultural knowledge, or to put oneself in the position of those who are *un*like oneself, becomes most fully exploited. As one freelance branding consultant told me:

[sometimes] you've got to put yourself in a different mindset ... I mean Vauxhall, I wouldn't have been the target market. Maybe for a Corsa, my mum's got a Corsa, so that was okay, so my mum is the target market for Corsas. So I just think, oh yeah, my mum, what would appeal to my mum? What would she like? What would her and her friends like? ... So you kind of, you put yourself into that, that consumer's head. (Sutton 2002)

This in turn will often involve a group of personnel from the consultancy speculating about who exactly the 'target consumer' is supposed to be, and what their lifestyle or tastes might include:

Very often you will sit down with your designers ... and say well what would the consumer be? ... What do they do in their leisure time? What sort of schools do their kids go to? What would they wear? Where do they shop? Would they go to Marks and Spencer's or would they go to Harvey Nichols? Things like that. So you can actually draw a profile. (Sutton 2002)

In this particular example, brand names provide a frame of reference through which both the target consumer – who is also a 'virtual consumer' (Miller 1998) insofar as they emerge almost entirely out of speculation and modelling – and their possible responses to a given branding exercise can be assessed. Ennis found similar examples in her own study, and notes that apart from basic demographic information, a list of 'brand allegiances' was often the only data provided about target consumers (Ennis 2005: 83). Designers and planners will then use these brand names as a springboard for further speculation about the target consumer's tastes, which will often lead them to consider other aspects of popular culture that may be relevant:

TV is actually quite good, you know, sort of documentaries and soaps and things like that. So you think, oh yeah, that's sort of like, Dot Cotton would like that ... some of it is guesswork, but *luckily we live in such a media-saturated world that you actually realize that you know quite a lot about other places and other cultures*, because it's there. (Sutton 2002, my emphasis)

In many ways, then, the 'creativity' to which many branding consultants and other marketing personnel allude might perhaps more accurately be described as a detailed knowledge of the media and popular culture, and the capacity to package and sell this knowledge as a distinct type of expert insight. This consumption of what is imagined to be 'other people's culture' was also reported by Ennis, who found that by 'collecting, consuming and engaging with the designed embodiments of the vernacular language of a remote audience [...] designers were able to expand the amount of audience groups within which they felt able to act as proxy members' (2005: 95). Ennis suggests that, as a result, designers and managers in the agencies she studied tended to construe the target audience for particular projects only in terms of consumption. Since they were rarely provided with any information about the target audience other than basic demographic information and 'brand allegiances', they lacked the ability to situate these 'allegiances' in any wider context, and were never able to construe the target audience as (for example) a social or political group (Ennis 2005: 83).

This was less true for the informants I interviewed, and particularly those working in larger organizations, who often had access to slightly more detailed 'social trends' or 'lifestyle' data and analysis, and were able to connect known patterns of consumption to broader social trends and to the various 'values' associated with particular social groups. Nonetheless, as I have also shown, many of those working in planning or strategic roles argued very explicitly that a reliance on research findings could inhibit their 'creativity'. In this context, they often relied on their own experience and pre-existing knowledge as a form of expertise through which such data could be 'creatively' filtered. This, they implied, was central to the successful integration of knowledge about both consumers and broad social trends into the resolution of a branding project or problem. One of the main ways in which this idea surfaced during interviews was when informants talked about how they processed data that was provided to them by an outside source. Here a branding consultant (who was dismissive of other people's 'addiction' to marketing texts) describes some research findings from the Henley Centre:

> what they talk about is kind of like identifying quite, yeah, quite real consumer trends that *seem to make some kind of sense in my life and the lives of people that are around me* and the world I appear to be in. It seems to make some sense. (Blackburn 2001, my emphasis)

Similar comments were made by other informants, suggesting that those working in design and branding increasingly position themselves, and are positioned by others, as 'proxy consumers' whose personal experience can be drawn upon as a valuable workplace resource. This is especially likely to be the case where there is insufficient information about the target audience and insufficient time or funds to conduct further research, and this in turn means that it may be particularly likely to occur in the work of freelance designers and consultants, or in cases where an agency or consultancy wishes to keep costs down in order to provide an affordable service to a potential client. However, it is not limited to these situations, and is also used by those with much greater access to research data as a form of 'pleasure in work' and as a means of buttressing one's own position within a competitive agency structure. While there are increasing pressures on agencies to provide clients with evidence of transparent research methods and consumer feedback mechanisms, the combination of financial and time pressures, and employees' own pleasure in playing the role of 'cultural expert', act as a countervailing force and create a situation in which, to use Ennis's own formulation of this phenomenon, branding consultants and

designers are 'not only testing through impersonation, [but] using impersonation in order to create' (2005: 92).

Taste Judgements

These accounts provide a picture of branding in which strategic and design solutions emerge at the end of a process during which both creative and strategic
personnel draw upon their own knowledge and experience in order to interpret
a brief and sell a proposed solution to the client. As with the attempts at 'product
semantics' outlined by Julier (2000), and the general 'substantiation of cultural
categories in goods' (McCracken 1988), these processes appear to be particularly vulnerable to error, in the sense that they rely very heavily upon the capacity
of key personnel to put themselves into the minds of target consumers, and then
to translate whatever values, ideas and meanings they find there into visual and
material form. They receive some help in this process from various kinds of
audience research and customer feedback, but in some ways this simply adds a
further layer of complication to the process, since they must then distinguish
which pieces of information are relevant, and decide how, if it all, these might be
incorporated into a design solution. As we have seen, personal experience then
very often becomes the means through which such choices are made, and
through which competing solutions or possibilities are evaluated.

The extent to which branding projects are therefore dependent on the judgements of a very small number of (often relatively similar) people does of course
vary. As we shall see in Chapter Six, larger international agencies often create
'panels' of project managers drawn from deliberately diverse backgrounds in
order to eliminate some of the most obvious dangers of this interpretative
approach. Nonetheless, the entire process does hinge on judgements made by
groups of people who are often relatively homogenous in background and, in
some cases, quite insular in approach. This can lead to some very pronounced
failures to 'connect' with the target audience. One informant, for example,
worked for an online recruitment site and described why the initial branding for
the site had eventually been changed, at great cost to the company:

> young people love it, old people don't, you know, don't think it's for them ... they
> think it's talking down to them, because of the look and feel, because it's so, I
> don't know, children's telly, bright and breezy ... [but] it doesn't even occur to
> you. You just think those look really nice colours, you know, you have no concept
> really of how people will take them. And also because our whole company is very
> young ... we had no one within our company who had actually put the older
> person's view ... It's hard to create a brand that has to include people that are
> older than you if you're not that age group yourself. (Fox 2000)

A similar phenomenon has been noted by Daniel Miller in his study of the
advertising industry in Trinidad, which found that the 'correct interpretation' of

an advertisement by consumers (that is, one consonant with that intended by the agency or client) largely depended on the extent to which they shared a similar class and educational background to those who had produced the advertisements (1997: 235–6). As Miller goes on to note, this discrepancy in perceptions does not always worry advertisers, since much of their output is, in any case, aimed at wealthier or middle-class viewers. However, class and educational background are by no means the only bases on which consumers are targeted, and the fact that those working in both the advertising and the design industries in Britain, for example, are overwhelmingly young and white, and that those occupying 'creative' roles are also overwhelmingly male,[10] means that there is plenty of room for error, particularly in a situation in which the resources for thinking 'outside' of one's own position consist largely of consumer goods and media content, with little or no information as to how these are contextualized in daily life.

The work of branding, as with the work of advertising, does therefore consist to a large degree in the making of judgements based on one's own taste and one's assumptions about the tastes of others. While such work may involve what Bourdieu calls 'the symbolic violence needed to create and sell new products' (Bourdieu 1984: 358), and may perpetuate existing – and indeed stereotypical – ideas about certain categories of people and their tastes, this does not mean that they will always be effective in strategic or business terms. Those working in branding do not necessarily mistake their own tastes for universally valid associations between ideas and things, but they do often have a rather inflated sense of their capacity to imagine themselves into the minds of others. This may limit the effectiveness of their work as a technique of brand management and communication, even while it does of course have very real effects on a broader visual and material culture.

A New Form of Symbolic Power?

Early parts of this chapter outlined some of the structural changes within the marketing industry, and socio-economic changes outside of it, that have in the past two and a half decades allowed designers and design agencies to reinvent themselves as fully fledged branding consultancies. The ability of these consultancies to compete with other symbolic intermediaries for the marketing budgets of large corporations was itself enhanced by the tendency of larger consultancies, particularly from the 1990s onwards, to offer more strategic and business-oriented design services; this in turn was happening at a time when advertising agencies were still very much caught up in notions of 'creativity' that were largely divorced from more explicitly commercial concerns. Most significantly, however, branding consultancies offered a more 'total' approach to communications, in which the *media* of marketing were considerably expanded. This has led to an enduring understanding of media as immersive and experiential and, most importantly of all, has rendered a far greater range of objects, spaces and surfaces as intentionally symbolic and communicative sites.

This was followed by a consideration of the ways in which this 'communicative-ness' of spaces and materials is actually achieved, noting in particular the sense in which branding (and re-branding) entails the work of *translation*, either from abstract values into material form, or else from one form or quality to another (e.g. from colour palette to material, from touch to sound). This kind of commercial synaesthesia relies in large part upon taste judgements and a knowledge of the conventional associations between different qualities, even though it is increasingly presented through the language of science, or indeed in some cases is actually subject to qualitative and quantitative forms of experimentation and measurement (Lury 2004). Many other forms of knowledge and expertise are selectively drawn upon in these processes, and business publications are an especially important resource for branding consultants when they present their work to clients, but ideas about personal or collective 'creativity' remain prevalent and powerful, despite the fact that this 'creativity' might more accurately be described in terms of a detailed knowledge of popular culture and of the disjunctures or equivalences of meaning between different 'brands' of cultural content.

Given all of this, the *effects* of branding should perhaps be construed less in terms of the 'effectiveness' of particular branding campaigns (which, as we have seen, are prone to considerable error), and more in terms of the impact of branding upon a wider environment. Specific branding strategies may not always 'work' in the ways intended, but the activities of branding consultants nonetheless have very tangible outcomes in terms of their impact upon the design of products, retail environments and other more mundane aspects of visual and material culture in both public and domestic spaces. The rise of branding is therefore closely associated with a situation in which more and more of the material of everyday life becomes communicative, and in which the symbolic or meaning-making properties of goods are less and less arbitrary or accidental. In the next chapter I will explore some of the implications of this shift.

CHAPTER 4

Branded Spaces

While the ability of branding to shift consumer perceptions in the precise ways intended may be an uncertain matter, the development of branding as a material practice has undoubtedly led to a greater degree of attention being paid to the objects, spaces and practices that support various types of encounter between citizens or consumers and branded products and services. The development of branding has in many cases led to the creation of new 'branded environments' (Moor 2003), perhaps most obviously in the sphere of retail, where powerful brands like Nike, Disney and Levi's have created spectacular flagship stores in major cities, designed to build brand loyalty by creating positive customer 'experiences'. High-end brands such as Prada and Helmut Lang hire avant-garde architects like Rem Koolhaas to create brand environments that 'augment' ordinary spatial experience and replicate the model of the cathedral or the museum (Manovich 2002), while chains like Starbucks create proprietary hybrids of retail and leisure and multiply these through strategies of 'clustering' (Klein 2000; Lury 2004). Even more mundane brands now pay considerable attention to the environments they create (for example through uniforms, delivery vans, retail spaces and so on) and increasingly seek to build brand equity through a multiplication of the services they offer and the spaces they can occupy in consumers' lives. All these efforts demonstrate the spatial ambition of many of the most enthusiastic proponents of branding, and their belief in the capacity of systematically designed materials and environments to convey values and to construct 'experiences' that may be commercially valuable.

Yet the use of branding techniques is not limited to these explicitly commercial environments, for in recent years it has been adopted as a form of strategic intervention in other spheres too. Branding has been applied to entire cities and regions, and is increasingly used by non-profit organizations such as charities in order to raise their public profile or increase their revenue. This chapter explores some of these new sites for branding, and the factors that have led to the adoption of these ostensibly commercial techniques within them. It uses these new developments to ask whether the extension of branding beyond the commercial realm represents a growing 'marketization' of those spheres of activity, or whether instead branding itself has mutated from being a form of capital accumulation to operating as a managerial technique for the patterning of information and the organization of institutional activity.

The chapter begins by considering two influential accounts of contemporary societies, namely that they are market societies, and that they are information societies. Although the logic of commoditization remains ever-present in contemporary societies, the broader context is often one in which non-commodified spheres have grown in scope, and in which both commodified and non-commodified realms are increasingly subject to logics of informationalization (Lash 2002). Some concrete instances of this, and their relationship to the rise of branding, are explored via four cases studies. The first and second of these consider the uses of branding in contexts that are made up of both market and non-market forms of exchange; a study of English Premiership football considers the relationship between the rise of branding and the alleged commodification of what is often considered to be a distinctive British 'cultural' activity, while an examination of the application of branding to the cultural life of cities explores its use in narrating local and regional 'values' as these are made more instrumental to a range of social and political as well as economic projects. The third and fourth examples look at the uses of branding in non-monetized or non-profit forms of exchange, focusing firstly on its use within charitable organizations and then on its use by various governmental agencies and departments. Both of these later sections pay particular attention to the strategic use of design in the context of neo-liberal forms of governance, and the chapter concludes by arguing that while it is often inaccurate to see the use of branding as a symptom of commodification or marketization, its deployment in new sites – and the extended range of tasks that it is now asked to fulfil – can often illuminate the changing social and political contexts in which these spheres of activity are enmeshed.

Market Societies and Information Societies

In many ways branding appears to be inextricable from market forms of exchange, both in terms of its early emergence from the late eighteenth and early nineteenth centuries, and especially in its consolidation as an industry from the late 1970s, a time that corresponds with the emerging neo-liberal consensus in Western and 'advanced' economies. Chapter Two argued that two of the major factors explaining the growth of corporate identity work during the 1980s were the series of mergers and acquisitions facilitated by the neo-liberal economic policies of Reagan and Thatcher, and the privatization of many of the goods and services previously provided by the state. During this period, institutions that previously had a monopoly on the provision of goods and services (e.g. telephone services) to the public were repositioned as private companies that had to compete with other private companies, and which therefore also had to create a distinctive and appealing corporate identity or 'brand image' to differentiate themselves from their competitors. At the same time, new companies were being created as a result of mergers, and these too made use of branding techniques to re-present themselves to their various 'audiences' (both external and internal) under a new guise, whilst also attempting to inculcate a new corporate sensibility in employees. In both cases, new private companies were increasingly aware that their major outputs were 'brands' of goods and services that could be valued on balance sheets and which therefore needed to be developed and protected.

Brands can also be seen as indicative of contemporary market society in the sense that they operate as legally protected forms of private property. Brands are often composed of things (designs, values, symbols, ideas, colours) that might not individually be conceived of as property, but which nonetheless take on the status of property as they are gathered into bundles of 'qualities' (Callon et al. 2002) and protected by increasingly stringent intellectual property legislation (see Chapter Five). This legislation guarantees the brand owner – or intellectual property holder – the exclusive right to derive material and other benefits from the exploitation of this new form of property, and it is partly for this reason that brands have come to be seen as emblematic of a general process of commodification, which is argued to proceed precisely through 'transforming into saleable objects social phenomena which were not previously framed in that manner' (Slater and Tonkiss 2001: 24).

There are, however, reasons why it may be erroneous to view brands only in terms of marketization and commodification. Firstly, there remains considerable dispute over the extent to which processes of commodification have in fact taken hold in those Western countries where the free market is usually assumed to be dominant. As Colin Williams (2005) points out, in recent years the spheres of non-exchanged work (i.e. 'subsistence' work such as housework and domestic care), non-monetized exchange (e.g. voluntary or community work) and not-for-profit monetized exchange (such as that which takes place in the public or not-for-profit sectors) have all grown in size relative to the commodified realm, yet such developments are often ignored by commentators, who rarely see them as 'economic' activities at all. This has a number of political implications, one of the most important of which is that social critiques focusing on issues of 'commodification' and consumerism may obscure more significant trends, such as the vast expansion of relatively invisible and unpaid forms of (non-market) work, which in many cases are undertaken by the poorest or most marginal sections of society.

In terms of the rise of branding, however, Williams' account draws attention to the role that brands play in spheres of exchange that are either non-monetized or monetized but not-for-profit. This might include the use of branding in charities and voluntary organizations, where many of the more formalized instances of non-monetized exchange take place, or in the public sector, where branding has been introduced with the aim of increasing efficiency in public administration and the delivery of public services, and to produce new 'brand identities' for local councils and government departments. In directing attention to these spheres, Williams' argument also invites a more general question, about how far the rise of branding is in fact tied to increasing commodification (understood in Slater and Tonkiss' terms as the transformation into saleable objects of 'social phenomena which were not previously framed in that manner') and whether instead it is more appropriately understood either as a process *internal* to the commodified realm, or else as a managerial or organizational technique that can, in certain political and economic contexts, be applied across a range of spheres, regardless of their commercial orientation.

The second reason for caution in the simple equation of branding with marketization and commodification can be found in accounts of contemporary societies that challenge the idea that they should be characterized as 'market societies' at all, and propose instead alternative descriptions or analyses. As Slater and Tonkiss (2001: 199) point out, the 'all or nothing' approach to market society, in which societies either are or are not largely organized through singular market principles, is in fact 'precisely the way of thinking about markets that makes least historical, social or even economic sense', since markets are embedded and contextualized, along with other forms of exchange, within 'complex social systems'. It is therefore more appropriate, they suggest, to look at 'instances of "market making"', which themselves must be teased out from 'the myriad and shifting exchanges in which it is contingently entangled' (202). Such an analysis would direct us away from sweeping claims about 'commodification' to consider instead the ways in which branding works in relation to *specific* conjunctions of social, cultural, political and economic forces that produce different configurations of market and non-market forms of exchange in different contexts at different times.

A slightly different perspective on this question is provided by Scott Lash (2002) in his account of an emergent 'information order'. For Lash, the 'informational regime of power' cannot be reduced to commodification, even if certain key aspects of this regime (such as the new centrality of intellectual property laws, explored in the next chapter) suggest that the logic of commodification is still very much in evidence. Rather, in information societies, 'both organic forms of life and the commodity are subsumed into the general informationalization of networks' (viii), and informationalization is increasingly the motor force behind commoditization, rather than the other way around. Seeing brands as 'prototypically informational' (3), Lash's account of information societies, like Williams' critique of the commodification thesis, invites us to de-couple branding from commodification, and to connect it instead to a wider range of social, political and economic activities and forms of exchange, which are likely to be increasingly informational, even if they are not always conducted for profit. If branding is, as Adam Arvidsson (2006) suggests, a form of management or 'political entrepreneurship', then it is one that is concerned principally with the meaningful patterning of information, and the intentional *design* of information such that it facilitates certain kinds of practice rather than others (Lash 2002; see also Haraway 1997). This is, as Arvidsson shows, precisely how branding works in relation to 'informational capital', but branding is by no means limited to the commodified realm. As the following sections will make clear, branding is now employed as a technique to support both individual and institutional forms of presentation and communication (Lash 2002), and to govern conduct across a range of fields so that it unfolds in particular ways (Rose 1999).

Commerce and Culture I: 'We're Not a Franchise, We're a Football Club'[1]

Sport in general, and football in particular, is one of the areas that is widely assumed to have become more commodified in recent years, and much of the basis for this assumption has been the visible intensification of marketing activity around the game, and the fact that clubs, teams and players have in many cases become brands, or brand names. Yet the extent to which these developments represent a 'commodification' of the game itself is questionable, and unpacking such assumptions demands an examination of the points at which branding and commodification coincide, and the points at which they diverge. To do this, I begin – following Slater and Tonkiss (2001: 202) – by assuming that the terrain of English football is a complex social and cultural formation in which 'instances of "market-making"' are, or have become, embedded. Branding, in this context, is arguably less about the *creation* of markets where none were present before (for this is usually an outcome of governmental interventions) and more a means by which newly 'marketized' actors can bolster their position and, in some cases, re-shape the structure of those markets. Equally, however, just as market actors from within and outside of the sphere of football often use branding techniques strategically to attempt to shape economic action, so too do non-market actors use both sport and branding strategically for a range of purposes.

Arguably the principal driver of commodification in English football was the series of regulatory changes in the 1980s, cumulating in the 1990 Broadcasting Act, which allowed broadcasters to bid for the exclusive right to broadcast live games.[2] This in turn allowed privately owned satellite channels to put up large amounts of money to prevent terrestrial broadcasters from showing live coverage of major sports events, turning television spectatorship of football and other sports from something that had been free at the point of access to something that had to be paid for. Branding, by contrast, has operated in football mainly in terms of the intensified use of marketing strategies by clubs to use their 'brand' as the basis for acquiring additional revenue from goods and services, as for example in the case of Manchester United's sale of products such as ketchup, champagne, wine, beer, cola, toothpaste and financial services (see Horne 2006: 33). Branding has certainly facilitated a higher degree of *commercial* activity by clubs, but it is not clear that this is the same as commodification, since the goods in question are not, for the most part, ones that would previously have been acquired through non-market means (Slater and Tonkiss 2001: 24). In this respect, branding is used to fulfil the fairly orthodox function – outlined in previous chapters – of providing the basis for line extensions, and for creating the means by which values assumed to be associated with one sphere of activity (buying or selling tickets to football matches) can be transferred into another (buying or selling toothpaste). This use of branding illustrates a point made by Don Slater, that 'marketing strategy is not – in the first instance – a matter of competition *within* market structures; rather, it is a matter of competition *over* the structure of markets' (2002a: 68, emphasis in original). The main way that branding works within football is thus to expand clubs' conception of the 'markets' in which they operate, allowing them to see themselves – and to be seen by others – not only as the providers of football matches but also as providers of, for example, financial services or toiletries. To reiterate, this does not necessarily entail greater commodification, but rather represents an attempt to intervene in the organization of market structures. It does this, or attempts to do this, by harnessing the affective investments fans make in their teams – their sense of loyalty, commitment, passion and so on – and using these as leverage to persuade fans to buy their brands of goods like toothpaste, ketchup and champagne rather than those of other companies (Figure 4.1). Branding operates, then, as an attempt to intensify the *symbolic* properties of mundane goods, and to make consumer choices in this area less and less arbitrary and more a matter of personal expression.

In fact, despite the growth of club-related merchandise and the expansion of clubs' commercial activities into new product and service areas, one of the most significant ways in which football has become related to branding is in the use of football-related marketing and sponsorship activities by *non*-sports-related commercial brands. The most obvious example of this is the ever-growing list of corporate sponsors for the FIFA World Cup, the sponsorship of English Championship football by Coca-Cola and the appearance of celebrity football players in advertisements for non-sports-related products and brands. Although the linking of sports personalities and sports-related values to non-sports-related commodities is not new (Silk et al. 2005), its significance to an understanding of branding is a further example of the ways in which broadly 'cultural' activities, and particularly those believed to have a wide appeal and a tendency to induce strong affective responses, increasingly form the substance with which brands work. As Adam Arvidsson argues, the purpose of brand management is 'to guide the investments of affect on the part of consumers' (2006: 93) and to attempt to harness consumers' 'ongoing production of a common social world' (in this case their love of football) and make this proceed in a way that 'reproduces a distinctive brand image, and strengthens brand equity' (2006: 74). Whether such management is actually possible is another matter, but the point is that the relationship of football, and sport more generally, to branding is increasingly one in which qualities that are assumed to characterize the game, specific clubs and players, and fandom itself, are sought by brands as sources of 'added value' for their products and as qualities that can be appropriated to direct action in some ways rather than others.

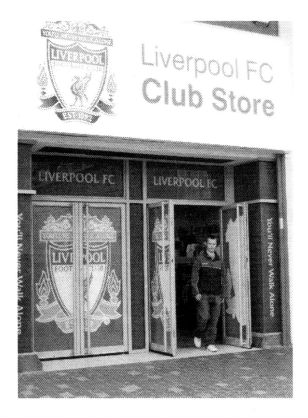

Figure 4.1 A Liverpool FC official store sells a range of club-branded merchandise.

The attempt to conceive of inalienable qualities and social phenomena (such as loyalty, commitment, passion) as things that can be measured, valued and, potentially, sold may look a lot like commodification, but it is important to remember that such accounts are not so much descriptions of what *actually* happens as performative claims made by marketing people embedded within particular institutional contexts. For these actors, sponsorship of high-profile sporting events, or endorsement from celebrity sports stars, is often a matter of gaining kudos *within* the organization, or of being seen to have outwitted one's competitors, rather than something that is known to change perceptions of brand. In any case, the attempt to manipulate the affective or 'cultural' qualities associated with football is by no means limited to profit-making activities, and in this sense it is perhaps more accurate to see it, following Yúdice (2003), as a further instrumentalization of culture for the purposes of governance. Indeed an analysis of contemporary sports policy in Britain provides a useful reminder of the ways in which sport has historically been, and continues to be, used not only by commercial operations but also by governments. John Horne, for example, shows that in addition to their continued involvement in the regulation and protection of sport, many governments have attempted to use sport as a form of 'cultural governance' (2005: 99). The UK Cabinet Office Strategy Unit's document Game Plan, published in 2002, identified two key objectives for the government in its 'use' of sport; the first was a 'major increase in participation ... primarily because of the significant health benefits and to reduce the growing costs of inactivity', and the second was 'a sustainable improvement in international competition, particularly in the sports which matter most to the public, primarily because of the "feelgood factor" associated with winning' (cited in Horne 2002: 100). Governments also attempt to use sport to improve social order, by 'dealing with community decline, identity (patriotism) ... racism and xenophobia', as well as fulfilling its more conventional role in nation-building and the control of the young (101). This calculated promotion of sport as a means to address social problems is often guided by an effort to reduce welfare spending and to avoid more stringent forms of regulation (e.g. of the content, labelling and advertising for foodstuffs) which are deemed risky because they might alienate or damage business interests.

Let us return, though, to the attempt to harness the affective dimensions of football fandom for the purposes of building brand equity. As Arvidsson points out, the major problem for brand management, and for informational capitalism more generally, lies in the successful appropriation of externalities (2006: 130; see also Slater 2002b). It is not only that the activities of the productive 'multitude' (in this case, football fans) must be steered in particular directions, but also that the qualities assumed to reside 'in' fandom must somehow be extricated and isolated and made to be compatible with other qualities, assumed to be qualities 'of' the brand. This attempt to translate one quality into another is fraught with problems, and it is by no means clear how it is supposed to occur. It is not obvious, for example, how an admiration for a football player like Thierry Henry might be translated into a desire to buy a Renault Clio (one of the brands with which he is associated) and nor, more broadly, is it clear how the various qualities, values, affects and affiliations associated with football can be disembedded from their personal and social context and re-embedded elsewhere. As Arvidsson notes, the qualities at stake 'lend themselves to measurement only with great difficulty' (2006: 134) and for this reason brand managers must rely on estimates and indicators whose use is secured by their legitimacy – that is, their acceptance by other actors – rather than their accuracy.

By contrast, fans' use of brand names for their own purposes is sometimes rather more successful, as in the formation by Manchester United fans of Shareholders United Against Murdoch (SUAM) and Independent Manchester United Supporters Association (IMUSA) in response to the club's acceptance of a takeover bid from Rupert Murdoch in 1998. Fans succeeded in getting the bid referred to the Monopolies and Mergers Commission, who ultimately outlawed it on the basis that it would damage the quality of British football by placing Sky in a monopoly position (Horne 2005: 105). Fans have not always been so successful in shaping their clubs' commercial activities (the failure of Manchester United fans to prevent Malcolm Glazer's loan-funded takeover of the club in

2005 highlights some of the limits to their power), but they continue to put up considerable opposition, in the form of protests, petitions and boycotts, for example, if clubs or other commercial operations attempt to use the club's name and reputation (its 'brand') in ways which they believe conflict with its social and cultural values. They also routinely engage in forms of activity that avoid the commercial imperatives of both their own clubs and other organizations, even if they do not explicitly set out to 'resist' them, for example by using pubs and bars as venues for collective football spectatorship after Sky's monopoly on live broadcasting rights came into effect, or by following matches via public radio or the internet. Club affiliation continues to serve as the basis upon which many non-monetized forms of activity are organized (as in the formation of pub teams and online fan communities, or demonstrations of civic pride), while the consumption of club-related merchandise itself often entails a deliberate attempt to 'de-commodify' items as they are embedded within different types of relationship and new 'frameworks of ownership, exchange and valorization' (Slater and Tonkiss 2001: 24). Again, to see consumption activities – such as the purchase of a branded club shirt by a parent for their child – as merely evidence of the 'commodification' of football culture is to miss the very important ways in which instances of commercial activity remain embedded in relationships and networks of activity that are *not* fundamentally commercial, and which often run counter to the aspirations of commercial actors.

There is little anthropological work that examines the ways in which sports-related goods (whether 'commodified' or not), and a broader material culture of fandom (Moor 2006), become embedded in non-sporting, and non-commercial, relationships and activities, but it is nonetheless clear that sport may be used as a means to resist commercial values, or to achieve non-commercial ends, even while it is produced as commercial spectacle (Horne 2005: 5). Furthermore, fans and other non-commercial actors such as governments have frequently been involved in forms of social and political action that attempt to 're-frame' football-as-commodity so that it incorporates its various forms of 'overflow' or externality back into the 'product'. This can be seen, for example, in activists' attempts to raise awareness of clubs' responsibility to take action against racism among fans, or governments' attempts to use football clubs to produce community cohesion or to increase young people's participation in sport. The broader point, however, is that by focusing more closely on specific instances of market-making, we see that branding is often less about commodification and more about the effort to reorganize markets and direct them according to 'emotional', affective or broadly cultural means. Similarly, while it is obviously important to be alert to attempts to further privatize the cultural and political dimensions of sporting activity,[3] it may also be important to attend to the increasingly strategic uses of both branding and sport itself by non-market actors who would use sporting cultures as a *technical* means to address entrenched *social* problems. As will become clear in some of the sections below, this is an increasingly common use of branding, and one that cuts across conventional distinctions between commercial and non-commercial spheres of activity.

Commerce and Culture II: Place Branding

In 1999 the city of Hull in the North of England appointed the brand consultancy Wolff Olins to help 're-brand' the city, and in so doing provided a high-profile example of a phenomenon that had in fact been growing for several years, of applying the principles associated with corporate identity work and branding to specific *places*. A number of other cities, particularly in Europe and North America, had taken a similar approach of including the redesign of a city's visual and material culture in broader projects of regeneration, and while aesthetic means have been used by cities for centuries in order to 'compete' with each other (Julier 2000), and the visual and material repackaging of cities like New York and Barcelona had attracted a good deal of attention, it was extremely rare for cities to hire external design consultants.[4] The branding of Hull, by contrast, was highly systematic and made what was, at the time, a very bold declaration that the city was a brand, and that it could therefore be shaped and managed just like other brands. Perhaps even more significantly, the branding of Hull was not undertaken primarily as a means of attracting tourists, but rather was aimed at internal audiences in order to build a sense of civic identity and purpose, and to raise 'expectations' among local residents.[5]

The principal motivation for the branding or re-branding of cities is, however, usually economic (in the broadest sense of the word), and the most familiar context for such interventions is the many post-industrial cities of Europe and North America whose economic fortunes have suffered as governments have no longer been prepared to protect national industries from overseas competition or provide incentives for private companies to remain within their borders. In this context cities have very often had to find their own ways of incentivizing private business, but have also had to look for new sources of income and investment, which they have sought variously from tourism (via 'destination branding'), by attracting new businesses or industries to the area or by seeking funding from both state and non-governmental sources. More significantly, perhaps, than the specific institutional *source* of new income is the fact that, in almost every case, the types of *people* that need to be won over are middle-class professionals, which means that the re-branding of cities almost inevitably foregrounds particular aspects of consumable culture as a means to achieve economic ends. Thus as Amin and Thrift (2002) show, businesses have become increasingly sensitive to the importance of 'soft' factors such as shopping, leisure and entertainment facilities in maintaining staff commitment, which makes such factors increasingly significant in decisions about business location. These issues of 'urban sociability' are argued to be particularly important in business services and knowledge industries, in which the core assets are precisely the capabilities of these middle- to high-ranking 'knowledge workers' (Amin and Thrift 2002: 74–5). As we shall see below, however, these potential workers are not the only people targeted by place-branding's renewed emphasis on the culture of cities.

The emphasis on the cultural aspects of city life in attracting new sources of investment lends itself to the use of branding consultancies because what these organizations purport to offer is strategic expertise in manipulating existing cultural variables ('heritage', 'values' and so on) and meshing these into new design schemes aimed at altering public perceptions. An example of this is provided in Julier's account of the redesign of Leeds city centre in the early 1990s, in which the appearance of a new series of 'urban furnishings' coincided with the Department of Health and Social Security's decision to move its headquarters from London to Leeds, bringing 1,500 new employees and their families into the city (Julier 2000: 117). Here, the design of seats, lighting poles, balustrades and decorative paving created a 'European modern' look, in which 'powder-coated steel, aluminium tubing and granite' provided 'a textural mix which would be equally at home in Düsseldorf or Rotterdam' (117). As Julier goes on to show, this slightly generic 'European modern' look, criticized by some as 'a disgrace in a city full of fine Victorian craftsmanship' (Powell, cited in Julier 2000: 118), was in fact designed precisely to leave behind the associations of a Victorian city and to attract revenue from those who would find the image of a continental European 'café culture' more alluring. The re-branding of Hull gave a similarly central role to these aspects of urban design, with Wolff Olins providing the city council with guidelines for future developments in architecture, interiors, streets and public art (Olins, n.d.: 6), while at the same time selecting particular aspects of the city's history, such as the fact that it had been the birthplace of abolitionist William Wilberforce or the place where Liquid Crystal Display technology had been developed, to be foregrounded as evidence of the city's essentially 'pioneering' spirit (6). What this means, in effect, is a dual effort to *narrate* the city in particular ways, and to use design objects to 'activate' this narration and encourage subjective identification (Julier 2005; Leach 2002). Design objects and buildings may thus function as a form of 'objectified cultural capital' for users of the city, which, as Julier notes, may or may not be incorporated into an 'urban habitus' through the performative reiteration and elaboration of cues set out by the built environment and other mechanisms (tourist literature, websites, urban 'furniture', leisure infrastructure) increasingly shaped by the activities of branding consultancies.

The branding of cities is, therefore, very much oriented towards the reworking, repackaging and re-presentation of both historical and existing 'cultural' qualities alongside a design programme that provides object-ive cues as to how the city should be narrated, both to and by internal as well as external 'audiences'. While these activities are often motivated by economic concerns (for example attracting the so-called 'creative classes' as the basis for future economic growth), they are also increasingly oriented around social and cultural concerns too. The context here is what George Yúdice calls the 'expediency of culture', in which 'culture' in its various forms is increasingly seen as a resource for achieving a number of social aims, including not only the creation of jobs but also increasing civic participation and multicultural tolerance, improving social conditions, enhancing education and reducing crime (Yúdice 2003: 10–12).

Yúdice acknowledges that the use of culture as a form of social control is not new, but points out that 'today it is nearly impossible to find public statements that do not recruit instrumentalized art and culture, whether to better social conditions ... through UNESCO-like advocacy for cultural citizenship and cultural rights, or to spur economic growth through urban cultural development projects and the concomitant proliferation of museums for cultural tourism' (2003: 10–11). In this context, the branding of cities is one means through which culture can be 'instrumentalized' for various ends, which are by no means limited to those that bring in private income. Julier, for example, shows how the re-branding of Barcelona in the 1980s and 1990s was not only undertaken in order to prepare for the Olympics and to attract tourism, but was also intended to give material form to Catalonia's 'metropolitan and nationalist' aspirations (2000: 126), using graphic design and the 'design hardware' of the city in the service of a broader project of 'Catalan-ization' (see also Julier 2005). This is perhaps the oldest use of public design, but one that should not be overlooked as renewed attention is paid to the role of branding in attracting investment to the post-industrial cities and regions of Western nations. For some cities, the priority may not be so much attracting private investment as instilling civic or regional sentiment and building a social consensus among governable populations.

There is thus an important sense in which branding projects for cities intervene in the visual and material culture of a place in order to work on the feelings, perceptions, attitudes and self-image of the existing population, as well as those 'outsiders' who might be persuaded to visit or invest. In the context of certain regeneration projects this might well be seen as 'a subtle form of *socialization* designed to convince local people, many of whom will be disadvantaged and potentially disaffected, that they are important cogs in a successful community' (Kearns and Philo 1993: 2–3, emphasis in original). And yet there is more to it than this because, as Yúdice notes, resources are increasingly allocated to cities and regions on the basis that such funds will be actively used to improve the lot of poorer or marginalized sections of local populations. As Wolff Olins points out in its report on the re-branding of Hull, one of the reasons why branding is so important to British cities is that they increasingly have to *compete* with one another for redevelopment funding, often provided by governmental or supra-national sources. In the European context, the EU's 'Capital of Culture' initiative is a case in point. Launched in 1985 with the aim of bringing EU citizens closer together, the programme grants an economic subsidy to the designated city in order to develop its cultural 'infrastructure', and in most cases successful bids have included 'urban revitalization', 'increased participation in culture' and 'community development' as principal aims. More specifically, target groups within the local population have tended to be identified, with 'young people ... elderly people, disabled people, ethnic minorities, the homeless and other disadvantaged groups' frequently named as potential beneficiaries (Palmer 2004). This does not of course mean that such groups *will* benefit in any tangible way, but it does mean that cities are increasingly required to *present* such marginalized populations as deserving, and to demonstrate these populations to be open to various forms of cultural intervention and education. One of the implications of this, as Yúdice suggests, is that the agency of groups seeking social justice or citizenship rights becomes more and more 'performative' as group-based political claims must increasingly be channelled towards 'cultural' forms of expression (Yúdice 2003: 23–4; see also Young 2000).

Conceived thus as one example of the instrumentalization of culture, branding entails both the management of cultural resources (which, for Yúdice, also implies the development of techniques and indicators to measure and predict the effects of various forms of 'investment' in culture) and the management and mobilization of populations. The branding of cities is concerned with providing a material and narrative basis from which a range of populations (often construed as 'stakeholders') may be motivated to think and act in ways that are consonant with the brand's ambitions; these ambitions are often forged with the interests of a relatively elite group in mind, or else entail such groups recommending what they imagine to be appropriate patterns of cultural and social 'development' for less advantaged groups (see also Blackshaw and Long 2005). As Hughson et al. (2005: 184) point out in their account of the use of sports in 'City of Culture' initiatives, one of the most disturbing aspects of such developments is their implicit or explicit separation of culture from the social, and the corresponding implication that *social* inequalities should be addressed through *cultural*, rather than political or economic, means. In this respect the use of branding in city regeneration projects is another instance of what Rose (1999) calls 'governing through community', whereby a range of techniques are mobilized to encourage forms of *self-*management and community development. As both Rose and Hughson et al. go on to note, however, the social roots of those cultural practices that branding seeks to manipulate always threaten to reappear, and may emerge in forms of 'incivility' or non-normative behaviour (which Rose terms 'anti-communities') that can only be dismissed as aberrations to a limited extent.

Not-for-Profit Branding: Charities

Non-profit forms of activity and exchange, as I noted at the beginning of the chapter, have in recent years grown in size relative to the commodified realm, and many of the formal institutional actors operating in these spheres have made increasing use of design and branding techniques. 22 per cent of the clients for UK design businesses are described as being concerned with 'Public administration, health and education' (Design Council 2005: 42), while 49 per cent of design agencies say that they do some kind of work for the public or non-profit sector (British Design Innovation 2005). Design and branding exercises are promoted in these areas as a means of cutting costs and increasing efficiency, communicating with diverse audiences and shaping behaviour both inside and outside of the organizations in question. The growing importance of branding and strategic design initiatives within not-for-profit organizations has a number of implications for the ways in which these organizations are perceived and managed, and relates closely to ongoing debates about the appropriate balance between the state, the private sector and the 'third sector' in providing key services to citizens. It also, however, draws our attention to the ways in which branding itself has extended its scope and taken on new functions as it moves from the commercial sector into new areas of social, economic and political activity.

According to branding consultant Susannah Hart (1998: 211), of Interbrand UK, 'at a time when commercial operations are seeking to establish brand values which are social or human, charities and other non-commercial organizations are ideally placed to exploit their inherent human and social values in order to extend their influence and increase their revenues'. The idea of 'exploiting' or otherwise manipulating one's values for strategic ends may seem at first glance to be antithetical to the work of charitable organizations, since the values of these organizations would appear to be an obvious and non-negotiable fact, with little need of embellishment. Yet in fact there is a good deal of evidence of a growing 'brand orientation' within charities, with most charity employees regarding their organization as a brand that should be valued and managed as such, and many charity managers employing 'brand-speak' in their day-to-day communications (Hankinson 2000). This represents a considerable change over the past ten to twenty years, since earlier research in this area (e.g. Tapp 1996) found little evidence of such practices. In the past five to ten years, in particular, many charities have undergone substantial branding or re-branding exercises, often using external branding consultancies. These developments in turn represent an extension of a series of trends that began in the late 1980s and early 1990s, in which charitable organizations began to recruit professional managers from both public and private sectors, and in which the services of management consultancies were increasingly targeted at voluntary and non-profit organizations as well as private companies.

There are a number of reasons for this shift towards a more 'professionalized' approach within charitable organizations, and for the embrace of branding in particular. Perhaps the most important of these is the substantial increase in the number of charities 'competing' for money and support, not only from the government and individual donors, but also increasingly from private corporations. Hankinson (2000: 207) points out that 187,000 charities were registered in England and Wales in 2000, and that this number was growing at a rate of 10,000 a year. The relative ease with which it is possible to register a charity in Britain is itself just one element of a broader series of policy changes around the voluntary and non-profit sector, set in motion in the 1980s under the Thatcher government, to do with the social role that charities were expected to play and the forms of funding available to them as a result. The neo-liberal tendency in government, which continued in Britain under the Labour government of Tony Blair, sees charities and other 'third sector' organizations as having an important role to play in delivering various types of welfare services and initiatives that would in many cases previously have been delivered directly by government agencies and employees. At the same time, a number of other sources of chari- table funding – e.g. from local government or metropolitan councils – have been cut (Batsleer et al. 1992). As a result, a good deal of government money has been channelled towards training schemes for charity workers and various types of non-profit organization, to build 'capacity' and skills for the future. The gov- ernment has also used tax incentives to stimulate private donations to charities, from both individuals and corporations, and has tried to encourage the private sector to recognise its 'responsibilities' and to form partnerships with charitable organizations (for example through cause-related marketing projects, see below). All of these changes have been accompanied by a greater degree of public scrutiny of charities, and by pressures from central government to make sure that money from private, public and individual sources is used in an effi- cient and effective manner. This new visibility, and the need to *be seen* to be acting in particular ways, obviously increases the appeal of branding techniques to non-profit organizations such as charities, since it frequently entails a combi- nation of promotional and managerial strategies that combine to create at least the appearance of a more 'professional' and efficient organization.

The uptake of branding initiatives and identity projects within charities has also been shaped by changing patterns of charitable giving, with an overall decline in the number of households making donations to charity. Donors them- selves are perceived to have become more 'sophisticated' (Hankinson 2000), in the sense that they, like the government, increasingly expect a greater degree of transparency and a higher degree of information about financial accountability and performance measurement from charities, while many charities have now started to imagine themselves as operating within a 'market', in which they compete not only with other charities but also with other ways in which poten- tial donors might spend their disposable income. Finally, the rise of cause- related marketing (CRM), which, as suggested above, has been stimulated by various kinds of incentive to private companies, is seen as an increasingly impor- tant survival strategy for charities in this new context, and as a way for charities to extend the scope of their operations and to encourage more people to get involved in their work. This development in particular has led to a need on the part of charities to 'market' themselves more aggressively to a range of audi- ences, and to find ways of communicating key values and aligning them with those of potential partners.

In this more complex environment, branding is perceived to help charities strengthen public awareness of what they actually do, to stimulate recruitment

of staff and/or volunteers, and to aid fundraising efforts (this is especially important for charities that receive little or no statutory funding). The growing significance of cause-related marketing as a future revenue stream for charities has
provided a particularly strong incentive for charities to develop strong and easily
'license-able' brand identities, through which key values can be communicated
quickly and reliably via logos and other design features. Such logos are now
licensed by charities to a range of goods, from wallpaper coverings to credit
cards and greetings cards, to provide revenue for the charity and new 'socially-
conscious' brand values for the licensor. In addition, many of Hankinson's
respondents (2000: 212) also said that branding helped them to create a shared
group ethos (or 'corporate identity') among staff, and to build trust among
increasingly sceptical potential donors. Branding was further seen by these
respondents as aiding them in their educational and advocacy roles, and in
giving them greater leverage with government and politicians in their parlia-
mentary lobbying activities. If politicians and government departments have a
clearer idea of what a charity does and the values it stands for, so the argument
goes, the more likely it is that these charities will be consulted and used as
sources of expertise in policy development.

Despite having its own specific set of motivations, in practice branding works
within charitable organizations in a manner that is very much akin to the way it

Figure 4.2 Oxfam charity shop, North London.

functions in other sectors of the economy. What Hankinson calls 'visual communicators', such as name, logo, websites, printed materials, media coverage
and the design of charity shops, are especially important, with the design and
branding of shops in particular being a major focus for various types of re-
branding activity. Oxfam, for example, hired Conran Design to redesign its retail
outlets (Figure 4.2), and is seen as exemplary in terms of the way in which it has
set out to 'revamp the entire shopping *experience* ... [and offer] an extended *range
of goods*, including its own brand "Free Trade" and the opportunity for customers to pick up printed materials about Oxfam' (Hankinson 2000: 213, my
emphasis). In other words, branding here, as in other sectors, works as the basis
for line extensions – for extending a charity's activities into other areas and
increasing its revenues – and through an attempt to translate abstract brand
values into material and experiential form. Even when branding exercises are not
undertaken *primarily* for commercial ends, the resulting brand identities often
enable charities to expand their commercial activities by applying their new
logos and design schemes to a range of products.

Yet branding is not simply a matter of visual and material cues because charities, like other organizations, are also increasingly alert to the 'behavioural communicators' that can be used in branding, which are assumed to provide
additional experiential evidence of the brand 'in action', and a more vital and
meaningful form of contact with the brand. Hankinson uses the example of
charities that consider 'professionalism' to be one of their key brand values, and
suggests that appropriate 'behavioural indicators' here might include speed in
answering phone calls, or a commitment to responding to recruitment enquiries
within twenty-four hours.

In many ways, however, external pressures from potential donors, commercial
partners and government departments mean that qualities like 'professionalism'
must now be developed and demonstrated by *all* kinds of charitable organizations.
This in turn entails the creation of various forms of benchmarking, performance
indicators and other types of self-auditing, and means that the 'values' that charities use as the basis for their branding activities are by no means always freely
chosen, and instead often reflect the actual or perceived needs and demands placed
by *external* actors. This continues to be a source of considerable anxiety within the
non-profit sector, and there remain important questions for charities about how far
the 'values' they promote should change to reflect external pressure and shifting circumstances (Stride 2006). Of course, such pressures do not only come from governments seeking to move the burden of welfare responsibility to 'third sector'
agencies, and may also include feedback from the beneficiaries of charities and
other concerned groups about, for example, the ways in which these groups are represented in marketing campaigns (disability charities and charities working in developing countries have had to deal with such questions in recent years). Similarly the
move towards a more 'professional' approach within the non-profit sector has been
applauded by some as a useful antidote to the self-righteous and often calculated
ignorance about matters such as financial planning, budgeting, credit control and

accountancy among various radical projects in the 1980s, where such skills were seen as inherently 'reactionary' and capitalist because of their use in the commercial sector (Landry et al. 1985). Nonetheless, there remains an important sense in which the values that charities promote are under increasing pressure to become more flexible and instrumental than they were in the past, with brand management itself increasingly operating as the major means through which such flexibility is to be achieved. As branding extends its role into new areas, it becomes caught up with important and ongoing debates about the role of the state in different areas of social provision for citizens, not least because it is often proposed as the 'solution' to the highly contentious new 'problems' posed by governments.

Branding the State

In fact, state and local government agencies have themselves become major adopters of design and branding techniques, which are argued to increase 'efficiency' in various ways, but also to help inculcate certain types of sentiments and feelings in citizens in their encounters with the agencies of government. The word 'branding' is often used cautiously in these spheres because of its connotations of manipulation and commercialization, but a range of governmental and quasi-governmental agencies now place a clear emphasis on 'design coherence', on the strategic use of design to achieve a range of outcomes, and on the manipulation of various kinds of feelings, attitudes, experiences and sentiments. All of these point to the increasing use of branding as a managerial technique for the governance of populations.

The London based Design Council has for some time been concerned to promote 'good design' as offering considerable advantages and benefits to public as well as private sector institutions. The main advantage proposed to the public sector is that of cost-cutting: good design, it is argued, can facilitate smoother transactions between citizens and the state and reduce the amount of time and money spent, and materials used, in the processing of various types of claims and other interactions. Lambeth Council in London, for example, hired the design consultancy Felton Communication in 1999 to redesign its logo and the layout of its council tax forms (Figure 4.3); the redesigned tax forms were issued in 2002–3, and in that year Lambeth reported the third highest increase in rates of council tax collection in England. A large increase in the number of payments made on time meant a reduction in the number of summonses issued, while an increase in the number of payments made by Direct Debit also led to greater efficiency and a reduction in the costs associated with the payment of bills (Design Council 2004a). Similarly, a research and design project conducted by Boag Associates on behalf of a cancer charity argued that redesigning the Disability Living Allowance claim form would minimise unnecessary helpline calls, eliminate the need for assessors for child cancer and similar claims and reduce the £40 million the government currently spends

Figure 4.3 The redesigned Lambeth council tax form (Felton Communication).

annually on reconsidering DLA claims. The director of the consultancy went on to argue that implementing similar design projects in other government departments could lead to 'better use of print and online delivery, potentially reducing print, storage and delivery costs ... [and] higher take-up of benefits and services, making agencies more likely to meet regulatory and standards requirements' (cited in Design Council 2004a).

The context for such arguments on behalf of design (and, in some cases, on behalf of the use of *private* design consultants who can take an 'objective' and 'strategic' view) is a growing 'audit culture' (Power 1997), in which it is assumed that government departments should attempt to mimic private companies by emphasising efficiency and savings in the delivery of goods and services. Indeed, public sector organizations are often compared unfavourably with private sector

companies who 'have long seen the value of clear, easy-to-use communications... [and] realise that good design has a measurable impact on sales and how
customers see their brands' (Boag, cited in Design Council 2004a). It is of
course the language of 'sales' that irks many commentators, particularly when
the 'savings' made are construed not as an additional source of revenue to be
invested in services but rather are diverted elsewhere within government or
redistributed to 'shareholders' (citizens) in the form of tax cuts. Here, once
again, the bureaucratic and managerial functions of design and branding cannot
help but become embroiled in debates about the appropriate role for the state in
social provision. Apparently benign injunctions about the role of design in
improving public service delivery and cutting unnecessary costs and wastage
have tended to be presented within a context that takes for granted an overall
diminution in the role of the state. Thus for example Katherine Raymond and
Marc Shaw (1996), in a paper for the Social Market Foundation, emphasise the
ways in which governments in Britain have historically ignored the potentially
socially beneficial effects of investing in good design (for example in the construction of public buildings), simply because there have not, at least until
recently, been appropriate accounting procedures in place through which initial
increases in capital expenditure might be weighed against savings in current-
account expenditure over time. This is surely an important insight, yet the
authors take for granted that newer techniques such as 'resource accounting' are
likely to be implemented in a context in which 'government departments are
purchasers rather than providers of these goods and services' – that is, in which
government employees assess designs put forward by private contractors, rather
than employing their own designers – and in which 'the public's tax tolerance
decreases' (1996: 5, my emphasis). If the *social* value of design and branding is
presented as inextricably linked to such *political* projects then it is hardly surprising if it is perceived negatively.

However, the emphasis placed by some of these design agencies on 'customer'
perceptions of both public and private 'brands' raises a further issue, which is to
do with the ways in which design and branding are used by government departments to influence both citizens' and employees' perceptions of their roles and
activities and to generate consensus about the appropriateness and legitimacy of
those activities. In fact, in recent years design and branding have been used, as
in more conventional commercial forms of corporate identity work, to communicate with internal as well as external audiences. When the Department for
National Heritage became the Department for Culture, Media and Sport
(DCMS) after the 1997 election, for example, it employed the branding and
corporate identity consultancy CDT to help define the new department's identity, to identify areas of poor communication or lack of employee understanding,
and to habituate employees to their new role. At the same time, the department
also clearly wanted to establish its own distinct profile within government (it
would, after all, be competing with other departments for resources) and to
create among the public a perception that DCMS was a 'dynamic and creative

force at the heart of government'. The project proceeded very much along conventional branding and corporate identity lines, with a seven-month period of research, questionnaires, interviews with staff and 'audits' of the department's publicity and communications materials, and the end result of the exercise, as in other branding projects, was a new 'identity mark' (or logo) for the department, an agreed palette of fifteen colours, a set of guidelines about how these should be applied, and a careful emphasis on the need for the brand to be coherent 'wherever it appears – from policy documents to business cards' (www.cdt-design.co.uk). And yet branding in this context works not only as a means to pattern and present information and to establish a coherent visual identity, but also – through its emphasis on research with employees and on 'redesigning' certain workplace practices – as a kind of managerial strategy that actively *creates* or assembles the new department.

The use of design by state institutions to shape the perceptions and behaviour of its citizens and workers has a long history, and is used not only to generate consensus or build legitimacy for specific departments and policies, but also to maintain the authority of the nation itself. This is perhaps most obvious in the use of dramatic buildings to intimidate citizens or to instil a sense of patriotism or national identity, and in the use of design and architecture in nation- and empire-building. As Dejan Sudjic (2004: 40) notes, the role of design here functions very much as 'a species of military uniform, a powerful way of signalling allegiances and aspirations, of rallying your own side, and intimidating the perceived enemy'. Design is also implicated, therefore, in the varieties of 'banal nationalism' that form the background to party politics (Billig 1995). Billig places particular emphasis upon the micro-*discursive* forms of nationhood that constitute such banal nationalism (the 'little words', used most frequently by politicians and the media, to 'remind us' of the nation), but he also notes the role of small objects, such as emblems and coins, in constructing something like a 'national habitus', with its own particular dialectic of remembering and forgetting (1995: 42). Designed *objects*, from dramatic buildings to small change, have thus always been involved in the constitution of national *subjects*. What branding adds to this, however, is a more systematic and planned approach, through the 'overview' provided by the independent consultancy, and the more totalising, and less piecemeal, take on communications that underpins branding as a discipline.

There is indeed some evidence to suggest that the planned and strategic use of symbols, insignia and other elements of design and branding to effect a type of 'corporate belonging' is now being extended to the relationship between the state and its citizens, and in ways that attempt to generate consensus about both particular forms of governance and about the nation itself. In 2004, the Institute for Public Policy Research (IPPR) and the Design Council jointly published the outcome of a collaborative research project investigating citizens' perceptions of a selection of their 'encounters' with the state and the role of design in mediating these encounters. The report paid particular attention to the role that design could play in aiding or inhibiting the governmental project of promoting 'active citizenship', as well as a general 'feelgood factor' about citizens' encounters with the state. As the then Home Secretary David Blunkett put it in his introduction to the report, 'if we can make these exchanges better *experiences*, we can start to use them as *opportunities* to ask people to get involved in other ways' (Blunkett 2004: 3, my emphasis). Openly acknowledging that one of the roles of design would be in 'symbolising political relations and representing collective identities' (2004: 9), and noting that many citizens' encounters with the state took place at a 'heightened emotional register', the project commissioned nine designers and design consultancies to 'redesign our encounters with the state in order to enhance a sense of citizenship' (63). As we have already seen, this type of rhetoric is typical of branding projects, in the sense that it attempts to take an actual or potential sentiment (the presumption that encounters with the state often take place in a 'heightened emotional register'), and to harness this for strategic ends (to 'enhance a sense of citizenship') through the use of design (by 'redesigning encounters').

Three types of 'encounter' were focused upon in this research: voting at elections, jury service and new citizenship ceremonies. These in turn correspond with three identifiable aims for potential design intervention. In the first example, the researchers addressed the question of public engagement with the formal political process (i.e. voting in national and local elections), which is argued to be facing 'something close to a crisis' in Britain (Cottam and Rogers 2004: 12). To this end, researchers questioned participants about their feelings about the voting process, while designers suggested a range of ways in which interest and a desire to participate could be stimulated. Secondly, there was the idea of using a formal, and mandatory, form of civic involvement (jury service) as a basis to ask people to get involved in other, informal, ways. Again, the focus of the research was on the sentiments of participants as they went through this process (annoyance at long periods of waiting around, pride at having done something useful and so on) and on the role of designers in ameliorating those parts of the process identified as frustrating or disappointing. In addition, however, the more positive moments and experiences in this process were conceived in this project as *opportunities* to tell citizens about other ways in which they could get involved in their communities. This in turn clearly relates to both a general tendency to shift some of the burden of social responsibility away from the state and towards voluntary forms of citizen participation, but also to a common concern within advanced liberal forms of government to establish a kind of 'stakeholder' approach to citizenship in which citizens are encouraged to imagine themselves as having social and civic responsibilities as well as rights (Rose 1999).

Finally, a more general and overarching concern of this project was to promote – and indeed to create, through design-mediated 'encounters' – a collective sense of *national* identity, at a time when such identities are deemed to be seriously weakening. As the authors of the report put it, 'as Britain becomes a less homogenous society, and old unifying ties of ethnicity, religion and kinship weaken, so we need to find new sources of common identity' (Cottam and Rogers 2004: 12). This search for a common identity is most obvious in the report's research on citizenship ceremonies. In this part of the report, three people were followed through the process of applying for British citizenship, waiting for a response and then finally preparing for their citizenship ceremonies, while at each stage their feelings about the process were plotted against its formal components. Thus one participant, Ron, who had been living between London and Trinidad for several years and had only been persuaded to apply for full citizenship by his sister, is described as initially cynical of the 'Americanized' nature of the process, but as becoming more excited as the day of the ceremony approaches, at which point he decides to buy himself a new suit and to invite his family and friends to attend. Yet when the day of the ceremony finally arrives, Ron is described as experiencing 'crushing disappointment' when he discovers that the ceremony won't take place in the impressive Town Hall but rather in the municipal buildings where people pay their taxes and parking fines. This kind of trajectory of sentiments – the series of emotional ups and downs that accompany a formal state process – is precisely what is conceived by this project as appropriate material for design intervention. Through the collaboration of specific actors – the Design Council, the Institute for Public Policy Research and the Home Office – at a specific historical moment in which both civic participation and the nation itself are imagined to be under threat and in need of help, spaces such as these emerge as appropriate sites for strategic intervention, and specifically for the use of design to work on the 'percepts and affects' of a governable population (Deleuze, cited in Rose 1999: 32).

Clearly the project described above was a research exercise rather than an ongoing programme, but it is nonetheless interesting to note the ways in which design and branding techniques are now floated not only as part of electoral strategies (the need to 're-brand' parties in order to regain voter confidence) but also as strategies of governance. While governmental efforts to use design to shape public perceptions and encourage particular forms of citizen behaviour are hardly without precedent, there is now evidence (for example from the case of the Department for Culture, Media and Sport) to suggest that the role of branding in *systematizing* such efforts is becoming more widely accepted within government. The actual uptake or implementation of such strategies is of course contingent upon political and other contextual factors; there are many reasons why current and subsequent governments may decide against redesigning the material culture of citizenship ceremonies, polling stations and criminal courts in a systematic or programmatic way. What I am pointing to here, rather, in addition to specific instances of branding being used within state institutions or governmental departments, is a longer historical process by which design and branding have become ever-more programmatic and strategic, and in which their use by non-commercial actors has become more widely accepted. The interaction of these longer-term processes with

specific conjunctures in which branding gets taken up in new institutional contexts is what implicates branding in the construction of types of 'citizenship' and
governance. At the same time, governance itself – as a process by which particular spaces or domains are conceived as amenable to strategic intervention, and
in which techniques are devised to mobilize forces within them (Rose 1999:
32–3) – is changed as the discipline of brand management endows it with additional resources and techniques.

Conclusion

In this chapter I have deliberately avoided using obviously commercial examples
to illustrate the ways in which branding works to shape particular spaces and
activities, and have focused instead on examples of the use of branding in contexts where commercial and non-commercial activities intersect, or where commercial imperatives are largely absent. My aim in taking this approach has not
been to downplay the importance of branding in creating new varieties of commercial space and experience, but rather to decouple branding from simplistic
ideas about 'commodification' and to reveal it instead as something more akin
to a managerial technique or resource that seeks to use broadly 'cultural' (in
both senses of the word) materials for a range of strategic ends. Thus even in the
most commercial of my examples – the marketing of branded merchandise by
Premiership football clubs – branding is not linked to commodification per se
but rather to an attempt to reshape particular markets (e.g. for toothpaste, duvet
covers or financial services) and to create a space within them. Again, it is not
clear that this kind of activity represents a 'commodification of fandom' so much
as the intensification of the symbolic-expressive potential of (for example) toothpaste consumption as new actors begin to compete within a given sector.

I have tried, in addition, to specify something of the social contexts from
which the use of branding techniques emerges in these domains. The imprint of
neo-liberal imperatives is very much in evidence here, with an identifiable regulatory and policy context emerging – at least in Britain and North America, but
arguably in many other countries too – in which a range of actors in various
social, cultural and public administrative spheres are under increasing pressure
to 'power up' towards ideals of professionalism and efficiency at the same time
as they are called upon to assume greater responsibility for the delivery of social
goods. In these contexts branding provides a way of harmonizing the visual and
behavioural 'outputs' of an organization as these come to be oriented towards a
wider range of real or virtual audiences (see Miller 1998), often in order to
compete with other similar organizations for contracts, funding and so on. This
pressure can be seen most clearly in the case of charity branding, but it is also
visible in the ways in which cities and local authorities are expected to present
their public spaces and populations for inspection by various non-governmental
organizations in order to attract revenue.

A similar impulse can be seen in the use of branding, and the growing emphasis on 'good design' more generally, within governmental departments and institutions. Again, the major rationale for such interventions is to cut costs and increase 'efficiency', which can be understood at least in part as one element of a more general project for the state to rationalize its efforts and spend a smaller proportion of its resources on the provision of key goods and services to the public. Within government, however, the use of branding has some further rationales, most notably to do with the attempt to pattern information and experiences, and thereby to inculcate certain behaviours and perceptions in citizens. Hence the redesign of council tax forms, for example, was undertaken not only to cut costs but also to affect public behaviour, while the Design Council research project outlined in the last part of the chapter was explicitly aimed at shaping a more 'active' citizenship and inculcating a more robust sense of national, as well as civic, identity. The use of branding strategies to shape public behaviour, whilst obviously sharing much in common with commercial branding techniques, alerts us to an emerging role for branding as a technique of governance. The 'branded spaces' created by these techniques are not simply designed to be attractive or profitable, but increasingly to 'make new kinds of experience possible, produce new modes of perception, invest percepts with affects ... [such that] through certain technical means, a new way of seeing is constructed' (Rose 1999: 32).

CHAPTER 5

Intellectual and Other Forms of Property

The rise of branding since the 1970s, and in particular the growing recognition of brands as assets since the 1980s, has coincided with a more general shift within advanced economies in which manufacturing components of the production process are increasingly outsourced to smaller companies or factories while the 'core' of major businesses consists in various kinds of information processing, research and design work, or 'creative' labour. Many larger Western corporations keep core business operations in their 'home' country, but outsource manufacturing tasks to low-wage parts of the world. As a result, there are many organizations for whom bundles of intellectual property rights – that is, exclusive rights to use and trade in certain forms of knowledge and information – may be the only, or certainly the major, forms of asset that are held. This is true even when manufacturing takes place in the same country as other parts of the production process. These rights in design and information are important because they contribute the greatest amount to the profitability of their business, often by protecting it from certain types of competition. To take the example (from Lash and Urry 1994) of the music industry, companies in this sector are less and less likely to own any of the factories that make the physical product (CDs or DVDs, for example), or even the recording studios in which music is produced, but instead own the exclusive rights to publish, copy and distribute the music made by artists and therefore to prohibit others from doing so.[1] Similar dynamics are in evidence in other creative industries such as publishing, but also in more mundane or 'non-creative' businesses too, while in some types of franchising and licensing agreements companies outsource not only manufacturing but also aspects of retail, distribution and advertising (Lury 2004).

In all of these examples what remains central is the brand, which itself emerges through the application of one or more types of intellectual property right. The major forms of intellectual property right are patent, copyright and trademark, but also include industrial designs, integrated circuits and Geographical Indications (see Chapter Six). Typically, patents can be applied to inventions, whereas copyright is used to protect literary or artistic forms of expression, although it is also used to protect computer software. Trademark is used to protect those qualities that distinguish the products or services of one company from another (May 2000). For many brand-name goods, the major form of intellectual property right is trademark, which protects the various words, signs and designs through which a commodity is distinguished from its competitors. Hence a washing powder like Persil will be protected by trademarks in its name, and perhaps also the colour and shape of its contents or packaging. In other cases, however, the brand will include additional forms of intellectual property protection, such as patent, copyright and in some cases various types of design right. Cosmetics ranges will usually be protected by several applications of trademark (for example the name L'Oréal and all the graphic signs relating to it), but may also be protected through patents on particular product formulae. The major significance of intellectual property rights for an understanding of branding is therefore that these rights allow goods to circulate on a competitive market by protecting their form, and sometimes their content, such that others are excluded from using those features that have been deemed to distinguish the brand from other goods. Trademark law is, as we have seen, particularly important in a context where these signs and designs have come to take on a greater role in identifying the brand in the minds of consumers, and in acting as vehicles for the 'values' it is supposed to contain. In essence, then, trademark law protects brands' profits by excluding other companies or individuals from using their designs and the 'sign-value' they produce.

The protection of corporate profits is not the only rationale for trademark law, since it is also supposed to prevent consumers from being 'confused' or deceived as to the origin and quality of a commodity (Lury 2004), and to provide an incentive for businesses to maintain the quality and standard of goods bearing their mark, thus offering additional protection to consumers. However, in recent years many authors have argued that this function of protecting consumers has come to be less significant as trademark law has instead focused on protecting companies' investments in design and marketing rather than consumers' interests in identifying the content and origin of goods. Indeed it has been argued that a whole range of consumers' interests and activities have been either marginalized or actively harmed by the increasingly stringent and business-oriented development of trademark law; some of these arguments will be explored below. Trademark law, like other forms of intellectual property right, has also become entwined with debates about corporate globalization, as it comes to protect the interests of multinational corporations seeking to capture new markets, often in the developing world or in emerging markets. Trademark and other forms of intellectual property are therefore caught up in debates about the power relations between states, and about the unequal global division of labour. One very obvious example of this role of intellectual property rights would be in the debates about the patenting of anti-retroviral drugs for people with HIV, but the law of trademark too is often the subject of international disputes.

To explore these matters further, I want to begin by outlining some of the basic features of intellectual property law, and to locate them in a longer history of property. Many of the premises of Western property law are themselves contentious, in part because they were developed at a time when Western nations were seeking to justify their attempts to appropriate New World lands from their native inhabitants. Some of these areas of dispute have resurfaced more recently in debates about intellectual property law. Having outlined some of the historical foundations of intellectual property law, I shall return to the present day and consider in more detail the role of intellectual property law in the contemporary global economy. Focusing particularly closely on issues pertaining to trademark, I will explore the ways in which the laws that protect brand names have been challenged and criticized on the basis that they de-legitimize the activities of consumers, as well as on the grounds that they replicate and further entrench the forms of inequality and dispossession upon which the initial forging of Western property was based.

The History of Intellectual Property in Europe and America

To understand how intellectual property law emerged, and the specific forms that it has taken, it is necessary to go back to the definitions of, and justifications for, private property put forward in the early modern period, since these definitions remain fundamental to the law as it exists today. Although early forms of private property had been established by the ancient Greeks, and consolidated further during the Roman Empire through a distinction between possession and property (Duchrow and Hinkelammert 2004), it was during the seventeenth century in England that private property was given a full legal justification. Prior to this point, both private and common property were recognized, but the shift from a feudal manorial system to a system of bourgeois private property entailed the large-scale enclosure of what had previously been a village's common land, and its transformation into the private property of landowners. During this period the idea of common property started to disappear and even, in some cases, to be seen as a contradiction in terms (May 2000). At the same time, the establishment of the basic principle of habeas corpus in 1679, as well as the Bill of Rights of 1689, emphasized equality before the law and the role of parliament in both representing the people and protecting their private property.

More crucially, however, this period was also the time of European imperial expansion, and this presented something of a legitimation problem for the new property-owning bourgeoisie. Where imperial expansion had previously been founded on the divine right of kings, the abolition of this right meant that new kinds of justification were required. Yet the principles of habeas corpus and of the Bill of Rights, which were so central to the bourgeoisie's economic ambitions, guaranteed the physical integrity of persons and of private property in the face of political authority. To take this seriously would mean excluding the forced labour of slavery, and the violent appropriation of the indigenous territories in North America, from the bourgeoisie's new territorial ambitions (Duchrow and Hinkelammert 2004). What this meant, in effect, was that there was a fundamental conflict between the bourgeoisie's ambitions at home, which were protected by habeas corpus, and their ambitions abroad, which were frustrated by it.

It was in this context that John Locke's *Second Treatise on Government* was published in 1690. For Locke, natural resources are given by God to mankind (sic) in common, and thus the original form of property is common property. However, Locke founds his idea of private property on its relationship to human labour. Each man, he argued, had a right to own their own labour, and the fruits of that labour, and this meant, for him, that private property could emerge as a result of the mixing of one's own labour with the common resources provided by God (Lury 2004). This principle, sometimes known as the principle of the 'labour of the first occupier', depends, crucially, on the idea that some forms of labour 'improve' upon nature, and may therefore be used as the basis for the conversion of nature into private property, while other forms of labour do not improve nature and therefore leave that nature as common property. It was this distinction that was applied by European colonizers in North America to justify the appropriation of land from indigenous people. These territories, the Europeans claimed, were 'wastes', left barren and uncultivated by people who showed no inclination to strive towards the 'workmanship ideal' of making efficient use of resources (Brewer and Staves 1995). Similar attitudes are present today when areas inhabited by indigenous and traditional peoples are referred to as 'wild' or 'wilderness', with no reference to the labour involved in maintaining such landscapes and conserving or enhancing their biodiversity (Posey 2004: 195).

There are, of course, many problems with this conception of property, most notably the ways in which 'improvement' is to be defined and the question of why this should in any case lead to private ownership. As Lury (2004: 106) puts it, 'even if labour can be owned and such labour is mixed with (common) resources, why should it automatically mean that the resource becomes the private property of the labourer? Why should the mixing of labour with a resource provide any private entitlement at all? Furthermore, if, as Locke argues, only activities that improve the resources are constitutive of property, how are such improvements to be recognized?' The picture is further complicated when we consider that the 'improving' labour that was supposed to occur as a result of colonization was in fact undertaken not by the new 'owners' of the land but rather, more usually, by slave labourers who were considered objects, rather than subjects, of property, and who therefore were disbarred from any claim on the fruits of their work. Later, Marx's objections to private property would rest on similar claims, that it was capitalist owners, rather than labouring workers, who reaped its rewards and that the alienation of the worker from the products of his or her labour meant that property could never be the expression of the human personality (see below), only its negation.

Making Intellectual Property

These early conceptions of property did, however, set the foundations for property law, not only in England but also in many other countries. These laws in turn have provided the framework for the development of *intellectual* property legislation. As Christopher May notes, Locke's account of property as the just reward for labour continues to operate as a central justification for intellectual property rights, on the basis that the effort expended to produce any knowledge or information should be rewarded with proprietary right in whatever is produced (May 2000: 7). This is supposed to encourage further intellectual activity by setting out a clear benefit – i.e. an intellectual property *right* – that can be converted into a monetary reward by exchange on the market.

In addition to this Lockean rationale, two further justifications tend to be made for the existence of intellectual property rights. Firstly, there is an ethical argument that sees (intellectual) property as an expression of the self. Deriving from Hegel's idea that people define themselves through their possessions and their (intellectual) property, including the possession of their 'capacities', the knowledge and ideas that go into 'intellectual' goods are seen as the expression of our identity. In this way, intellectual property rights recognize the sovereignty of a person over their thoughts; as May (2000: 7) puts it, 'the expression of self through the creative act ... should be protected as this represents the product of selfhood and is the property of the self'. Secondly, intellectual property rights are justified on the basis of potential economic outcomes. Here, it is held that it is only by allocating a monetary value to a particular resource (in this case information or knowledge) that it will be used to its best advantage and will encourage further useful developments (May 2000.). As May puts it, this argument rests on the idea that in allocating a price through the market, 'users' of intellectual property will constantly be forced to assess the return that use generates, and will therefore think of ways to maximize that use. This in turn will promote a more efficient use of resources, as well as innovations in mode of use.

Both of these additional justifications for the existence of private (intellectual) property present further ethical questions, that apply equally to material and immaterial property, but part of what is so interesting about intellectual property is how justifications devised in the seventeenth and nineteenth centuries for material property (and indeed, as we have seen above, for the seizure of land from the native inhabitants of new colonies) have been applied to this relatively new kind of property without any real modification. The various forms of intellectual property (such as patent, copyright and trademark) are justified, most often, by one or a combination of the rationales outlined above, and pay little if any attention to the significant differences between, on the one hand, material and immaterial things, and, on the other, the particular historical, economic and political contexts in which intellectual property now operates. As May points out, the major contradiction lying at the heart of the political economy of intellectual property is that the marginal costs of reproducing knowledge and information (unlike material goods) are low to non-existent, yet it is treated as though it is scarce and costly (May 2000: 42). Whereas material forms of property cannot be in two places at once and therefore cannot be used by two people at the same time unless those people are themselves in the same place, the use of information, techniques, skills and so on does not preclude use 'at the same level of intensity', and in a different location, by someone else. Intellectual property law, therefore, aims to 'establish some form of *constructed scarcity* which is achieved through the use of previously legitimated justificatory schemata of property' (2000: 45, my emphasis).

What all of this means, in effect, is that one of the underlying rationales for the legal protection of private property – i.e. that it prevents creators and owners of a good from being dispossessed of that good at the hands of malicious others – no longer applies, since ownership or use by one person is not compromised if that good is also 'owned' or used by another. In this context, earlier justifications for property, such as 'just rewards' or 'self-expression', appear to grow in importance, since they seem to provide a continuing *moral* basis for the construction of intellectual goods as a scarce resource even when they are not so in reality. Thus as we have seen, intellectual property is justified on the basis that it provides an incentive for future productive activity, or that it acknowledges and represents the sovereignty of the individual over their thoughts and ideas. However, as critics of intellectual property point out, such an argument tends to assume that financial gain (through the right to exchange one's intellectual property on the market) is the most appropriate, or indeed the only, way in which effort can be rewarded or further activity encouraged. By contrast, critics argue, the only protection for those who want to limit the use of their ideas should be secrecy or non-disclosure, while the 'reward' for their efforts should be reputation or fame rather than the ability to restrict others from using their ideas (May 2000: 62).

Yet as these critics acknowledge, the 'self-expression' or 'just reward' arguments for intellectual property are in any case something of a smokescreen, since the major beneficiaries of intellectual property law tend not to be private individuals and 'creators', but rather large corporations, who have the capacity to turn these abstract rights into active and tradable properties, which can then be protected by law. Such companies have an interest in asserting the moral rights of 'creators', but only insofar as those rights are alienable (they can be exchanged and purchased by corporations) and exclusive (others can be prevented from using them), and can therefore become the basis of a profitable monopoly. In other words, although intellectual property is periodically justified by ideas such as 'just rewards' or 'self-expression', the principal function of intellectual property *law* is to facilitate the continuing expansion of profit-making activity. This is particularly so since the incorporation of intellectual property into the international trade regime organized by the World Trade Organization (see below). In this context, contradictions that emerge from the application of earlier justifications for property to the contemporary situation (such as the validity of the 'single author' model in a context where 'innovation' is largely incremental and based on the manipulation of existing knowledge) tend to be glossed over as powerful groups mobilize substantial resources to ensure that the benefits of private ownership continue to accrue to them even while the objects in which they trade change (May 2000: 43; 50–1). This glossing of moral and ethical contradictions is, of course, bolstered by the taken-for-granted bottom line argument about intellectual property's role as a stimulus to economic activity and growth, and by the international lobbying efforts of powerful nations and corporations.

Intellectual Property in an Age of Post-Fordism

One of the ways in which this fundamentally economic motivation for protecting intellectual property along the lines established for material property has manifested itself in recent years is in the fact that international agreements in this area have been interested primarily in *trade-related* aspects of intellectual property, to the exclusion of other concerns. Hence the signing of an agreement on Trade-Related Aspects of Intellectual Property Rights (the TRIPs agreement) at the Uruguay round of the General Agreement on Tariffs and Trade (GATT) in 1994. This expanded the scope of intellectual property governance considerably, by bringing intellectual property into the broader international trade regime overseen by the Word Trade Organization (WTO) – which was formally established as the successor to GATT the following year – and by attempting to establish a tighter and more effective mechanism for resolving intellectual property-related conflicts (May 2000: 67–8). Although much of the substance of the agreement simply enshrines already-existing conventions on intellectual property (such as those enacted in the Berne Convention for the Protection of Literary and Artistic Works, and the Paris Convention for the Protection of Industrial Property), and the actual character of intellectual property was only somewhat modified, the significance of the agreement lay in the extent to which it was freedom of international trade, rather than any other kind of concern, that established the parameters of the debate, and on a near-global scale. Thus as May (2000: 70–2) points out, although the agreement does not represent a direct legal structure to be incorporated by states into their national legal systems, it does stipulate that national legal frameworks for intellectual property must meet the general requirement to 'avoid the creation of barriers to legitimate trade' (cited on p. 70) and to enact stricter border controls with regard to goods in which intellectual property rights are embedded (such as CDs, software, clothes and so on). What this means in practice, as we shall see below, is that although relatively few things are actually prohibited in this formula, few things are protected either, leading to a situation in which groups seeking to assert their own version of rights or to challenge the terms of the agreement have often had to proceed through various types of illegal activity.

Patents and Generic Drugs

One of the major areas of dispute following the TRIPs agreement was in the area
of pharmaceuticals, where the more rigorous enforcement of laws on patent
meant that sick people in poorer countries could not afford medication for serious
illnesses such as HIV and tuberculosis because the licenses for patents were too
expensive for their national governments, and the brand-name products were too
expensive for individuals. Thirty-nine pharmaceutical companies filed lawsuits
against South Africa, whose national laws continue to permit compulsory
licensing of patents without the patent-holder's consent, and it was in this context
that a further round of trade talks was started in Doha, Qatar, in 2001. These led
to an agreement that patent laws could be suspended in the case of threats to
public health. However, as some commentators have pointed out, the outcome of
these talks did not in fact involve any change to the wording of the original TRIPs
agreement (which had not, in any case, explicitly ruled out the possibility of
ignoring patents when public health was at stake), leaving open the possibility of
future challenges to practices such as those of the South African government
(Yúdice 2003). Furthermore, this particular 'concession' to developing countries
took place in the context of a broader set of trade negotiations, and was seen by
many to have been deliberately calculated to persuade poorer countries to sign up
to a deal that also included allowing EU countries to maintain their agricultural
subsidies and the United States to hold on to textile and garment quotas. Thus
although the relative success of the South African and other governments in
avoiding prosecution by large pharmaceutical companies gives some grounds for
optimism that considerations beyond the strictly economic may be taken into
account in the regulation of intellectual property at an international level, the
broader context remains one in which the trading activities of powerful nation-
states and large multinational corporations are prioritized and protected, while
any contestation of such rights may have to proceed, in the first instance at least,
through 'illegal' behaviour on the part of disadvantaged groups or states. What is
more, other forms of activity that infringe the TRIPs agreement are open to punishment through economic sanctions or import tariffs, while the fact that the fundamental category definitions of property and ownership have remained
unchanged means that economic and cultural activities that do not conform to
these definitions may be vulnerable to forms of expropriation similar to those that
characterized earlier histories of dispossession.

Indigenous Knowledge

A further area of ongoing concern, where resonances between current practice
and earlier histories of dispossession are very much in evidence, concerns the
ways in which ideas about intellectual property rights are applied to traditional
or indigenous knowledge. These debates, which tend to focus in particular on

the 'bio-prospecting' activities of largely Western corporations, throw into relief
the continuing significance of eighteenth-century definitions of property for
present-day politics. At the heart of many of these debates are attempts by large
multinational corporations to patent naturally occurring substances, which are
often found in relatively under-developed parts of the world. Such substances
may already be widely used in their native lands, but multinational companies
are now spending vast sums of money trying to identify these naturally occurring substances (which may include cereal crops, plants and marine organisms)
and to patent part or all of those substances for use in their own businesses. The
most sought-after, and most immediately lucrative, substances tend to be staple
cereal crops with a wide commercial value, such as maize, rice, sorghum and
millet, and many of the genes and gene sequences of these crops are now
patented and owned by large agribusiness companies (Vidal 2000).[2] One of the
major growth areas in bio-prospecting, however, is in the use of plants and other
organisms with possible medicinal qualities. Here, individual prospectors, multinational companies, national government agencies and universities are all
involved in collecting plant and animal samples from across the world and, in
many cases, applying for patents on their use.

Debates about the ethics of such activities tend to hinge on two key arguments. Firstly, those involved in bio-prospecting tend to argue that such substances are part of the 'common heritage of humankind', that they are not
'owned' by the communities that live in a particular region, nor by their national
governments. Plants with potential medicinal benefits, they argue, should be
made available for testing and development, and those who are able to track
down such plants and make them available on a wider scale (through 'innovation' in extraction and processing, and the commercial ability to distribute the
results on the market) should not be prohibited from doing so. For their part,
representatives of those who live in these areas and who may have made use of
the various plants and other substances for many generations, see this as little
more than theft, in which resources that they have cultivated carefully, and used
responsibly, for a long time are taken away, with little or nothing in the way of
compensation, and in some cases to be sold back to them at near-prohibitive
prices. Indeed it is this latter fact – the ability to control the circulation of a particular resource, and thereby to hold the exclusive right to derive profits from it
– that is particularly problematic from the point of view of critics. As Vandana
Shiva (cited in May 2000: 104) puts it:

[after] centuries of the gene-rich south having contributed biological resources
freely to the north, third world governments are no longer willing to have biological wealth taken for free and sold back at exorbitant prices ... as 'improved' seeds
and packaged drugs. From the third-world viewpoint, it is considered highly
unjust that the south's biodiversity be treated as the 'common heritage of
mankind' and the return flow of biological commodities be patented as the private
property of northern corporations.

One of the significant features of these debates from the point of view of the historical emergence of intellectual property law is that it has even become possible for large multinational corporations to patent naturally occurring substances in the first place. As May (2000) points out, it is unclear in many instances whether the company seeking a patent has in fact 'innovated' in any meaningful way, or whether they have in fact simply 'westernized' traditional methods and exploited Western-designed laws to protect such use. In the case of the Neem tree, for example, which is traditionally found in rural parts of India, and is widely used medicinally, in toiletries, and in timber, food and fuel, a number of US and Japanese multinational companies have been able to patent various chemical elements used in exploiting the products of the tree. This means that not only are they able to establish intellectual property in natural resources, but also that they are able to do so in the face of existing knowledge about that resource's use and in spite of the fact that it already has a widespread social currency. As a number of commentators have pointed out (e.g. Vidal 2000) it seems that the ability to patent naturally occurring substances, even down to the smallest microbe, is limited not so much by whether any innovation has taken place, but rather by the abilities of specific actors to negotiate the complexities of patent laws. In this respect, companies with large budgets for patent lawyers stand to benefit the most.

The second major feature of these debates is the significance of the fact that only certain categories of legally established individual (including, as we have seen, corporations) are able to become rights holders. In other words, ideas, resources and techniques held *in common* cannot actually be recognized as property, and therefore cannot be protected by intellectual property law. As May points out, this goes back to the fact that the idea of common or communally held ownership of resources dropped out of property law in the seventeenth century, but what it means in the current context is that even when the historical expertise and husbandry of nature by specific social groups (such as rural farmers or indigenous peoples) is recognized as embodying 'a significant intellectual contribution' (as was acknowledged in the Convention on Biodiversity Conservation), the intellectual property laws that might protect such stewardship of natural materials cannot recognize 'ownership' other than in terms of the 'legally constituted individual'.

Taken together, these facts mean that the historical dispossession of indigenous people at the hands of Western nations is replicated in two specific ways. Firstly, arguments for the validity of bio-prospecting tend to assert that the resources they seek constitute the 'common heritage of humankind' and, in support of this claim, that they are found in areas of 'wilderness' which have no owners. As Darrell Posey (2004) points out, this ignores the fact that these 'wild' areas are in fact very often *managed* landscapes whose biodiversity has been protected over millennia precisely through practices of sustainable use and the creation of conservation areas. Furthermore, by ascribing no value to the knowledge and stewardship of indigenous and traditional peoples, contemporary bio-prospectors, and the governments and corporations that fund them, assume that such areas and resources are there for the taking, thereby replicating the concept of *terra nullius* ('empty land') that allowed colonial powers to expropriate 'discovered' land for their empires (Posey 2004: 203) from John Locke's time onwards. What follows from this, secondly, is that only certain categories of person (the 'legally constituted individual') can be recognized as potential owners, and this in turn depends not only on the *nature* of labour being recognized in specific ways (what intellectual property laws sees as an 'improvement' is also one that is trade-related) but also on the particular organization of that labour, so that in order for something to be legally protected it must be traceable to an individual owner rather than held in common over generations.[3]

Piracy and Counterfeiting

A further area of conflict in relation to international intellectual property law is that of counterfeiting and 'piracy'. According to Sodipo (2004: 126), piracy is defined as the 'unauthorised recording, copying or broadcasting of any article the subject matter of intellectual property protection, on a commercial scale and for profit', while counterfeiting refers to 'the unauthorized copying of the trademark, labels or packaging of goods on a commercial scale, in such a way that the get-up or lay-out of the cover, label or appearance of the goods closely resemble those of the original'. Thus conventionally piracy refers to articles (such as books, DVDs, computer games) covered by copyright, while counterfeiting refers to goods protected by trademark, although of course both categories are usually brand-name products and many brand-name goods are covered by multiple forms of intellectual property protection. The apparent proliferation of these activities, and the accompanying rise in the number of pirated or counterfeited goods sold, is in many ways a natural outgrowth of the fact that intellectual property law seeks to create a false scarcity in categories of things which, by their very nature, are relatively cheap and easy to produce. Moreover, as I shall suggest below, the scale of response to these activities by Western governments and corporations, as well as their difficulty in enforcing the laws that protect them, illustrate very clearly the centrality of branding to contemporary capitalist accumulation strategies.

The fact that much, although by no means all, of the *production* of counterfeit and pirated goods takes place in relatively poorer parts of the world (and in poorer parts of the 'first world') suggests that such activities should be understood at least in part in the context of the contemporary global division of labour, in which, as we have seen, badly paid and relatively low-skilled manufacturing work takes place in poorer parts of the world while the design and research components (which are both better paid and add most exchange-value to the product) tend to take place in richer areas. In fact, much counterfeiting takes place in the same factories or locations where 'legitimate' merchandise is

Figure 5.1 Clothes with unauthorized logos.

produced, with legal merchandise being produced during the day and counterfeit produce at night (Mertha 2005: 171). In other cases overruns from a legal
production operation are simply sold on to counterfeiters to maximize the
factory's profits, while of course many instances of counterfeiting simply entail
the unlicensed addition of more-or-less well replicated signs and logos to
'generic' goods (Figure 5.1). In any case, what counterfeiting in these contexts
seeks to do, in effect, is to harness some of the 'added value' of the brand name,
for manufacturers rather than trademark owners and retailers, as a kind of sup-
plement to the low-wage manufacturing work that frequently forms the mainstay
of that local economy.

An understanding of the inequalities that underpin such a system is no doubt
part of how such activity is justified by those who take part, but there are additional reasons, both contemporary and historical, why those in poor or developing countries might be resistant to Western attempts to enforce stringent
intellectual property laws in the areas of copyright and trademark. As Sodipo
(2004) points out, many of the intellectual property regimes that operate in
developing countries, and particularly those that were formerly the colonial possessions of European nations, were originally imposed to protect foreign interests in those countries rather than to stimulate or protect local economic
development. Not only have these laws tended to ignore or disregard local conventions about communal, rather than individual, property ownership, they

were also sometimes introduced in ways that deliberately made it easier for foreign, rather than local, applicants to register (Sodipo 1997: 36) or with the intention to protect the trading activities of foreigners rather than stimulate local economic growth. As Sodipo goes on to note, if the initial purpose of the system was not to influence technological or economic progress locally, then it is hardly surprising that the system will now be seen as irrelevant to local people. In this regard, it is also worth noting that some authors (e.g. Ben-Atar 2004) have argued that America's industrial power was itself built in large part upon the widespread piracy and smuggling of mechanical and scientific innovations from Europe during the early republic, with federal and state governments not only knowing about, but actively encouraging, such activity.[4]

As with the issuing of compulsory licenses for patents, flouting intellectual property laws in the areas of trademark and copyright is in any case often a matter of social or economic necessity. Sodipo shows that in Nigeria, for example, the scarcity and overpricing of pharmaceuticals contributes directly to problems of drug counterfeiting, while the low value of Nigerian currency on international markets means that books imported from the UK for educational purposes are prohibitively expensive and therefore frequently reproduced illegally by local printers (2004: 144–5). Equally, the failures of trademark laws to protect consumers in line with their justificatory claims is also a factor in the widespread acceptance for counterfeit goods. Not only do trademarks fail to indicate 'origin' in any meaningful way, but they also increasingly fail to provide any useful guarantee of quality or consistency to consumers, who in some countries have very few direct rights of redress should the contents or quality of a good change or deteriorate (Sodipo 2004: 72). This tallies with a more widespread perception among critics that although the scope of trademark law has expanded in recent years, it has done so in ways that protect trademark owners more than consumers. Specifically, the use of trademark law to protect consumers from 'confusion' as to the origin of products has receded, while its use to prevent the 'dilution' of a company's distinctive image (and hence its investments in design and promotional activities) has increased (Lury 2004: 108–9). The direct social or economic value of trademark law to *consumers* then becomes somewhat unclear, as trademarks increasingly operate more vaguely as 'ciphers for linking the product with what is expected, known and associated with *the mark*, either by way of experience, reputation or advertising hype' (Sodipo 2004: 72, my emphasis).

Perhaps the most important factor, however, in explaining the growth of counterfeiting and piracy is the fact that there is simply an enormous market for these goods. These 'unsatisfied market demands' (Sodipo 2004: 143) may occur for a number of reasons, but the main reason is the combination of intensive marketing activity by rights holders (which creates demand, or at least awareness) and the fact that the goods in question are usually priced so highly that many people cannot afford to buy them. While prices for 'original' or 'legitimate' goods may be kept artificially high to cultivate a brand's 'prestige' or to prevent consumer dissatisfaction at unequal pricing arrangements, the fact that distin-guishing brand features (such as labels and buttons on clothes, or inlay sheets for CDs and DVDs) are in reality easy and cheap to copy and reproduce (espe-cially in low-wage areas) means that demand will be high and substantial profits virtually guaranteed. Furthermore, demand for such goods is hardly limited to poorer parts of the world. The high numbers of Western tourists visiting coun-tries known for the easy availability of high-quality counterfeit goods, and their disappointment when such goods are not available,[5] suggests that the world's poor are by no means the only people interested in liberating the signs, designs, meanings and affiliations inscribed on goods from the profit-seeking enterprise of first-world corporations, nor the only people from whom profits can be made. These consumers are hardly 'deceived' or 'confused' as to the origins of these goods, and are well aware that trademark law protects corporate investment above all; for them, these goods have a social value that does not need to be met only by 'authorized' versions of a particular item or brand. The significance of these social uses for brands and trademarks will be discussed in more detail in the next section.

Anti-counterfeiting Activity: Strategy and Rationale

Unsurprisingly, piracy and counterfeiting activities have drawn a strong response from multinational corporations and their national governments, and one of the more recent developments is the attempt to draw parallels, and in some cases to assert a causal link, between piracy and counterfeiting and other illicit activities such as drug trafficking and terrorism. This in turn is used to justify increasing military surveillance of areas in which counterfeiting and piracy is argued to take place. George Yúdice (2003: 36), for example, shows that the United States has been able to lead a transnational surveillance network in spying on inhabitants of Ciudad del Este in Paraguay, by claiming that software piracy in that area is linked with drug trafficking and terrorism, and that merchants have connections with narcotraffickers and Middle Eastern terrorist networks. As Yúdice points out, these arguments tend to take the form of vague allegations rather than con-crete proof, but by linking the proceeds from the sale of counterfeit goods to the funding of militant Islamic groups, both transnational corporations and national governments have been able to naturalize and justify the use of national police and military forces to protect the interests of companies trading in intellectual property, whilst also creating a rhetoric in which economic security and national security appear to converge.

Of course not all anti-counterfeiting activity involves US-style military surveil-lance, but elsewhere the growth of piracy and counterfeiting in large emerging economies has led to new types of collaboration between representatives of transna-tional corporations and local law enforcement agencies. Mertha (2005), for example, suggests that although US pressure on China to strengthen its intellectual

Figure 5.2 A café in Wood Green, North London, borrows the name and design style of the Warner Bros. comedy series *Friends*.

property laws has at some points been so successful that foreign copyright holders have (once again) been afforded greater protection than Chinese citizens, and TRIPs-compliant provisions were in place in China even before TRIPs actually came into effect, the problem is one of enforcement. Recognizing the substantial financial incentives for workers, and particularly rural or migrant workers, to engage in counterfeiting work, and the fact that the economic and social wellbeing of entire communities may depend upon counterfeiting, foreign corporations have increasingly hired private or quasi-private investigation agencies, both foreign and Chinese, to locate counterfeiting operations, and have then used these agencies to persuade official governmental enforcement agencies to join them in raids. This in turn often involves bribes, side payments and various other incentives such as (in one of Mertha's examples) lavish banquets, karaoke evenings and 'hostess' entertainment for local officials (2005: 165–6). However, even here the rather piecemeal success rate means that foreign companies have recently started to pursue alternative strategies, such as the collective prosecution of counterfeiters (Watts 2005) or the creation of lobbying groups (such as the 'Quality Brands Protection Committee') to protect their interests by direct appeal to the Chinese government (Mertha 2005: 205).

Corporations' and governments' assessments of the amount of money 'lost' to business through counterfeiting does, then, tend to provide the basis for various kinds of anti-counterfeiting intervention, whether it is the lobbying of GATT (and later the WTO) for intellectual property to be included in its international agreements, or the military surveillance of particular regions deemed to be hotbeds of piracy. What tends to get glossed over in such assessments, however, is the fact that money made from counterfeit goods precisely does *not* tally with what 'legitimate' trade might have earned. As Sodipo (2004: 151) puts it, 'it does not follow that if ten copies of an illicit recording are sold for a quarter of the original price, the loss to the industry is ten copies multiplied by the price of the original copy, or even the total cost of the illicit copies, [since] there is no guarantee that purchasers of the illicit copies would have bought the original at the original price'. Indeed, it is precisely because the 'original' versions of pirate and counterfeit goods are usually prohibitively expensive to the majority of the world's population that there is a market for the 'copies' in the first place. What we see, then, is rather a mixture of corporate greed at the prospect of how much money *could* be made if everyone in the world was part of their market, and fear that the prestige (and therefore profitability) of their goods will be compromised if they become too widely available to people, regardless of income and status.

The Meaning of Trademark

This latter motivation for controlling the circulation of pirated and counterfeit brand-name goods – that the reputation of the 'original' will be compromised – is rarely mentioned in corporate petitions to governments and international organizations, but within business circles the relationship between counterfeiting, perceptions of exclusivity and profitability is more explicit. The authors of one business text advising brand owners on protection against counterfeiting take the example of fake Rolex watches, and note that:

> although it is unlikely ... that the Rolex company may have lost a sale to a poten-
> tial real customer, Rolex is nonetheless damaged because there is a palpable *degra-*
> *dation of its brand* when it is so widely available in ... a counterfeit format. Brand
> exclusivity is due in part to its relative scarcity ... Imagine, if you will, what would
> happen if everyone suddenly started wearing fake Rolexes – the pleasure of
> wearing a real one would be diminished. (Hopkins et al. 2003: 12, my emphasis)

In fact, the prevalence of counterfeit goods threatens brands on several levels. The relatively cheap, and perhaps low-quality (or 'obvious') fakes threaten brands by diminishing their exclusive appeal, but the more expensive, and often higher quality counterfeits (what Hopkins et al. call 'true fakes'), which may have been manufactured in the same factories, or with the same materials, as the 'originals', threaten brands by taking business away from the brand owners at the same time as they reveal the size of the premium that the 'authorized' brand owner has charged.

Profits and Values

Corporate profitability does not, therefore, always depend solely on securing the widest possible market for one's goods, but rather may also involve some degree of manufactured scarcity. For some luxury brands in particular, profitability is guaranteed less by the volume of sales than by the tightly controlled perception of exclusivity that allows enormous premiums to be charged. This in turn means that maximizing profits involves a calculation that balances the size of the premium and the size, nature and distribution of the market. A further example of this type of accumulation strategy can be seen in the increasing number of 'limited edition' versions of well-known brands available to consumers, in which the announcement of exclusivity, careful promotion and distribution only through selected outlets allows brand owners to charge much higher prices for these goods than for their more widely available counterparts (Lury 2004).

What should also be clear, however, is that consumers have a significant part to play in the creation of brand values because their 'investments' in brands (in both senses of the word) are not only a source of profit but also a source of meaning and association that can harm as well as help the brand. To put this another way, the damage done to a luxury brand's 'exclusivity' when it is circulated on a wide scale is not simply a matter of numbers; rather, the popular adoption of an allegedly 'exclusive' brand means that the brand becomes intimately associated with the mundane and the ordinary rather than the elite and the particular, thus altering the associations that the brand owner has tried to cultivate. As brands become assets in their own right, and brand 'equity' is measured according to reputation as well as recognition, companies have started to pay much more attention to public perceptions of their brands, and the people or practices with whom those brands become associated. As the following example illustrates, a number of actors may have an interest in tracking the mutations in a brand's reputation and appeal:

Tania do Nascimento, a contestant in the hit TV show Big Brother, is probably not a customer that Burberry would have chosen to flaunt its products in front of an audience of millions. When the shop assistant, who has dated a number of minor pop stars and football players, stepped into the Big Brother house four weeks ago, her suitcase included a Burberry bandanna and bikini, which she has worn with pride ever since. Famous for boasting about her sexual exploits and vowing to spend the £70,000 prize on breast implants if she wins ... retail consultants and brand gurus fear that pictures of a Burberry-clad Tania ... may not enhance the cachet of the luxury brand best known for its famous plaid. 'Burberry is supposed to be an aspirational brand. Are people on Big Brother aspirational?' asked Richard Ratner, an analyst at Seymour Pierce, the City investment bank. The company's profits have soared in recent years ... but more recently it has been adopted by D-list celebrities, topless models and minor actresses ... 'As soon as you go down the mass market road you lose control of

who wears your product,' said John Williamson of Wolff Olins, the brand strategists. (Fletcher 2003)

There is no suggestion here that Tania's Burberry clothes are counterfeits; in fact
the implication is that it is she who is the 'fake'. Simply by being herself she is
supposed to be a threat to the value (and therefore profitability) of a brand that
has invested heavily in creating the aura of exclusivity. The fact that she has
probably paid the full market price may be some compensation for the loss of a
different kind of 'value' that her attachment to the brand represents, but she has
nonetheless played a small part in shifting the popular associations of the brand
in ways that are beyond the company's control. In a context in which the 'sign-
value' of commodities is assumed to be central to the realization of exchange-
value, examples like this are very telling, for they show how far sign-value is itself
the outcome of the (often unintentional) activities of consumers as well as producers. Indeed, for all that brand managers spend a good deal of time and effort
trying to ensure that 'the becoming of subjects and the becoming of value coincide' (Arvidsson 2006: 93), such control is not always possible and brand managers are further frustrated by the fact that it is hard to predict what the
outcomes of these intermittent fluctuations in sign-value might be for the longer
term profitability of the brand. This frustration is of course compounded by the
fact that it is not only counterfeit but also 'legitimate' versions of branded goods
that may be the source of these fluctuations.

Trademarks as Resources for Self-making

Trademarks and other forms of intellectual property may of course be incorporated into individual lives in a number of ways, and some of the uses of brands
by individuals and by groups of consumers will be explored in the next chapter.
The point here is that consumers' uses of brands are increasingly an object of
concern *for corporations*. As we have seen in previous chapters, brand owners are
often very keen for consumers to endow their brands with personal meanings,
and to form attachments to the goods produced under the brand name, but they
are also interested in guiding these meanings and attachments so that they
unfold in ways that are consonant with the brand image that they have tried to
cultivate (Arvidsson 2006). This is particularly so when consumers' uses of
brands move out of the private sphere, and into public media such as television
and the internet. Public 'subversions' of the brand, such as those described
above, are particularly troublesome for brand managers, because their effects are
hard to predict and cannot be contained within domestic spaces or private life-
narratives.

Corporations may go to considerable lengths to guide consumers' uses of
brands and to prevent them from altering brand 'meanings' too fundamentally.
While various forms of advertising tend to be used to promote the 'official' form

of brand identity, companies also employ PR professionals to counter negative publicity and, as we have seen, spend considerable time and money trying to shape the perceptions and uses of brands through the creation of dedicated 'brand environments' and through attempts to build a particular 'context of use' into the product itself (Lury 1997). Increasingly, however, companies also have to deal with more elusive forms of publicity that are harder to control. Rosemary Coombe (1998: 144), for example, suggests that 'trademark rumours' are a natural response on the part of the public to the 'simultaneously pervasive but incorporeal presence of corporate power' in the public sphere, and that such rumours are hard to counter because they often involve a complex relationship between empirical fact and historical truth. Thus the various rumours alleging the Ku Klux Klan's involvement with various American corporations or, more recently, reporting Tommy Hilfiger's alleged displeasure at his brand's popularity among African-American consumers may be empirically false but have tended to articulate broader social truths about the relationship between capitalism and white supremacy. The effects of these and similar rumours are hard to quantify, but the efforts made by manufacturers and brand owners to counter their influence or disprove their claims suggests that they are often taken quite seriously, and particularly, of course, if the groups among whom such rumours circulate are also part of the brand's target market.

The problem for brands is that such rumours tend to move through unofficial and seemingly subterranean channels. The internet has recently become particularly important in facilitating the circulation of trademark rumours and stories, although its use to publicize and comment upon the activities of corporations and brand owners has produced some new developments too. Coombe and Herman (2000; 2002), for example, trace some of the key moments in the history of trademarks on the internet, from the era of 'cyber-squatting' and struggles over domain names to the more sustained attempts to track 'trademark wars' and to highlight instances of intellectual-property-based censorship on the web. They draw attention to the increasing use of corporate names in the metatags of websites, so that people using search engines are likely to come across a company's detractors as well as its official site, as well as to the fact that many corporations have attempted to respond to this by buying up potentially insulting domain names; phone company Verizon Communications apparently registered the domain name verizonsucks.com very shortly after the company itself was formed (Coombe and Herman 2002: 936). They go on to draw particular attention to the widespread attempts by companies to limit and control the use of their brand names, as well as various websites' responses to this. In one fairly well-known example, in 1998 Colgate-Palmolive repeatedly threatened to bring legal actions against the ajax.org website on the basis that it had infringed its trademark (used on a range of cleaning products produced by Colgate-Palmolive), and that this infringement would both 'dilute' the brand's goodwill and lead to consumer 'confusion'. The company eventually backed down, and this was partly attributed to the online petition gathered on ajax.org's behalf, but also to the fact that the site's webmaster had temporarily reinvented himself as an amateur trademark lawyer, responding to Colgate-Palmolive's threats with a compelling argument against the validity of the company's claims:

> [...] the top-level domain 'org' was created for the establishment of free and non-profit organizations, of which the AJAX organization is one. The 'com' domain is reserved for commercial ventures such as your corporation. Furthermore, I hope you understand that the word 'Ajax' is the name of a historical/mythical figure, and as such is not a unique trademark such as 'Cheerios' or 'Pepsi'. (cited in Coombe and Herman 2000: 603)

The author of the letter went on to point out that since the website made no mention of either Colgate-Palmolive or its products, the likelihood of consumer 'confusion' was fairly small, and that a brief perusal of any phonebook would bring up several companies operating under the Ajax name. As Coombe and Herman show, this is only one example of countless corporate attempts to police the online presence of their brand names, which tend to proceed less on the like-lihood that their arguments would be upheld in court, and more on the basis of intimidation and the inability of small, non-profit website owners to fund their own legal defence. However, one of the ironic outcomes of these actions is to fuel an 'emerging popular legal culture' (606) and, combined with the more obviously dialogic opportunities created by digital technology, to stimulate further social and cultural activity in which symbolic forms – and especially those ostensibly controlled by corporate brand owners – are deployed and reworked in the making of communities and identities.[6]

Trademarks and Personhood

To draw this discussion of intellectual property to a close, I want to focus on one final category of intellectual property rights, namely the 'image rights' and 'pub-licity rights' accorded to celebrities. These examples illustrate the ongoing sig-nificance of the relationship between intellectual property and legal definitions of personhood, and the highly asymmetrical outcomes of protecting cultural icons or activities as principally *commercial* goods. Celebrity names and images are, in Coombe's (1998: 89) words, not simply marks of identity or mere com-modities, but also 'cultural texts ... floating signifiers that are continually invested with libidinal energies, social longings and ... political aspirations'. As such, the names and likenesses of celebrities are also very often part of a society's cultural heritage, visual and material objects that 'resonate with meanings that exceed the intentions or the interests of those they identify or resemble'.

For precisely these reasons, however, celebrity names, images and other asso-ciated signs also have a significant potential economic value. As Coombe notes, in an era of standardization and rationalization, the celebrity 'aura' has a 'potent force' and one that is easily capitalized upon as a source of economic value. The fact that celebrity images, 'no matter how often they are reproduced, are ... tied to a specific individual and the substantive duration of a life history' means that consumers may form attachments to celebrities and celebrity images that exceed those induced by even the most beloved brand names, seeing them as embodying their own aspirations for 'recognition and legitimacy', and as human points of connection to a broader social history of which both celebrities and ordinary members of the public are a part. Celebrities that fulfil these functions might include explicitly political figures like Gandhi, Che Guevara or Malcolm X, but also people that have challenged social norms and expectations, people who have excelled within particular fields, people who have overcome discrimination and disadvantage or simply those more 'mundane' celebrities whose life stories appear to resonate with those of particular publics.

However, unlike ordinary members of these publics, celebrities have considerable scope to use the various laws of intellectual property to protect their names and images, and specifically to protect against the 'misappropriation' of their names or likenesses for commercial purposes. In Britain this right has developed through common law into a specific 'tort of the appropriation of personality', while in the United States the 'right of publicity' emerged as a category of the right to privacy (Coombe 1998: 90). Such laws are most often used to protect against the unauthorized use of celebrity names and images in the advertising of commodities, as for example in the 2002 case where Formula 1 racing driver Eddie Irvine successfully sued radio station TalkSport for manipulating an image of the driver so that it appeared that he was listening to, and therefore endorsing, TalkSport Radio (Bent 2003). Yet as Coombe points out, such laws have also been used to prohibit the distribution of memorial posters, novelty souvenirs, magazine parodies, and the presentation of nostalgic musical reviews, television docudramas and satirical theatre performances, thereby compromising free speech and intervening in what many would regard as legitimate cultural activities, simply on the basis that they are also – often only tangentially – commercial activities.

In addition to these 'protective' laws, celebrities may also make use of other intellectual property provisions to pre-emptively protect their name and image and to lay the basis for using it as a future source of revenue. Hence many celebrities have registered their names as trademarks: the footballer David Beckham had, by the end of 2003, registered the names Beckham, David Beckham and Beckham 7 (the number on his shirt when he played for Manchester United) in eight different categories of goods, including clothing, jewellery, leather goods, toys and sporting goods and cosmetic and cleaning preparations. He had also registered a graphic representation of his 'trademark' free kick, and given notice of his intention to register the name Beckham in four food and drinks categories (Milligan 2004: 162). Many other celebrities have made similarly wide-ranging registrations of their names – singer Britney Spears has registered her name as a trademark in the category of inflatable furniture as well as phonograph records (Ferguson 2005) – and the general tendency here is for celebrities to maximise the potential value of their images wherever possible, and to prevent others from doing so (May 2000).

Part of what is so interesting about the legal structure that protects these moves is that it depends, to an ever greater extent, upon a criterion of public recognition as the basis for asserting intellectual rights. As Coombe (1998: 91) notes, 'increasingly, it seems that *any* publicly recognizable characteristic will be legally legitimated as having a commercial value likely to be diminished by its unauthorized appropriation by others'; what this means in practice, however, is that celebrities are able to expropriate *social* knowledge and *public* significance as private property, even though it is precisely the activities of the public, in 'recognizing' the celebrity, that create celebrity status in the first place. Hence while a celebrity footballer like David Beckham may serve as a role model or 'moral compass' for young people (Wicks et al. 2006), the role of the public in creating this situation is unrecognized in legal terms, even though it creates the means by which his likeness can be exploited as a mode of capital accumulation and, increasingly, *only* made available to the public through branded goods and licensing agreements. 'Ordinary' members of the public, by contrast, have been much less successful in efforts to establish image or privacy rights, which suggests that being publicly or socially 'valued' (i.e. recognized) has now become a precondition for certain forms of legal protection (May 2000). In fact, as we have seen, there is a significant conflation of different forms of value here, since the general emphasis on 'trade-relatedness' in intellectual property legislation tends to favour those 'legal individuals' who can turn intellectual property into economic value over those who may have actually created the social value upon which intellectual property depends in the first place (May 2000).

Conclusion

This chapter has outlined the role of various types of intellectual property in providing both content and protection for brands, and has noted in particular that the forms of protection offered to brand owners (as opposed to consumers) by intellectual property law have been considerably extended in recent years. This has taken place both through the growing tendency in case law to favour a 'dilution' rather than 'confusion' definition of trademark infringement, and also through the international framework provided since 1994 by the TRIPs agreement, which emphasizes 'trade-relatedness' as the principal focus for international interventions in this area. In this latter respect, I have also noted the extent to which the formulation of contemporary intellectual property law facilitates the replication of the types of exclusion and dispossession that accompanied the original making of Western 'property'.

I then turned to the issue of piracy and counterfeiting and suggested that the growth of these activities is due in large measure to the artificial scarcity inherent in the making of intellectual property, but more specifically to the fact that many pirated or counterfeit goods (such as music, books, clothes and medicines) are items that have a wide social appeal, often as an outcome of aggressive marketing activity on the part of multinational corporations, which cannot be satisfied under the current terms of international trade. Many poorer communities depend upon employment in counterfeiting work for their survival, and on the purchase of counterfeit or pirated goods to satisfy their needs as well as their wants. In these contexts, acceptance of counterfeiting activity may be further compounded by the (not unreasonable) belief that intellectual property laws are constructed in such a way that they tend to favour the profit-making activities of individuals and groups that already have considerable resources at their disposal, rather than those who do not.

An additional reason for the relatively widespread acceptance of pirated or counterfeit goods is the lack of obvious benefit, in many instances, of buying an 'original' version. This is particularly true in cases where the use-value of a good resides either in its intellectual content or in its sign-value, both of which can easily be replicated without significant damage to other owners. These issues also, however, draw attention to the specific kinds of use-value contained in branded, as opposed to generic, goods, and to the ways in which publicly recognised trademarks and brand names are incorporated into the meaning-making activities of individuals and groups. In the latter parts of the chapter I have paid particular attention to activities that intentionally or unintentionally *alter* the sign-value of brands, but it is also important to note the more mundane ways in which branded goods are used to confer not simply status, but also value and meaning, upon their owners. This in turn takes us back to the issue of possessive individualism which, as we have seen, underpins both historical and contemporary formulations of the relationship between property and personhood, as well as providing the rationale for the existence of intellectual property itself. In Locke's account, property is intimately linked with freedom; as Jane Gaines (1991: 19) puts it, 'property is premised upon freedom, the ownership of oneself and one's own labor', and hence 'if you can't own yourself you can't own other property, and if you can't even own property, then how can you possibly be said to own yourself?'

If modern personhood is defined in large part through the disposition to possess, and if communal or collective forms of ownership lack any kind of public or legal recognition, then the specificities of both individual and collective life narratives increasingly depend upon the ownership of branded goods, both licit and illicit, for their expression and recognition. For what brands confer is precisely not the generic and the ordinary, but the specific and particular. This is perhaps most obvious in the case of celebrities, whose stories are 'shared' through television and magazines (and the various forms of image rights and licensing agreements through which such 'sharing' is regulated), but also increasingly through branded commodities – modelled, as John Frow (2003: 68) points out, on 'the effect of unity of a person' – and the forms of domestication and tactile appropriation that these make possible. That these money-making activities are legally recognized and protected while the activities of the celebrity's (or brand's) audience are not is indicative of the partial and uneven recognition of the public interest under most intellectual property regimes. Yet as we have seen in this chapter, the public's appropriation of brands – whether they are celebrities, clothes or music – continues to exceed the boundaries set for it by an increasingly stringent international intellectual property system.

CHAPTER 6

National Brands and Global Brands

The early chapters of this book explored some of the ways in which national and imperial themes were incorporated into brand identities, both through branded packaging and in the design of branded goods themselves. In some cases, I argued, these branded goods did not simply express or reflect broader political preoccupations, but played an active part in the circulation of popular national and imperial consciousness, bringing national or imperial imagery and concerns into the most mundane forms of consumption. This was particularly the case in Britain, where opportunities to display British goods (whether in shop windows or international exhibitions) were also opportunities to promote Britain and its Empire, but it was also true for the United States, where the iconography of the city, or futuristic space-related themes, were part of a concerted effort to arrive at an 'indigenous' style for national production (Woodham 1997). Equally, however, many manufacturers in the United States were quick to see the potential of a more 'international' style to aid the marketing of their goods overseas, and later British branding consultants such as Wally Olins would argue that corporations wishing to compete in an international economic arena without protected markets should seriously consider shedding the national connotations of their brands.

Yet Olins also noted reasons to be cautious in the development of overarching 'global' identities; 'people', he warned, 'don't like it when their roots are torn up and thrown away in the interest of some homogenizing force for neatness' (Olins 1978: 50). Although strong and clear brand identities could provide 'reassurance' in a rapidly changing world, he argued, trends towards regionalism and devolution were becoming more important and should be taken seriously. How far are such trends still in evidence today, and what has their impact been upon branding and marketing? The export activities of some Western corporations and brands have been argued to lead to a homogenization of both cultural practices and public spaces (Ritzer 1993; Mathiason 2006), and powerful transnational corporations have been heavily implicated in the (sometimes forced) opening of national markets to greater international trade and investment. Companies like Merck, Pfizer and DuPont were key players in getting the international harmonization of intellectual property laws onto the agenda of the

Uruguay round of GATT/WTO talks, and critics of the current international trade regime have drawn attention to the role of such corporations in driving down the wholesale prices of goods and the wages paid to manufacturing workers (e.g. Klein 2000), not to mention the trade and investment-related conditions attached to proposed aid programmes for poorer countries (Buckman 2005). How, if at all, have corporations responded to such debates in their marketing strategies? How far are consumers aware of these issues and to what extent does it influence their consumption choices?

Both large and small corporations have, unsurprisingly, been eager to exploit the new openness of international markets, and have paid considerable attention to the means by which they can successfully establish their brands in those markets, and gain the edge over local or international competitors. As in domestic markets, the ultimate unpredictability of consumers' uses of, and responses to, brands has in no way diminished companies' attempts to control and shape these factors. Many of the debates within business and marketing circles still revolve around the extent to which a relatively uniform 'global' branding and marketing strategy is appropriate for particular goods, or whether instead a more 'localized' approach is preferable (see e.g. Van Gelder 2003; Usunier and Lee 2005). Similar questions have been raised about whether brand names should be synchronized across markets, how franchises should be managed, and so on. But these debates increasingly proceed in tandem with a more explicit attempt on the part of corporations to locate and understand the *cultural* meanings that become attached to branded goods as they circulate in different contexts. At a time when corporations increasingly draw upon information about consumer trends and tastes in the construction of brand identities and business plans, consumer perceptions of the national or regional origins of goods – and the values they associate with these areas – are often factored into corporate strategy in ways that create new opportunities for commercial activity, as well as new risks to be negotiated.

What this means in practice, as we shall see below, is that while national governments continue to argue about the terms of international trade, and in particular about the vulnerability of poorer countries to new rules on international investment and the trade in services (see Buckman 2005), commercial organizations operating at a range of different scales, as well as non-commercial actors and political parties, are themselves increasingly focusing on the cultural dimensions of globalization as part of their own branding strategies. At the same time, the representations of consumer trends and tastes made by corporations in their strategic and research activities rarely reflect the full range of ways in which brands are used by consumers. Brands are not only used to aid routine consumption decisions or to register consumers' identification or dissatisfaction with the activities of particular corporations; they are also used to symbolically connect consumers to particular places, to represent individuals and families as 'normal', to distance consumers from what they imagine to be 'mainstream' tastes and to mark relations of inclusion and exclusion, among many other things. In this respect, the national and international connotations of particular brands are only one among a number of elements influencing the choice and use of goods, although as the latter parts of this chapter will suggest, they are often folded into these other dynamics in interesting ways.

Global and National Brand Strategies

The first section of this chapter, however, focuses on the production of brand identities and uses a number of examples and case studies to illustrate some of the ways in which companies and their marketing agencies have begun to grapple with issues arising from shifting relationships between national 'bases' and international, or potentially international, markets. As we shall see, although there are relatively few truly 'global' brands, there are certainly companies operating in particular market segments who are attempting to harmonize their brand identities and marketing activities across borders, often by deliberately removing potentially 'national' connotations and associations from goods and services and from the promotional complexes surrounding them. Equally often, however, brands seek to consolidate their 'national' identity and domestic markets, or to cultivate national qualities as integral characteristics of their brands, on the basis that these can be used effectively as promotional tools in an international market. This has led in some cases (such as that of Geographical Indications and 'Protected Designation of Origin' status, see pp. 126–30) to the creation of profitable local, national or regional monopolies. Such examples reflect the continuing, and in some cases growing, salience of national identities in the context of globalization, and also provide an insight into the ways in which commercial operations attempt to calibrate different possible configurations of global, national, regional and local characteristics of goods with reference to what is known or perceived to be known about the attitudes of consumers in particular markets.

Global Marketing Convergence and its Limits

I want to begin, then, by looking briefly at some of the ways in which the globalization of markets allows for branding and other marketing activities to become more synchronized and used in a relatively uniform fashion across different territories. This, after all, is the kind of activity that many people assume leads to a kind of 'cultural homogenization', or to the gradual eradication of meaningful differences in cultures and public spaces in different parts of the world. This is also the kind of development that many in the business world had anticipated, and indeed hoped for, in the early stages of a more intensified period of economic globalization, since it was imagined that companies would in the future be able to exploit substantial economies of scale in the production of their advertising campaigns and other marketing material. This is not necessarily how things have unfolded, as we shall see, not least because the majority of exports from North America and Europe continue to flow to other countries in those same regions (World Trade Organization 2005). Nonetheless, a number of companies and advertising agencies remain committed to the attempt to harmonize marketing output, with the aim of achieving greater economies of scale in the longer term.

One of the first things to note is that the extent to which the synchronization of marketing output is possible depends in part upon the particular market segments involved. In certain product categories (such as foods and alcoholic drinks, for example), markets are widely assumed, by both corporations and marketing agencies, to be predominantly national in character, and to be driven by local conventions or taste differences (Denehy 2005). In such markets, profitability for large multinational corporations may sometimes depend less upon the export of brands from one country into new markets, and more upon their ability to purchase brands that have already established strong reputations and a large market share in those territories (although this may in some cases be constrained by national laws and regulations). Similarly, while the export of brands like McDonald's lends itself to arguments about cultural imperialism and homogenization (Ritzer 1993), such cases are, in some product categories at least, less common than the purchase and maintenance of national and local brands by transnational corporations, who can then use these brand names as the basis for future marketing activity and brand extensions into new or related product categories.[1] Cases like this illustrate why brands increasingly drive mergers and takeovers, but are also indicative of the perceived difficulty of establishing new and 'foreign' brands in contexts far from their place of origin, where other brands may have already gained considerable customer loyalty and become integrated into routines of everyday life.

Of course many 'foreign' brands already have an established presence or reputation in particular countries for geopolitical or historical reasons, such as European colonization and its legacies, or the massive expansion of international exports by America during and after the Second World War. In these cases, expansion from one product category into another is easier, and so, potentially, is the harmonization of branding activity across different national markets. Yet whether such harmonization actually takes place also depends upon other local and institutional factors. In the first instance, it may depend upon the perception of key players *within* an organization as to whether such harmonization is desirable or strategically appropriate, and this is likely to vary according to the beliefs of key personnel as well as on the particular product category in question. It also depends upon the advice given by marketing and branding agencies; some advertising agencies, for example, are known to favour the international harmonization of marketing content more than others. Large international agencies tend, unsurprisingly, to be particular proponents of such an approach, but even within this kind of structure national or regional offices are in some cases able to retain control of particular campaigns. They are particularly well placed to do this if they have previously run campaigns that have been perceived to be successful, if the national market in which they operate is the dominant one within a given region, or if the brand has been 'indigenized' by consumers to such an extent that they believe it to be a 'national' brand (Denehy 2005).[2] Within Europe, for example, if a brand is particularly strong within one country then the qualities assumed to define this market will tend to be prioritized within advertising campaigns, and less attention will be paid to local or national differences within other, less developed, markets in the region. This will lead, in some cases, to the production of television advertisements aimed primarily at one market but dubbed into several different languages so that they can be used in neighbouring countries.

As some advertising practitioners point out, the risk in taking such an approach is that it will actually compromise the ability of the brand to grow and expand in these less developed markets (Denehy 2005). Nonetheless, many large brands and marketing agencies *do* aim towards a greater integration of brand identities across national borders, in essence trading these risks against the cost savings for themselves and their clients. What is notable, however, is that they rarely believe that truly *global* campaigns are possible, and aim instead to shift from national to supra-national or regional campaigns. This in turn will often entail a 'lowest common denominator' approach, in which agencies explicitly aim to reduce the advertising output for a given brand to as few 'versions' as possible without these becoming entirely unintelligible to specific national markets. Describing the strategy for Olay skincare products within the Europe, Middle East and Asia 'region', for example, Micky Denehy of Saatchi and Saatchi's London office points out that the agency currently runs two separate advertising campaigns for the brand, but aims in the longer term to bring these two campaigns together. Indeed, according to Denehy, the advertising campaign in the Middle East region is 'deliberately set on a target to *educate* those consumers, to bring them along ... initially by making it a very straightforward "this enriches your skin", but behind it we know where we want to get to [which] is making women feel better about their skin' (Denehy 2005, my emphasis).[3] The end goal of this multi-stage campaign, then, with all its attendant suggestions of cultural 'lag', is to be able to use the same script and narrative across all markets. Although the agency would still end up shooting two or three different versions of the same advertisement (using different models), there will still be both considerable production savings and, perhaps more importantly in the longer term, a global brand with a global 'message'.

In terms of how this regional harmonization is achieved, two things are important to note. The first is that large agencies like Saatchi and Saatchi can and do put together multinational teams (what they call 'tribes') of account directors and creatives to produce 'non-national' campaigns that are acceptable – or at least, not actively alienating – to multiple markets. Hence Denehy describes the creative team for Saatchi and Saatchi's campaign for Toyota as comprising up to eight different nationalities, who are tasked to work together over a period of time to develop 'truly non-national ideas' and to eliminate themes that rely on local or national idiom or humour. The second, and arguably more important, factor facilitating this synchronization is the fact that conventional advertising often makes up a decreasing proportion of overall marketing activity, and that other means are increasingly used to address what are imagined to be local or national issues. Thus, as Denehy notes, large multinational companies like Procter and Gamble are withdrawing a good deal of their spending from 'above the line' (mostly television) advertising campaigns and putting it instead into 'below the line' marketing, particularly new 'point of sale' techniques to be used in shops.[4] Similarly, Denehy notes that although the overall brand 'message' for a company like Visa is the same in most countries in Europe, part of what makes this possible is the growing use of below-the-line methods for more strategic local campaigns, such as, in Britain and other European countries, the use of direct mail and credit card statements to encourage people to make more of their smaller purchases by credit card. What this means is that the regional harmonization of brand identities in advertising is often accompanied by a more differentiated approach within national contexts through non-advertising (and heavily design-led) techniques. There is, in short, an impulse to save money on the more expensive parts of marketing activity (i.e. television advertisements) through synchronization, but to transfer such savings to other aspects of marketing activity (such as direct marketing and other 'below-the-line' options) that are increasingly seen as more effective. This does not mean that there is no 'homogenization', but rather that such homogenization usually takes place regionally, rather than globally, and that it tends to be restricted both to particular product categories and to those aspects of marketing that often make up a decreasing, rather than increasing, proportion of overall marketing activity.

Re-making National Markets

The balance between national and non-national elements in marketing campaigns remains, then, an important strategic concern for branding consultants and other marketing professionals, and reflects assumptions about particular product categories (whether or not they are fundamentally 'national' in character) as well as about markets themselves. For global brands operating in product areas deemed to be driven by local or national market dynamics, integrating some element of national specificity into marketing campaigns can be an important part of efforts to fend off competition from more locally embedded rivals, and to distance oneself from claims of cultural homogenization. In Britain, for example, global food and drinks brands like Coca-Cola and McDonald's have in recent years attempted to imbue their marketing efforts with a 'local' or national sensibility through involvement with various football-related activities (Figure 6.1), including sponsorship of Championship football (Coca-Cola) and the training of local football coaches (McDonald's). These

campaigns are not limited to Britain, and both brands are involved in the sponsorship of football in other countries and at international level; the point, rather,
is that while much of the television advertising for these brands remains non-
national, their other marketing activities have increasingly been oriented towards
forms of activity, such as football, that are assumed to be characterized by deep-
seated local or national affiliations, with all the affective intensity that goes with
this (see Chapter Four).

Figure 6.1 Billboard advertisement for Coca-Cola used in England during the football World Cup 2006.

In some cases, however, the national connotations of a particular brand may
be a cause for concern and may become the subject of efforts on the part of the
brand to shift its perception among a particular market or part of a market.
During the late 1990s Guinness, for example, conducted substantial consumer
research which found that young people in Ireland, and particularly those in the
sought-after 18–24 age group, had a very negative view of the brand, which they
associated with older generations of Irish people and with the dominant institutions of government, the national media and the Catholic church. Broader social
and economic shifts in the country were argued to have caused a split between
the 'old Ireland' and a 'new Ireland' (Patel 2001), and Guinness appeared to be
associated by young consumers with the 'old' Ireland from which they wanted
to distance themselves. Furthermore, these consumers were found to be highly
media-literate and increasingly disengaged from Guinness's advertising campaigns, which typically circulated through established national media channels.
For this reason, national television and press advertising were believed to be part
of the problem rather than part of the solution, since they simply replicated the
process by which younger consumers became ever more alienated from the
brand.

Guinness was understandably concerned about these shifts,[5] and in 2000
began a marketing campaign aimed at re-branding Guinness within this market

of young Irish consumers through non-traditional means. It hired the London office of international marketing agency KLP, which specializes in 'experiential' marketing campaigns, to produce a music-related marketing strategy aimed at changing perceptions of Guinness among young Irish consumers. Between 2000 and 2003 Guinness staged four two-day music festivals in County Meath, modelled on the Glastonbury and Reading festivals held annually in the UK, bringing together international artists and bands, including many Irish acts. Most of the publicity for the events was conducted in 'ambient' form, through the use of flyers in bars and clubs and internet chat forums, and there was a deliberate attempt to circulate information through 'word of mouth' rather than conventional media (see Moor 2003 for more details). Coverage of the festival by niche media (such as music and lifestyle magazines) based *outside* of Ireland was actively sought, since these were assumed to be more 'credible' sources of information for the target market, while deliberate attempts were made to exploit differences *within* the target market (e.g. distinctions of 'hipness') as a way of building a reputation for the brand even prior to the event.[6] Coverage by national media *after* the event was considered useful in so far as it might create demand for subsequent festivals and related music events, but the main aim was to engage the target market through 'their' media and spaces, and by avoiding 'mainstream' coverage at most stages of the promotional campaign (Musselbrook 2001). These media, to reiterate, were both 'below' the national (flyers in clubs, bars and on the street) and 'above' it (British or international style and music publications), despite the fact that it was a *national* market that was being targeted.

The agency employed to design and produce the events has run similar 'experiential' marketing campaigns in other parts of the world for other drinks companies, including a DJ tour sponsored by Pepsi in Eastern Europe and music festivals sponsored by Smirnoff in Kenya.[7] Such developments are of interest in their own right, of course, and relate to the growing tendency to create branded environments and experiences, outlined in previous chapters. What is interesting here, however, is the specific combination of national and international elements used in such strategies. The aim of the Guinness re-branding campaign was not to *displace* the historical connection between Guinness and ideas about Irishness, but rather to remove the association between Guinness and the so-called 'old Ireland', and to replace this with a reworked notion of Irish identity with which it was believed that young consumers would have more of an affinity. This in turn was achieved in large part by re-situating the brand within the context of a more international music scene, and a more international – but also less mainstream – set of media.[8] This did not preclude holding on to the potentially positive or useful aspects of the link between Guinness and national pride or loyalty, as was evident in the prominence given to the idea that Guinness was providing Irish citizens with a festival to 'rival' those held in England. Similarly, later stages of the re-branding campaign involved a series of live events designed to showcase young Irish musical talent and thus to demonstrate Guinness's 'commitment' to the

Irish music scene. Nonetheless, the broader context in this and similar campaigns is that although they may ostensibly be aimed at a 'national' market, they increasingly seek to locate that market through a configuration of local and transnational, as well as national, media and spaces, which in turn will reflect a company's perception of the extent to which the nation itself is constituted out of a combination of, or interaction between, national, international and subnational elements.

National Brands and the Global Division of Labour

Presumed national affiliations and identifications may, then, be very much retained in contemporary marketing strategies, either because a particular brand, its parent company or its marketing consultants have chosen to approach each national market separately or, as we shall see in some of the examples below, because the national connotations of a brand are themselves considered useful marketing tools as the brand circulates in other markets. Emphasizing a brand's national origins is not a new phenomenon, however; Chapter Two described how integral national and imperial themes were to early brand identities, and how these in turn sometimes fed back into national consciousness itself. The marketing of goods based on implicit or explicit comparisons with those produced in other countries is also an ongoing theme (Molotch 2003), and many brands continue to conduct 'country of origin' surveys to assess how consumers respond to goods originating in different parts of the world (Lury 1997). Such approaches have, if anything, become more important as markets have become increasingly international, and as companies increasingly seek to avoid negative consumer perceptions that could damage brand 'equity'. International markets have also led producers to search for new points of product differentiation, and in some cases to develop strategies through which the meanings conventionally associated with places can be transferred to objects.

This section focuses on one specific version of this phenomenon, involving the US-based clothing company American Apparel and its efforts to use national qualities in the exploitation of a niche market (see Littler and Moor 2008). Initially set up as a wholesale business providing high-quality T-shirts for printing, the company has since become a retail brand with 145 stores in eleven countries and sales that have doubled or nearly doubled every year since 2002 (Dean 2005).[9] What makes the brand especially interesting is that its identity has been built in large part upon a marketing strategy that emphasizes its 'ethical' credentials and contrasts its American production base with the outsourcing activities of its competitors. Specifically, the company's ethical claim rests upon the fact that it does not outsource manufacturing to low-wage areas outside of the United States, but rather manufacturers all of its goods under one roof in Southern California, where it pays a 'fair' wage to employees who are often migrant workers from Mexico, and who, the company claims, might otherwise be subject to considerable exploitation in 'sweatshop' conditions.

In positioning itself in this way, American Apparel inserts itself into long-standing debates about the relationship between *global* flows of people, capital and goods, and *national* cultures and identities, and engages directly with the anxieties that such flows generate (Bender and Greenwald 2003). In addition, by emphasizing its 'sweatshop-free' status, the company evokes a broader historical understanding, prevalent in the United States and other Western nations, of sweatshops as essentially a 'foreign method of working' (Bender 2003) opposed to, rather than continuous with, the American factory system, considered a model of efficiency and civilization. And by conjuring up such associations at a time when citizens are increasingly anxious both about the loss of 'American' jobs to overseas production facilities and the exploitative labour conditions upon which such outsourcing may often depend, the company is further able to key into patriotic sentiments that derive much of their potency from ideas about the moral superiority of America and other 'developed' nations (Littler and Moor 2008). All of this entails a series of careful rhetorical manoeuvres in which the historical, and indeed contemporary, existence of 'sweatshop' working conditions *within* the United States must be simultaneously evoked and then attributed to 'foreigners', whilst the 'foreign' workers that make up much of American Apparel's manufacturing workforce (i.e. Latino/a migrants) must be construed as appropriate beneficiaries of this new company's ethical mission because of their capacity for upward mobility through American values of meritocracy and hard work.

American Apparel's multinational workforce, and its largely Latina manufacturing workers in particular, are indeed crucial to the construction of the company's place-based brand identity, which emerges not only through its national appellation but also through copious references to the fact that its products are 'Made in Downtown LA'. Assessing the reasons for the large number of clothing manufacturers based in Los Angeles, Bonanich and Applebaum (2003: 157–8) suggest that it is not only the availability of cheap (i.e. immigrant) labour and the well-developed regional infrastructure that explains its value to the garment industry, but additionally the global cultural significance of the region, which ensures a ready-made market for its cultural products. They argue that the 'mystique of the location of origin' ('images of sun and surf ... people who are wealthy and glamorous') adds value to the goods produced here, since these acquire in the popular imagination some of the reputation of the place and its characteristics (see also Molotch 2003). American Apparel adds a further element to this configuration by drawing attention to the historically multi-ethnic quality of Los Angeles and its proximity to the Mexican border. Photographs of the company's staff and of different parts of LA's downtown area adorn the walls of its stores from London to Tokyo, while its international website contains many images of the Los Angeles workforce and short worker biographies and testimonials. In this way, the huge domestic market for goods that are 'Made in America' can be supplemented by an international market of young, middle-class consumers who are also attracted by both the promise of a more transparent chain of production and an implicit celebration of the role of 'life-enhancing' marginal populations in the lives of global cities (see Yúdice 2003; Castells 1998).

There are, perhaps unsurprisingly, certain contradictions that emerge in the company's position, which creates brand value, and considerable profit, out of its pro-immigrants' rights position, while nonetheless remaining privately owned and non-unionized. The company's CEO, Dov Charney, has made frequent pronouncements about the value of migrant workers to the Californian economy and the fact that these workers lack the legal recognition that would entitle them to proper rights and benefits. As part of this campaign (which, as I have suggested, is a significant part of the company's *brand* strategy) Charney has expressed support for a policy floated by President George Bush prior to the 2004 elections to grant currently undocumented workers temporary work permits or 'guest worker' status. Yet this policy proposal is by no means widely supported, since it would expose migrant populations – many of whom have lived in the United States for many years – to a much higher degree of state surveillance, which could lead to forced return at a later stage when their presence is deemed surplus to economic requirements. Cast in this light, American Apparel's support for this particular policy proposal looks very expedient, and illustrates the asymmetry between the company's interests and those of its workers; while the company can derive a competitive advantage from employing migrant workers at a 'fair' wage, it does not actually need its workers to be permanently, or legally, settled, and it can derive international brand value from its Los Angeles location and Latino/a workforce regardless of the latter's *actual* legal status or domestic circumstances.

Examples such as this suggest that the contemporary global division of labour not only offers considerable economic advantages to those companies who outsource aspects of production to low-wage parts of the world, but also creates new opportunities for those brands that are able to exploit the ethical gaps in these arrangements as a new market niche. 'Ethical' trading initiatives of various kinds can be seen in a range of sectors, such as agriculture, where there is a growing market for organic seed varieties and other organisms (Hudson 2005: 51), while in the UK the supermarket Waitrose has attempted to consolidate its reputation for 'fair play' in its sourcing practices through the creation of the 'Waitrose Foundation', which channels some of the surplus value extracted at various points in the supply chain back to South African farmers who produce its citrus fruit.[10] Yet as the company admits, the project – which allocates grants for educational and health projects via its board of trustees – is not linked to the broader Fairtrade Foundation, but rather is a 'Waitrose branded product'. As a proprietary form of 'ethical trading', it does not have to abide by externally formulated rules, but rather, like American Apparel, can set its own terms of 'ethical' conduct and market them in such a way that they create brand equity for the entire company (whose commodities extend well beyond citrus fruits), while the project as a whole further tightens its control over the supply chain.

The recognition of such activities as a new market niche illustrates very clearly that it is possible to acknowledge and even partially respond to the inequities of the current global division of labour, while still leaving its wider structures intact. Indeed one might argue that companies pursuing this approach in fact *depend upon* wider structures remaining in place, and on the general lack of response to international labour conventions, as the basis of their own competitive advantage. In a context in which relatively educated and well-off consumers across the globe are becoming more aware of the divisions and inequalities upon which their freedom to consume depends, companies like American Apparel are able to use national myths and stories, and apparently novel configurations of the chain of production, as a means to both reassure and derive profit from those consumers who have the economic and cultural capital available to re-imagine their own place within those structures. Needless to say, such a situation, in which responsibility for 'ethical' behaviour in matters of trade is devolved to individual companies (who can use it to create brand equity) and consumers (who can use it as a source of cultural capital), is very much of a piece with a neo-liberal or free-market agenda that sees very little role for the state and international organizations other than as facilitators of such market encounters.

Geographical Indications

Exploiting the potential of these new niche markets depends, then, to a large degree upon an appeal to the cultural, as well as economic, capital of wealthier consumers; that is, to the knowledge and skills that enable them to make 'appropriate' selections from a range of choices. This knowledge is especially important in a context in which commodity chains have become longer and more complex, and in which information about the provenance or origins of particular goods is both more detailed and harder to disentangle (Hughes and Reimer 2004). Under these conditions, an understanding of the complicated transnational networks through which commodities are assembled and distributed may become an additional mechanism for the display of cultural competence, while from the point of view of major corporations such understandings can be harnessed as a source of brand value and as a way of offsetting the risks posed by cheaper competitors.

Assumptions about the relationship between country of origin and the nature or quality of goods date back to the earliest forms of international trade, where the acquisition and ownership of 'exotic' foreign goods became a source of distinction for wealthy consumers in western European countries who were the first to feel the benefits of the expansion of international trade (Mukerji 1983). Such forms of distinction persist to this day, but the 'insider knowledge' on which they depend has not only become more complex and hard to unravel, but has also frequently mutated into stereotype and rumour. This has been particularly true with increasing international competition in trade, as Western corporations have sought to maintain historical advantage in particular trade sectors in the face of a gradual dissolution of favourable trading relationships with former imperial dependents. One example of this is the threat posed to European and American manufacturers of electronic goods by the emergence of a strong Asian electronics industry from the 1970s onwards. The negative associations with these goods in the minds of many Western consumers, at least for a certain period, emerged as much out of stereotypes about 'Asian sweatshops' and assumptions about the inferior quality of components as out of any historical reality. Governments have often allowed such rumours to flourish and have played an important role in encouraging 'patriotic' forms of consumption to lessen the impact of competition from abroad whilst taking advantage of it through liberal trade laws at an international level.

Brands have also, as noted in the previous section, made explicit efforts to build 'national' or place-based qualities into their products. One example of this is the Swiss watch company Swatch, which, as Celia Lury (1997; 2000) has shown, has not only incorporated references to its national home in its name (an amalgam of the words 'Swiss' and 'Watch'), but has also flagged up the 'transparency' of its manufacturing process in many of its design features. Nicolas Hayek, one of the senior executives at Swatch, has argued that 'if you can surround your product with your own culture ... it can be a powerful advantage ... Europeans and Americans are damn happy if you can show that their societies are not decadent – that every Japanese and Taiwanese worker is not ten times more productive or more intelligent than they are' (cited in Lury 1997: 87). Cases like this, where there is an explicit effort to imbue brands with 'cultural' elements of national identity, add a further level of complexity to debates about relations of production in an international market, since presumed knowledge about contemporary practices – the 'quality' of Swiss watch-making, for example – cannot help but remain embedded to a certain extent in stereotypes about some places and implicit or explicit comparisons with others.

For those nations able to avoid negative stereotypes, however, the circulation of 'national' brands on global markets may open up new possibilities for exploiting national identity and reputation and showcasing it on a wider stage (Figure 6.2). Such attempts to trade on the historical connotations of, or stereotypes about, particular places and the goods produced there have in recent years acquired a significant degree of international legal protection, through the use of exclusive 'Geographical Indications' on goods, often known in Europe as 'Protected Designations of Origin' (see Gangjee 2006; Parry 2006; Rangnekar 2004). Geographical Indications are protected as intellectual property under the TRIPs agreement (see Chapter Five), which permits member countries to protect goods that include 'indications which identify the good as originating in the territory of a Member, or a region or locality in that territory, where a given quality, reputation or other characteristic of the good is *essentially attributable to its geographical origin*' (World Trade Organization 1994, my emphasis). Hence

Figure 6.2 Advertisement for Guinness at a bus stop in central London.

'Parmesan cheese', for example, can only be produced under the authority of the Parmigiano-Reggiano Consortium of producers in Parma, Italy. Additional higher level protections are provided for wines and spirits, where the regulations allow WTO member states to prevent the use of 'their' geographical terms by producers in other countries, even when the *actual* country of origin is also indicated (e.g. Champagne that is clearly identified as 'Made in Australia' rather than France) or where the indication is qualified by suffixes such as 'kind', 'type' or 'style' (e.g. 'Champagne-style drink').[11]

More recently, some WTO member countries have attempted to extend this higher level of protection to all types of goods, a move that is argued by some to be justified by provisions in the Doha Declaration, although this is contested by others. In 2005 the European Union proposed an amendment to the TRIPs Agreement so that all categories of goods would be eligible for the higher level of protection, and also be covered by a multilateral registration system currently being negotiated for wines and spirits. These proposals for extension are supported by a number of countries, including India, Jamaica, Kenya, Madagascar, Mauritius, Morocco, Pakistan, Sri Lanka, Switzerland and Turkey, who argue that extending the higher level of protection would help them to market their products more effectively by differentiating them from those of their competitors, and preventing these competitors 'usurping' their geographical terms. By contrast, those opposing extension, including countries such as the United States, Australia and Canada, but also Chile, Colombia, Ecuador, Guatemala, Honduras, Panama, Paraguay and the Philippines, argue that extension would interfere with their own entirely legitimate marketing practices, and that accusations of 'usurping' are inappropriate given that many of the products, production methods and geographical names at stake were brought into these countries by migrants, who have used them in good faith for considerable periods of time.

The contours of this debate are quite complex, since the higher levels of protection have so far tended to favour European producers, even though their extension is supported by many developing countries and Geographical Indications are seen by many commentators as having the potential to promote rural development and protect indigenous knowledge (Rangnekar 2004). In the area of wines and spirits, European producers have been able to prevent 'New World' producers from using geographical indicators such as Champagne, Port and Hock, and some European countries have even sought to lay claim to generic winemaking words such as 'reserve' and 'vintage' (Denny and Elliott 2002). At the same time, the fact that countries such as India, Jamaica, Mauritius and Kenya support the proposals for extension suggests that the protection of Geographical Indications might help the international trading ambitions of historically disadvantaged countries, who have nonetheless developed reputations in particular areas of production, and who without protection might see the 'goodwill' associated with their reputations exploited by other countries. The debates around this topic do not look likely to be resolved anytime soon,[12] but what is significant about these discussions is the attention they draw to the continuing importance of place-based marketing under conditions of economic globalization. Perhaps even more notably, they highlight the relevance of *historical* trade-related reputations of particular countries (themselves forged out of unequal, and often exploitative, economic relationships) for the *contemporary* marketing activities of corporations, and the apparent willingness of international intellectual property agencies to protect these.

Assumptions that globalization would lead to a homogenization of cultures and the absorption of cultural differences have, in recent years, received considerable criticism, with authors noting, for example, the vigorous defence of national identities and the emergence of new nationalisms, as well as the processes of heterogenization and indigenization at work in the consumption of globally available goods and technologies. Assumptions about the vulnerability of smaller nations to global economic cycles, instability due to global financial speculations and a higher level of dependence on foreign exports have had to be qualified to take account of the fact that, for some nations, globalization has also opened up new opportunities for state agency, and specifically for the creation and export of commercially valuable representations of nationhood (True 2005). New Zealand, for example, has been able to exploit its historical reputation for being 'pure', 'clean' and 'green' and package these values as a brand that can be attached to a range of goods and services, from kiwifruit to the provision of film locations (True 2005). What is also clear, however, is that the ability to act is this way is highly unevenly distributed. While some countries have been able to exploit (or fabricate) distinguishing 'cultural' qualities and production methods as a source of legitimate marketing advantage, other countries have been forced to adopt generic economic models – such as structural adjustment policies – that flatten out existing differences between places and pay no attention to local contexts or needs (see Miller 1998).

The implications of this for marketing and branding are twofold. Firstly, despite evidence that some brands are seeking to 'de-nationalize', and indeed to 'homogenize', their images in order to exploit economies of scale in certain aspects of marketing output, it is also the case that many brands are seeking to exploit the historical relationships (or perceived relationships) between places, people and goods for competitive advantage and for the purposes of building brand equity. Secondly, such associations between places and goods in many cases emerge from historically unequal or exploitative economic relationships, such as those put in place by the European conquest of the 'New World', by the IMF and the World Bank, and more recently by the WTO. Such inequalities are often compounded by new trade and development rules that consolidate these associations into specific marketing *rights* based on a very limited conception of the relationship between place and 'culture'. This in turn means that while some countries are able to use national brands as routes to economic development, others are prevented from developing new areas of comparative advantage and remained trapped, in international trade terms at least, as providers of generic labour.

The Uses of Brands: Consumers

Such legacies also make themselves felt in the sphere of consumption, where brands may become connected to particular spatial qualities and to perceived relationships between people and places at different geographical and historical moments. Work in anthropology has emphasized the realm of consumption as a space in which value is attributed and in which all manner of relationships may become elaborated and reconfigured, and recent interventions have stressed in particular the need to study chains of consumption and modes of provisioning as well as chains of production (see e.g. Hansen 2000; Gregson and Crewe 2003; Raghuram 2004). Furthermore, the success of brands like American Apparel, above, has in large part been due to the existence of a growing popular discourse that encourages predominantly Western consumers to act in ways that deliberately and consciously *reflect upon* what is known about aspects of the chain of production and incorporate these into consumption practices. Brands have played a significant part in this attempt to address consumers as activists

(Daunton and Hilton 2001), whether in the form of the 'anti-brand' politics of writers like Naomi Klein (2000) and organizations like Adbusters, or the emergence of an agreed Fair Trade logo and discussions of the 'ethical' credentials of various brands in national media.

Brands and Migration

Just as traders have for a long time highlighted the national or 'cultural' qualities of their goods, the current context is not the first in which particular forms of consumption have been encouraged as a means to address international, as well as national, concerns (see Littler 2008), or to re-make the connections between different parts of the globe. Similar issues were outlined in Chapter Two, where it was shown that both commercial and government-funded institutions in Britain encouraged the consumption of Empire produce as a means to hasten post-war economic recovery and to ensure future growth, as well as to prop up Empire itself. In the nineteenth century some parts of the anti-slavery movement in Britain emphasized the need for boycotts of slave-grown produce as a means to register opposition to the slave trade and to deprive its products of a market (Ware 1992: 72–3), while more recently the emergence of a 'green capitalism' and corresponding 'green consumerism' has sought to persuade Western consumers that the purchase of particular brands of goods constitutes a form of international political action in its own right (Ware 1992: 245–8).

Examples such as these involve a very explicit attempt to imbue consumption practices with a political or moral purpose, yet an ethical impulse can often be traced even in those consumption activities that appear relatively unselfconscious or habitual. Indeed as Howard and Willmott suggest (cited in Barnett et al. 2004), practices of thrift and a concern with price and affordability are perhaps the most fundamental ethical issue for the majority of people on a limited budget seeking to feed or clothe a family or loved ones. This has become an especially pressing issue as the costs of meeting basic survival needs have increased, in many countries, more rapidly than incomes (Lodziak 2002). However, even apparently mundane forms of provisioning can be opportunities to enact a practical ethics and to counter alienation. As Daniel Miller (1998: 192) puts it, in ordinary and mundane forms of consumption 'the smallest social groups, even individuals, confront objects that, in their production, express the very abstraction of the market and the state. Yet, through purchase and possession, people can use those objects to create worlds that strive to be specific and diverse precisely because we wish to escape from our sense of alienation from the[se] vast institutions.'

Consumption, from this point of view, is not only a habitual practice (Appadurai 1996) but also has a ritual quality: 'hardly ever about individuals or subjectivities ... it can be better understood as a ritual ... devoted to the construction of key relationships and the objectification of devotional love' (Miller

1998: 194). Yet what drives such ritual behaviour, and the worlds it seeks to create, varies a great deal. Arjun Appadurai, for example, has argued that changing patterns of migration have had a significant impact upon the kind of work that consumption is called upon to do. The 'deterritorialization' brought about by the movement of populations, he argues, creates new markets for a range of products that 'thrive on the need of the deterritorialized population for contact with its homeland' (1996: 38), and brands with strong place-based associations, or those with a 'strong element of nostalgic identification' (Miller 1997: 106) are often able to expand their export activities considerably by catering to the needs of these populations. This clearly creates another incentive for the exploitation of place-based qualities described in preceding sections, although elsewhere Appadurai is careful to note that the play of the imagination is such that place-based identifications do not always correspond to actual historical experience in any straightforward way; people use the place-based and cultural connotations of commodities in highly idiosyncratic ways, and in some cases the 'invented homelands' that emerge from these long-distance and commodity-mediated relationships may, when combined with what Appadurai calls the 'internal colonialisms of the nation-state' (1996: 38), be exploited by national governments for a range of political ends.

Indeed although Appadurai's analysis of the relationship between migration and consumption emphasizes the need for 'invented homelands', his work also highlights a new set of potential roles for brands when he notes that migration itself throws up critical questions about social and cultural reproduction in new locations, and specifically the 'politics of *representing a family as normal* ... to neighbors and peers in the new locale' (1996: 44, my emphasis). Such questions, he argues, are particularly vexing in a context in which both points of departure and points of arrival are in 'cultural flux'. While the consumption of brand-name goods from a place of origin may indeed be experienced as a necessity for deterritorialized groups, this rubs up against a further need to 'fit in' to one's current home, and to demonstrate one's viability as a new subject of a particular nation and one's commitment to that place (see also Pun 2005).[13] This is particularly likely to be the case in situations where there is anxiety about the arrival of migrant populations or hostility, perhaps even violence, towards these migrants from 'host' populations. We have seen in Chapter Two that 'patriotic' or nationalistic consumption has often been construed as one of the responsibilities of capitalist citizenship in various nations (see for example Ewen and Ewen 1982), but this may not only be an external imperative to consume the brand-name goods of a new nation, but also a more subjective need to avoid appearing too obviously different. Although migrant populations may require connection to their homelands for the purposes of ontological security, their movement through the public spaces of their new homes may also require them to fit in – either through the consumption of national brands or in some cases through visible commodity signifiers of global capitalist citizenship.

Sub-national Distinctions

Consumption practices may therefore be animated by pressing 'local' concerns as much as by broader transnational horizons or histories, and are likely to illuminate intra- as well as inter-national dynamics and distinctions. As Arvind Rajagopal (2001: 317–18) points out, in a context in which consumer society is more or less coterminous with society itself, the ability to consume and the choice of things consumed may offer 'a gauge of the distribution of power and the patterns of participation … [and] of the nature and quality of citizenship available, and the benefits it makes possible'. Holding this in mind, an attentiveness to the inter- and intra-national distinctions at play in practices of consumption is helpful in thinking about how and why particular types of branded goods become desirable or meaningful for consumers at given times, and why the national or international 'origins' or connotations of those goods may become significant.

To begin with, then, consumption choices clearly reflect differences *internal* to nation-states, perhaps the most obvious of which relate to distinctions of class and status. In the following example, taken from Beverley Skeggs' interviews with working-class women, Skeggs describes the ways in which knowledge of the connotations of different items of brand-name clothing is used in processes of distinction and the search for 'respectability':

> [For Jane C] having the right labels becomes a construction of 'rights' (as opposed to 'wrongs') … Every item comes with a label which signifies her knowledge and her difference … Jane C's desire to own the right objects includes herself. She knows the clothing signifiers of working-classness such as shell suits and she is careful to mark her distance from them. Clothing and objects are experienced intimately: they signify the worth of the person. This is not just about difference but also about deflecting associations of negative value. They are ways of distancing oneself from the pathological and worthless. (Skeggs 1997: 86)

Here class divisions within the nation provide the backdrop to consumption choices, which relate not only to the *economic* necessity of finding affordable clothes on a budget but also the *social* necessity of finding goods that will help the subject to avoid negative judgement from others. Certain brand names are attributed with a protective quality that can deflect negative associations, in a context where being deemed 'worthless' is an ever-present danger, but also in which both embodied cultural capital (knowledge about the connotation of different brands) and objectified cultural capital (the brand-name goods themselves) are imagined to offer some protection.

In more middle-class contexts, however, brand-name goods may be marked with connotations of negative, rather than positive, value. Gregson and Crewe's work on second-hand consumption practices (Gregson and Crewe 2003; Gregson et al. 2000), for example, shows that although these practices are often motivated by concerns with thrift, they are also seen by many consumers as encoding a good deal of knowingness and skill. Second-hand shopping, with all the time and effort of searching and sorting it entails, deliberately elevates cultural over economic capital (2003: 100), thus undermining the attempts of other consumers, such as those described in Skeggs' work, to 'buy' cultural capital in objectified form through brand-name commodities. For some consumers, the authors suggest, 'the more outlandish and obscure the site of purchase, the more symbolic value comes to be invested in particular purchases and the greater its 'boast' value' (Gregson and Crewe 2003: 100). In these contexts, brand names – especially those with a 'mass market' resonance – tend to be avoided and denigrated. Consumers searching in retro shops for home furnishings describe shops like Ikea as providing 'unrisky form of prescribed taste' for 'lazy shoppers' (101), while large shopping malls were also 'abhorred, loathed and universally avoided within this group ... despised for their prescriptive practices and regulation of taste'. Such mass-market brands thus figure as a limit case for certain groups of consumers with the cultural capital to 'constitute taste with certitude and without anxiety' (101–2). For those lacking this cultural capital, by contrast, brand names are often useful in authenticating purchases as coming from a 'good' source and for offsetting the perceived risks associated with second-hand shopping (their connection to unknown other bodies, the danger that people will think you don't have much money). These risks are, needless to say, felt much more keenly by some people than others.

At one level, then, brands or their absence in consumption practices are clearly related to *intra*-national distinctions based on inequalities of class, gender and, as we have seen above, to ethnic or national origin. The national or place-based connotations of brands are often folded into these distinctions in ways that emphasize critical distance and knowingness as well as the forms of identification highlighted by Appadurai and others. Hence in Alison Clarke's study of 'nearly new' sales of children's clothing, one middle-class mother in North London rejects a polyester Disney nightdress sent to her by family members in America because she considers Disney merchandise to be 'exploitative and non-educational' (2000: 87) and because she dislikes synthetic materials. While such choices undoubtedly reflect the application of range of tacit skills to the caring work associated with motherhood (89) they also imply not only the display of cultural capital but also its reproduction, as the informant in this case explains to her six-year-old daughter why she is not allowed to own an object that otherwise holds an 'unsurpassable appeal' for her. To the extent that such knowledge is bound up with broader constructions of 'good mothering', these local responses to 'global' commodities are themselves to be understood as actions that imply judgements about other consumers and the choices they make.

Thus although brand choices may be motivated by a range of moral or ethical concerns, this does not necessarily make them benign. In Britain during the 1970s and 1980s, for example, many young, male football fans were part of the 'Casual' subculture, which was known in part for its preference for 'designer' clothes and brand-name goods, many of which, in turn, were more usually associated with continental Europe, and with middle- and upper-class leisure spaces, such as tennis (Tacchini, Ellesse), golf (Slazenger, Pringle) and country sports (Burberry, Aquascutum) (Armstrong 1998). Although many of these brands are thought to have been 'discovered' by fans through their travels to watch their teams play in European competitions, their use and display has been understood in terms of an attack on middle-class privilege and a desire to challenge the 'snooty-nosed middle classes' (Hewitt and Baxter 2004: 195). In other words, the use of 'foreign' brand-name goods was made meaningful in more 'local' contexts where it was construed as a way of challenging implicit taste hierarchies that reserved certain forms of bodily adornment and dress for more powerful social groups. Yet this subculture was also founded, arguably, upon exclusionary forms of fraternal association (Moor 2006), with brand-name clothes frequently used to taunt and humiliate other fans, and to mark territorial claims and boundaries. As one of the informants in Hewitt and Baxter's account of football and fashion explains, with regard to the choice of footwear for Casuals, 'Nike were shite … too American, and hence too commercial', whereas 'Puma were the business, as were Reebok with that British flag that reminded you that you were part of a scene that was a white working-class British phenomenon and there's fuck all wrong with that' (cited in Hewitt and Baxter 2004: 193). The use of brand names in this context might have been motivated by a desire to challenge certain forms of hierarchy and privilege – that is, to counter a particular form of alienation – but it was by no means incompatible with their use to shore up other types of hierarchy and privilege elsewhere.

A second example of this more exclusionary mobilization of brand names can be found in the forms of popular economic nationalism that have often accompanied attempts at trade liberalization. I have alluded to this above in the brief discussion of European manufacturers' responses to the emergence of a globally competitive Asian electronics industry, but it can also be seen very clearly in the actions of consumers. As Dana Frank (1999) shows in her history of various twentieth-century 'Buy American' campaigns, ordinary consumers have regularly responded enthusiastically to government- or union-led efforts to contain the impact of trade liberalization and rising imports from foreign countries through 'nationalist shopping' and anti-import mobilization. Furthermore, these allegedly 'patriotic' acts have frequently descended into widespread anti-Asian racism and the invocation of older forms of anti-Asian sentiment, often linked to the Second World War. Thus for example the demise of large parts of the American automobile industry from the late 1970s and early 1980s led to the expression of hostility not only towards Japanese car firms but also to Japan and to all other Asian nations (1999: 162–3), and to the emergence of a war-infused rhetoric of 'beating the Japs', resisting 'invasion', and so on. During this period racist stereotypes about 'cunning' and 'sneaky' Japanese economic strategy were both promoted and condoned by the media and public figures (227–9), while the movement from depictions of an 'economic war' to suggestions of a real war led to divisions between ordinary people, in which many people (but especially those involved in the automobile workers' union) scrutinized their fellow workers' buying behaviour for evidence of 'unpatriotic' activity (165).

In many of these examples, the relationship of 'global' or foreign brands to specific national or local contexts is not one of 'takeover' or homogenization, but rather a more subtle process by which brand names are incorporated into the service of a range of personal or social concerns (the making and re-making of class distinctions, the practices of motherhood, and so on). What is more, brands often become significant in their new contexts not through their adoption but in fact through their rejection, where they come to stand in for the ability of individuals to resist broader structures or processes that might otherwise be experienced as beyond their control. This is perhaps most obvious in the case of popular economic nationalism (and, one might argue, in some forms of anti-globalization activism), where government actions or changes in relations of production are experienced at the level of citizens and consumers as the activities of brands and the people or places to whom these brands become attached. Hence particular brands or national-branded goods may be avoided while at the same time others become, or become perceived as, indexes of fellow citizens' assumed allegiances and beliefs.

Brands and the State

These kinds of consumer responses to, and uses of, brands are, as I have suggested in previous sections of this chapter, something that large corporations increasingly seek to track and measure, through consumer research, 'country of origin' surveys and similar techniques. National or regional governments, too, may have an interest in following such developments; states have often been involved in efforts to encourage nationalistic forms of consumption, or have attempted to influence the extent to which exchange activities become connected to the pursuit of national or imperial projects, as in the case of the Empire Marketing Board, outlined in Chapter Two. State actors have also influenced the consumption of particular brands by choosing, or refusing, to impose trade sanctions on other countries during times of war or political unrest, and states' involvement in international trade talks – including the alliances they do or do not forge with other nations – also have an impact upon the volume and type of commodities entering and leaving their countries.

One example of this is states' rules on foreign direct investment. In India, for example, foreign direct investment in the retail sector is currently only permitted for 'single brand' stores and for franchise operations. This means that large supermarket-style retailers (like Wal-Mart and Tesco) are kept out (Figure 6.3). The measure is designed to protect smaller local retailers, although major European and American brands such as Zara, Nokia, Gap and Nike are able to either operate their own stores or else to license their brand names and associated

Figure 6.3 A Tesco supermarket in Malaysia. Rules on foreign direct investment mean that foreign-owned supermarket-style retailers are currently able to operate in some countries but not others (© Tesco plc).

proprietary techniques and procedures to Indian retailers, who then run their stores for them as franchise operations. This has led to a significant expansion of the Indian retail sector and to the growth of large private retail groups, such as Planet Retail, who make much of their income from opening stores such as the Body Shop and Mothercare in major Indian cities (Ramesh 2006). It also means that other Indian retailers, from small market stall holders to large supermarket chains, are often able to capitalize upon brand awareness of Western goods among wealthier Indian families by selling single items or product lines from British stores. Although this situation is unlikely to continue indefinitely, state intervention has nonetheless been able to exert some influence over the terms by which Western brands develop in India and over the people to whom the benefits of this development accrue.

In political terms, however, many states are facing challenges to their authority, not only from the 'outside' in the form of international laws and regulations, but also from inside their own borders, in the form of various kinds of internal dissent and the claims of what Appadurai describes as 'groups with ideas about nationhood' (1996: 39). In this context, according to Appadurai, 'the nation and the state have become one another's projects', with those groups seeking 'nationhood' trying to capture or co-opt state power, while states at the same time seek to monopolize ideas about nationhood. For both of these projects the 'ideoscapes' and 'mediascapes', of which brands comprise a part, are useful resources. One of the key examples of this dynamic in Appadurai's account is the way that various states seek to produce or exploit fears of 'Americanization' or 'commoditization', particularly in relation to their own internal minorities, as a way of quashing dissent and propounding of a view of external threats as more dangerous and urgent than their own hegemonic strategies. Yet such dynamics are also visible within the United States itself, where some commentators have argued that a fear of outsiders, and particularly of international terrorism, has been stoked and exploited by those inside the country for both political and commercial ends, creating a distraction from significant internal divisions while creating new market opportunities for a range of commercial operations, from book publishers and media channels to technology producers and private security firms (Harris 2006). Such dynamics can also lead to a revival of familiar forms of economic nationalism, which again can be exploited for political as well as commercial ends.[14]

As Appadurai also notes, however, states that might find it politically expedient to play up the risk of 'homogenization' through external economic and cultural influences very often find themselves pressurized to remain open to those very influences because of forces of global media, technology and travel, as well through their membership of organizations like the WTO. This in turn is argued to fuel consumerism and the desire for (often Western) goods in ways that may sit rather uncomfortably with the nation-state's own projects. These desires for foreign goods may in turn become 'caught up in new ethnoscapes, mediascapes, and, eventually, ideoscapes, such as democracy in China, that the state cannot tolerate as threats to its own control over ideas of nationhood and peoplehood' (1996: 40). The state in this sense must become the 'arbitrageur in this *repatriation of difference* (in the form of goods, signs, slogans, and styles)' (42, emphasis in original). Some countries, however, have greater power at their disposal with which to argue for special exceptions and the protection of national privileges in matters of international trade. Both the European Union and the United States have been notoriously intransigent in their attempts to protect their right to subsidize their own producers and to get special treatment in the forms of exemptions for what they deem to be 'sensitive products', while France in particular has frustrated other nations with its insistence on protecting its own cultural products (such as television, films and music) and attempting to exempt them from general trade rules. Not only is such power to 'resist' trade liberalization unevenly distributed among nations, it can also be disingenuous in its appeal to the protection of 'cultural diversity'. As Alison Beale points out, French and Canadian efforts to protect 'cultural diversity' in international trade forums are more appropriately seen as attempts to protect their own national capital interests rather than 'national identity' as such, and this does nothing to protect nonprofit arts initiatives nor to defend internal minority cultures in any serious way (cited in Yúdice 2003: 223).

Figure 6.4 The We Are Londoners, We Are One promotional campaign was launched by the Greater London Authority after the bomb attacks of 7 July 2005 to 'show that the people of the capital were proud to be part of a united city' (© Belinda Lawley).

Finally, states can also employ local versions of commercial design and branding techniques for their own non-commercial ends. Some of the examples in Chapter Four illustrated the ways in which the British government has made use of design and branding techniques – and independent branding consultancies – not only to increase efficiency in the delivery of public services and to create new identities for government departments, but also as part of efforts to inculcate a more 'active citizenship' and to find 'new sources of common identity' at a time when presumed ties of ethnicity and religion are weakening (Figure 6.4). This use of branding as a technique of governance involves concerted, and coordinated, efforts to work on the 'percepts and affects' of governable populations (Deleuze cited in Rose 1999: 32), and its use is becoming more common, in part for the reasons outlined by Appadurai, above. Bhatt (2001: 188–9), for example, details some examples of the branding of Hinduism by nationalist groups inside and outside of India during the 1980s, as part of a broader 'political semiology' of Hindu nationalism involving the 'loading [of] affect onto symbol'; while Rajagopal (2001) describes the emergence of what he calls 'Retail Hindutva' – including the commodification of religious objects and imagery in the form of stickers, buttons and armbands, as well as other popular cultural forms – as an element of efforts to foster popular participation in, and acceptance of, a Hindu nationalist version of Indian identity. In both cases such commodification and branding activities existed alongside a more ambivalent relationship to the foreign brands introduced by free markets, seen by some within these groups as threats to their own plans for a strong national state (Rajagopal 2001: 63).

Conclusion

Although large multinational companies unquestionably benefit from their overwhelming location within powerful nations, who lobby on their behalf for beneficial international trading arrangements, the brands owned by these companies frequently operate within specific national contexts as emblems of an ever-present threat of Americanization or homogenization, which can in turn be used to conceal what may, in reality, be more pressing threats from forces internal to a particular nation or state. These forces may, as we have seen above, make use of the same types of marketing techniques as these commercial organizations, while some of the larger and more geopolitically powerful emerging economies have retained some power to control the pace at which international trade, and foreign direct investment, proceeds. Yet as other examples in previous sections have made clear, the ways in which branded goods are actually *used* in specific national or local contexts does not in fact suggest global assent to a unified Western 'mindset' of consumerism, so much as a tactical and selective incorporation of particular goods into more locally embedded projects, whether intra-class distinctions, efforts to become 'metropolitan', the consolidation of links with 'home' or efforts to accrue cultural capital through an assertion of distance from the commodified realm. Consumption remains, then, a site at which alienation from state or market institutions may be countered, and more personal or social projects be pursued, even if such projects are by no means guaranteed to be benign.

Brands, however, remain attuned to the place-based connotations of their goods, and in some cases have responded to the globalization of markets with deliberate efforts to play up their *national* specificity and to use this as the basis for the promotion of goods (both commodities and, increasingly, destinations) abroad. This continues despite the fact that some global brands appear to be aiming towards a harmonization of their imagery in order to cut costs, and to establish a unified brand 'message'. Such developments suggest that the alleged opposition between political logics concerned with nationalism and capitalist logics of globalism may not be so strong as once claimed, and indeed that the two forces may often serve the same material ends (True 2005). Yet the power to legally protect the place-based connotations of goods often depends upon historically unequal global trading relationships, and may end up reinforcing such divisions by creating regional monopolies and barriers to entry for other economic actors (Pike 2006). Attempts by companies operating in more developed markets to promote their brands on the basis of their 'ethical' credentials may similarly depend upon historically grounded assumptions about the relationship between place of origin and product quality, in ways that are sometimes facilitated by the absence of any internationally agreed legal rules or benchmarks against which such claims might be assessed. Indeed both of these cases suggest that the 'problem' of branding in an international context is less a matter of the homogenization of cultural meanings and practices, and more a matter of the uneven, and often hypocritical, ways in which national governments and international agencies approach the regulation of trading rights and responsibilities. The future for both national and 'global' brands, in other words, looks set to depend not only upon the economic and political barriers to 'free' trade, but also upon the legal framework that determines the kinds of histories, reputations and qualities to which particular brands are able to lay claim.

CHAPTER 7

Conclusion

This book has made a number of claims about brands and branding: that they organize forms of economic activity; that they render a greater array of materials communicative and informational; that they attempt to give concrete physical form to abstract values and concepts; and that they try to influence the perceptions and behaviour of customers and citizens. It has also argued that brands are objects of research and measurement, and that their development is bound up with changing definitions of, and uses for, the laws of intellectual property. Brands often incorporate ideas – and stereotypes – about particular places, cultures and histories, and their circulation across national borders sometimes gives rise to concerns about the shape and form of an increasingly global order, as well as – in some cases – creating new resources for the construction of meaning and for forms of connection between groups. In this final section of the book, therefore, I want to review some of these claims, and to consider once again what the rise of brands can tell us about business, politics, consumption and culture in an increasingly global era.

The Business of Branding

The early chapters of this book were concerned with the economic context for brands, the means by which brands get produced and the ways in which branding and re-branding exercises are conducted. These chapters traced the emergence of corporate identity consultancies and the development of brands as assets, and linked these to the rise of more design-intensive forms of production, to the growing number of mergers and acquisitions from the 1980s onwards, as well as to the rise of the service sector in advanced capitalist economies. These chapters may, perhaps unavoidably, have given the impression of a smoother and more linear trajectory for the rise of branding than was actually the case, although Chapter Two tried to illustrate the unevenness of the development of industrial design in Britain and America, and the social, economic and political reasons for this. Branding, as I noted in the first chapter, is an ongoing process because it is constantly receiving new inputs and updates, and a contingent process in the sense that it does not take the same shape, or have the same effects, in every context. Chapter Three drew particular attention to the many resources and types of knowledge and expertise utilized by branding consultants in their work, including focus group and survey findings, marketing and business books, industry journals and supposedly 'scientific' testing and experimentation processes. These are combined differently by different actors, who often claim to employ their own creativity and intuition in the interpretation of branding texts and the findings of research, and in the application of these to specific cases. Of course there are reasons to be sceptical of such claims to personal style and creativity, for these are often territorial claims designed to boost one's position within an organization or to distinguish oneself from others working in similar occupations. Yet nor should such claims be dismissed out of hand, since they point to something that is well known about the practices of capitalist organizations, namely that they are embedded in the practicalities of business life (Carrier 1998; Thrift 1998), which includes the particular orientations and projects of specific actors in specific institutions. This means that branding ideas and principles are applied differently in different contexts, and that those working in branding consultancies and design agencies are rarely able to implement some 'pure' form of branding logic – even if they wanted to, and even if such a thing could be identified – because they constantly rub up against the constraints put in place by other actors (lack of money for research, lack of information about consumers) and the more general constraints of operating in 'real time' rather than the abstract time of templates and models (Thrift 1998).

The first chapter suggested that since branding now operates as a fairly powerful conceptual abstraction, it is also useful to consider how far it also operates as a form of political and economic virtualism – that is, a 'practical effort to make the world conform to the structures of the conceptual' (Carrier 1998: 2). As Carrier and Miller (1998) point out, however, for such conceptual abstractions to become instances of virtualism, they must be granted the power and the means to be implemented in the real world in a generic or acontextual fashion. There is currently little evidence of such power and influence; branding is perhaps the most dominant form of marketing discourse currently in circulation, but it still lacks the institutional power of many other species of economic thought, and it does not only change the contexts in which it is applied, but is also itself changed by those encounters. There are, at the same time, some branding consultants who are more immersed in, and more committed to, the abstract conceptions of branding prevalent in business and marketing publications, and who display a relatively greater disposition to see these implemented in a 'pure' form. A number of the informants cited in Chapter Three have subsequently gone on to set up their own smaller consultancies – guided, no doubt, by their own interpretation of what branding is 'really' about – but even with the power that comes from running one's own business they are still likely to come up against all manner of practical constraints, including lack of funds, time constraints, resistance from clients and many other contextual factors that demand recognition and incorporation.

What we might consider, instead, is how far branding is likely to remain central to corporate strategy in the future, and with what kinds of effects. I noted in Chapter Six that some countries' rules on foreign direct investment have so far tended to privilege single-brand stores and franchise arrangements rather than multi-brand outlets, and this suggests that brands are likely to remain important drivers of economic expansion for the next few years at least. It also suggests that the trend for retailers to tighten their control over the supply chain by manufacturing their own brands – and by promoting these through carefully designed 'branded environments' – is likely to continue. Equally, of course, design and branding consultancies will probably have to continually diversify, rework and update what they offer if they are to remain competitive, and it will be an important task for economic sociologists and others to assess the mutations and impact of branding and strategic design initiatives as they expand into new areas and consolidate their institutional power. Indeed one of the main arguments of this book has been that there is an ongoing need to track the social, political and economic uses of design as it becomes increasingly central not only to corporate profitability but also to a wider range of social and political initiatives (such as those outlined in Chapter Four). This will involve looking beyond the world of conventional advertising – even though the changes wrought on advertising agencies by branding, experiential marketing and strategic consultancy are interesting and important – in order to consider the sometimes more mundane, but far more wide-ranging, work that now gets accomplished under the heading of design.

The Materiality of Branding

This book has also, through its attention to design, placed considerable emphasis on the *materiality* of branding, and has tried to dispel any idea that the outputs of its activity are simply abstract signs, logos and buzzwords. I have argued, to the contrary, that branding consultants – and especially the many branding consultants with backgrounds in design – are highly attuned to the materiality of communication, and to its tactile and immersive qualities. As such, branding consultants play an important role in the production of increasingly communicative surfaces, spaces and objects, and in the attempt to imbue relatively mundane categories of things with symbolic and informational content. This, of course, has been an ongoing trend over the past few years, linked to a more general shift in marketing practices (Slater 1997) as well as to processes of informationalization (Lash 2002; Manovich 2000) and the longer history of creating communicative surfaces in art, design and architecture (Colomina 1994; Venturi et al. 1977). Nonetheless, the work of branding has now become a major driver of this trend, to the extent that its work involves making perceptible changes to a product or service and its environment or 'ambience', and the translation of abstract values from one sensory form to another. Branding is underpinned, in other words, by the belief that the material content of clothes, car upholstery, uniforms, urban furniture and the design and layout of buildings, among many other things, can embody brand values and 'narrate' them to others with demonstrable effects on practice, and in ways that are often deemed to be socially and politically, as well as economically, useful. My claim has not been that this necessarily works in reality in the ways intended and conceived by planners, but rather that branding is above all a material practice, and that branding consultants – to a much greater extent than other types of marketing personnel, and in ways that have often been overlooked by the disciplines of sociology and cultural studies in the past – have the power to change our environment and everyday sensory experience.

Brands and Politics

The latter chapters of the book have addressed some of the more explicitly political dimensions of branding. Branding has become more of a political concern in recent years, firstly, because it has in some cases driven changes in the definition and scope of intellectual property laws and been linked to the international harmonization of those laws, their increasing trade-relatedness, and with more concerted efforts to enforce such laws at a global scale. Secondly, branding has become an explicitly political matter because it has been linked by those in the anti-globalization or 'global justice' movement to questions about the global division of labour and about consumers' responsibility for acting or speaking about such issues through their consumption practices. One of the outcomes of this latter development, as I noted in Chapter Six, has been the creation of new market niches for companies seeking to exploit the ethical gaps and anxieties created as global inequalities become more extreme and more visible. As part of this trend, there also appears to have been an increase in the number of companies seeking to engage with public concerns about 'fair trade' in only selective or one- or two-dimensional ways, and to do so individually rather than in concert with international organizations and benchmarking initiatives. Thus American Apparel, one of the examples from Chapter Six, claims to be an 'anti-sweatshop, anti-brand' company that pays its workers above the minimum wage, but provides little evidence to verify such claims and will not allow its workers to join unions (it also has a bad record on sexual harassment). Similarly the British supermarket Waitrose has set up its own 'Fair Trade Foundation', but it operates in only one product category (citrus fruits) and is not part of the official Fair Trade network. In instances such as these, branding is not the opposite of ethical trade, but rather the point of it – companies can build brand equity through selective engagement with those aspects of the fair-trade discourse that appear to have most effectively caught the public's attention. My point in using these examples has not been to single them out for particular criticism – they are, in many ways, more responsible than their competitors and their contributions to discussions of business ethics are not to be overlooked. Rather, the point has been to show that the broader structure remains one that allows, even encourages, such selective engagements with ethical matters, and that this has the effect of skewing debates about ethics towards individual decisions and brand choices, rather than broader systems and structures. This may mean that the forms of exploitation entailed in the production of non-branded commodities, whether sold directly to consumers or exchanged between companies, remain virtually invisible to all but the most dedicated activists. Similarly the labour and environmental exploitation involved in the making of car parts, mobile phones and computer processing chips (for example) often remain invisible as mainstream media focus on the more spectacular (and often more feminized) examples of high-fashion clothing and domestic food purchases.

There are, in any case, reasons to be cautious about a situation in which ethical behaviour becomes a matter of market exchange between private individuals and companies, rather than a matter for national governments or international institutions and agreements. Apart from the fact that this is precisely the route that neo-liberal governments would like to see taken (for it makes ethical behaviour a matter of individual 'freedom', and avoids too many awkward confrontations between government and big business), it also means that ethical practices will be limited in scope and uneven in distribution. Any individual consumer item is invariably made up of many different components, practices, relationships and structures, and expecting consumers to unravel these complex commodity chains (Hughes and Reimer 2004; Gereffi and Korzeniewicz 1994) and distinguish between their different components is a lot to ask, even if it has recently become something of a middle-class obsession. Under such conditions, 'ethical' goods and services (which are also usually *branded* goods and services) will continue to function like luxury goods – that is, goods we place more value on as we become richer – and like positional goods, where 'the practical devices through which a universalistic responsibility is made possible is also a means of socially and culturally differentiating certain classes of persons from others' (Barnett et al. 2004: 9).

Reversing such a trend will have to involve an effort to harness genuine and positive forms of consumer concern about relations of production and distribution and to direct these towards the more mundane, but probably more effective, forms of political engagement embodied in pressure groups and lobbying organizations that work with governments and institutions rather than merely advising individual consumers on the 'right' brands to buy (and the ones to avoid). This will be difficult insofar as the appeal of market-driven forms of politics may depend to a large degree on the absence of more substantive initiatives elsewhere,[1] but it is not impossible and groups like the International Labor Organization and (in Britain) the National Consumer Council, Oxfam, Action Aid, the World Development Movement and many others lobby governments and international institutions to make international trading rules fairer. Understanding why these kinds of political engagement are sometimes less appealing than lifestyle practices and individual consumption projects would also entail an acknowledgement on the part of those who take an avowedly 'anti-consumerist' approach of the benefits of capitalist commodities that accrue to those who can afford them (Miller 1998). A related point is that concern about exploitation at an international level should not detract attention from the vast inequalities in wealth and opportunities within, as well as between, nations. Neo-liberalism has produced growing inequalities between rich and poor *inside* nation-states, and social mobility has stagnated, and in some cases actually declined, since the 1970s (Blanden et al. 2005). In this context, access to mass-market goods may feel like a particularly pressing concern for those at the lower ends of the social scale, not only to negate a sense of alienation from the market and the state (Miller 1998) but also as part of efforts (such as those outlined in Chapter Six) to 'fit in', to represent one's family as 'normal' (Appadurai 1996), to appear 'respectable' (Skeggs 1997) and so on. To repeatedly propound an 'anti-consumerist' agenda (which often takes the form of an 'anti-brand' agenda) without reference to the different contexts in which consumption takes place or the different social tasks it fulfils is lazy thinking at best.

Of course, this does not mean that consumption is always a benign activity; Chapter Six outlined some of the ways in which the consumption of branded goods is linked to various types of status competition and symbolic violence, as well as the ways in which the consumption of some brands and the avoidance of others has been incorporated into exclusionary nationalist formations. Similarly, just as certain types of political and economic organization are partly responsible for allowing wealthy Western consumers to use their consumption practices as a type of class and status competition, so too can the export of such forms of governance lead to wealthier groups in non-Western countries using the consumption of branded goods in a similar way. Older or more entrenched forms of social stratification are not replaced by new divisions based on the 'freedom' to purchase one type of commodity rather than another, but are often compounded by them; certainly they provide the framework through which markets and their values are subjectified and locally embedded (Rajagopal 2004). As neo-liberal economic policies are introduced – and sometimes imposed – in new and different social and political contexts it is important to recall the various ways in which the consumption of some brands and the avoidance of others has historically been used to bolster, rather than diminish, exclusionary forms of association and to give moral weight to xenophobic or absolutist nationalist political campaigns. The broader point, however, is that there is rarely a straightforward or singular meaning to consumption practices; they are inevitably embedded in *specific* social formations and relationships and will tend to register – and act in relation to – the fully ambivalent and conflictual nature of such relationships, rather than offering a straightforward route out of them.

At a global level, however, it is the terms of international trade, rather than trade itself, that presents the biggest problem for the poorest nations. In terms of branding, the nature of property rights, and especially intellectual property rights, are an especially pertinent issue. As was suggested in Chapter Five, contemporary intellectual property laws protect trade interests above all else, and this tends to benefit the owners of such rights (usually corporations) rather than consumers of intellectual property-heavy goods or even the actual creators of those goods. The increasing importance of intellectual property rights to the profitability – and brand-based equity – of corporations also puts populations in poorer parts of the world under higher levels of surveillance, as corporations seek to neutralize the threats to their profitability represented by counterfeiting and piracy activities. Yet the market for counterfeit goods continues to expand, as consumers in all parts of the world show acceptance of, and demand for, counterfeit goods. This acceptance is particularly common when trademarks appear to protect the marketing and promotional investments of corporations rather than representing any kind of relationship to consumers or guarantee of quality or service, pointing once again to the significance of the shift in the functions of brands from being a guarantee of quality to the consumer to operating as an additional mode of capital accumulation for corporations (Lury 2004).

Many of the most important political debates today involve, directly or indirectly, questions about intellectual property and its regulation, and there are many interesting accounts of the functioning of the international intellectual property regime and its relationship to issues of economic development, free speech and 'cultural rights' (see Coombe 2004 for an overview). While it may not be realistic or even desirable to abolish intellectual property rights altogether (as some working in this area claim), there remains a good deal of work to be done in publicizing their effects and challenging their current definition, scope and application. The apparent tightening of trademark laws to protect the promotional investments made by producers over the rights of consumers has already led to renewed concern about corporate power to control public expression; some critics have responded by proposing a strengthening of the category of 'the generic' rather than the proprietary, and a more active promotion of the idea of 'generic expressivity' (Dreyfuss, cited in Lury 2002b). Such efforts have taken on renewed vigour as corporations have increasingly sought to use more aggressive and pre-emptive means to protect their brand assets through overzealous application of trademark laws. Unsurprisingly, some of the biggest anti-corporate successes in this area have taken place on the web. Although digital technologies have provided commercial organizations with new opportunities to circulate their brands and new ways to monitor 'unauthorized' uses, they also create opportunities for more dialogic encounters between producers and consumers, and for faster and more effective collective efforts to promote free speech and to resist corporate censorship. Furthermore, such battles have in turn given rise to an emergent popular legal culture on the internet, with growing confidence in its own ability to challenge corporate excesses and create a new 'ethics of propriety' (Coombe and Herman 2002).

In addition to providing new battlegrounds between consumer groups and corporations, current formulations of intellectual property law have also in many cases drawn attention to the relationship between current international trading regimes and historical forms of expropriation and dispossession, as well as the definitions of property that have been used to support these arrangements. Some of these debates were outlined in Chapter Five, which looked at issues such as 'bio-prospecting' and the uses of indigenous knowledge, and in Chapter Six, which discussed the uses of Geographical Indications and the fact that historical associations between particular places and certain categories of products – in most cases formed out of European colonial conquest and its legacies – are now protected as a legitimate marketing advantage under the 'Geographical Indications' provisions of the TRIPs agreement. Partly because of these developments, many critics of intellectual property propose a rehabilitation of notions of 'the commons' that were in use prior to this period and remain implicit (although not usually legally enforceable) in some non-Western property regimes. The problem, however, remains one of balancing a desire to promote free speech and creativity – the motivation for many anti-copyright activists – against the growing need to protect certain forms of indigenous knowledge against theft by powerful multinational corporations (Coombe 2005); generalized conceptions of 'the commons' are likely to be inappropriate in such contexts, where the idea of a 'common heritage' of mankind is currently used to justify various types of expropriation (such as bio-prospecting by Western institutions) rather than prohibit them.

Brands and Culture

Perhaps most significantly in terms of the key themes of this book, the fact that allegedly 'national' qualities of commercial goods are still being debated, promoted and offered international legal protection tells us something important about the ongoing salience of national identities for marketing in general and brand values in particular, as well as about the continuing resonance of imperial structures in current trading arrangements. The first two chapters of the book noted that national and imperial themes were an important influence on some of the earliest brand identities of mass-produced goods, and that they provided some of the first examples of 'cultural' values and meanings being inscribed on the surface of commodities. Current debates about the nature and scope of Geographical Indications – with all the post-imperial legacies of place-based reputation, and over- and under-development, that they embody – are highly suggestive in terms of the ways in which historical inequalities between places and peoples have come to be recast as potential sources of promotional capital that can now be protected by intellectual property law and regulated by structures such as the WTO. The continuing use of 'country of origin' surveys by manufacturers and marketing specialists in their preparation of brand identities also testifies to the importance of such dynamics, which appear to remain powerful even while some brands and marketing agencies seek to promote themselves as 'global' or non-national entities, and to deliberately *dis*-embed themselves from their national moorings.

Yet as we have also seen, branding now encompasses an enormous range of supposedly 'cultural' values, and is widely used in *non*-commercial projects. Some of these are also, implicitly or explicitly, aimed at exploiting or promoting national feeling and sentiment; Chapter Six noted the uses of corporate branding techniques by various Hindu nationalist groups in India in the 1980s (Bhatt 2001; Rajagopal 2001), and Chapter Four noted the British Design Council's government-supported efforts to use design to effect a more 'active citizenship' and to renew a sense of national identity. Branding is also used by charitable organizations, where it is proposed to help fundraising efforts, to raise a charity's profile within government and to increase revenue through an extension of its licensing and merchandising activities. Thus although the rise of branding is unquestionably tightly linked to new forms of capital accumulation, it is also part of a wider context in which 'culture' is used strategically for the purposes of governance. Within branding, this 'expediency' of culture (Yúdice 2003) operates in two specific ways. Firstly, branding makes use of culture in the sense that it harnesses the productive potential of design and creative work in general in an attempt to shape the perceptions, feelings and behaviour of its target populations. As such, it works with an understanding of aesthetics as both judgement and as a more general 'disposition to sense acutely' (Bull et al. 2006). These dispositions are attributed to both producers and consumers, with the former charged with working upon the latter, often through processes of imitation, identification or intuition, but also through experimental or technical means.

Secondly, branding makes use of culture in the sense that it attempts to work on and through people's ongoing production of a common social world, and to insinuate itself into the webs of meaning that these common social practices create (Arvidsson 2006; Moor 2003). This is most obvious in 'viral' marketing and in attempts to build communities of interest around brands (e.g. Nike running clubs, various types of fan communities) but its roots lie in a broader understanding on the part of marketing agencies and other institutions that particular consumption decisions – and other activities that require us to make choices – are embedded in social and personal networks of meaning and value. The presumption that consumers have *affective* connections to brands means that both consumers and brands are approached as more susceptible to institutional manipulation and direction. It is because of the 'heightened emotional register' in which some types of activity take place, in other words, that they are deemed especially appropriate sites for strategic intervention by designers and brand management teams. Such interventions may be aimed at building brand equity and establishing long-term profitable relationships, or at inculcating a 'feelgood factor' and changing one's disposition towards the state; the point is that the discourse of branding has consolidated itself to the extent that a much wider range of sites and activities are now considered suitable for design-led interventions.

In making these claims about the work of branding, I have deliberately avoided linking branding too tightly to issues of commodification or consumerism. Although branding and related marketing activities are certainly important elements in the process by which new categories of goods and services are created and brought to market, they are not the principal drivers of this process, and their function is more usually that of attempting to influence the choices made *within* markets that are already established. One of the principal commercial functions of branding, as we have seen, is as a means for firms to compete with one another over the organization of those markets so that, for example, Amazon can compete with more well-established electrical retailers to sell DVD players, or supermarkets can compete with financial services providers to supply insurance. For similar reasons, branding is rarely a simple matter of consumerism, since for the most part it is not branding that compels us to purchase goods and services rather than making or doing them ourselves, but rather the pressures of employment and its effects upon the time and energy left over for autonomous production (Lodziak 2002). These logics precede branding, which, again, operates more usually as an attempt to influence our choice between one brand of (for example) ketchup, toothpaste or jeans and another, rather than as an attempt to dissuade us from making these things ourselves. Indeed, in terms of debates about commodification and consumerism, it is pertinent to note that not only have the spheres of non-exchanged work and non-monetized exchange actually *grown* in size relative to the commodified realm in recent years (Williams 2005), but also that the divergent practices included in these spheres reflect increasingly stark inequalities of wealth and income. Whereas the non-exchanged work undertaken by lower income groups is usually a matter of essential routine tasks that they cannot afford to 'commodify', the non-exchanged work undertaken by more affluent groups – often, paradoxically, those who make most noise about the pernicious effects of 'consumerism' – very often reflects a deliberate choice by those groups to distance themselves from the 'mass' cultural connotations of the commercial realm, by de-commodifying those activities deemed most pleasurable, 'creative' and rewarding. Needless to say, the 'de-commodification' of activities like home decorating is, however, often made possible only through the commodification of other, more routine, chores such as housework which others can be paid to conduct on their behalf.

None of this is to say that brands themselves are not political objects, and that they are not cause for concern; they are, as I have already suggested, significant elements in various types of competitive consumption and in the status-seeking activities of various class fractions. We should also be wary of corporate attempts to restrict the meanings and values that proliferate around brands, and the fact that it is, in reality, difficult to control these flows of meaning (Durant 2006) does not mean that corporate efforts to seek legal protection for their own version of what a brand 'represents' should not be vigorously resisted. Similarly, at a time when branding and marketing are increasingly recognized by the law as drivers of economic growth and development, changes in trademark law that protect the interests of established corporations more than those of the public or of individual producers and consumers, that produce monopolies and create entry barriers for new economic actors, or that consecrate historical or existing inequalities between regions as legitimate sources of marketing advantage, are all a major cause for concern. Finally, the growing use of elaborate branding strategies by political parties in their efforts to get elected should not distract us from the more pervasive, but less spectacular, ways in which design and branding have attached themselves to strategies of governance and become embedded in governmental attempts to secure popular assent to their own versions of nationhood or institutional efforts to subject particular spheres of social activity to more intense scrutiny and intervention.

Brands may not always work in practice in the ways intended by those who create them, but the effort to cultivate brand identities, and to use these as a means to organize production, exchange and management, structures a growing range of social and political as well as economic activities. Such efforts often produce substantial material changes in the look and feel of many types of environment, circulating in both public and private spheres as the designed embodiments of various institutional projects and aspirations. Our own engagements with brands – what we think of them, how we use them, which ones we like and which ones we avoid – reflect not only our tastes but also, very often, our ability to make choices in the public sphere at all. It is, increasingly, through the appropriation of these designed objects and spaces that the particular configurations of structure and agency made available to different social groups – and the wider social forces that these embody – are made meaningful and integrated into everyday life.

Notes

CHAPTER 1 THE RISE OF BRANDS

1. As for example in the incorporation of branding and product design sections into established advertising agencies such as Saatchi (see Chapter Six) and HHCL (Armstrong 2006). For a discussion of viral marketing see Goldsmith (2002); for an outline of 'experiential' marketing see Pine and Gilmore (1999).
2. Adam Lury, a former director of the advertising agency HHCL, argues that business texts such as these are usually a key part of a consultancy's marketing strategy, or else are published by industry professionals seeking consultancy work (A. Lury 2001).
3. Lury has also developed accounts of branding that emphasize its potential role in the reorganization of categories of 'nature' and 'culture' (2000; 2002b).
4. Here I am borrowing Nikolas Rose's (1999) phraseology in his description of the fabrication of 'governable spaces'.

CHAPTER 2 THE BRAND IN HISTORY

1. Early urban theorists such as Georg Simmel (1971) and Louis Wirth (1995) had noted the role of commodities in the forms of association that characterized city life. Wirth in particular observed that 'the close physical contact of numerous individuals necessarily produces a shift in the mediums through which we orient ourselves to the urban milieu ... typically our physical contacts are close but our social contacts are distant ... *we tend to acquire and develop a sensitivity to the world of artefacts*' (Wirth 1995: 70, my emphasis).
2. Constantine (1986: 200) argues that it was not always easy to impress a specifically imperial ideology on British consumers, who were used to being at the centre of an international as well as imperial economic system. One example of this is the apparent refusal of both shopkeepers and customers to believe that Californian tinned fruit was not an Empire product.
3. Hine (1995) gives the example of CD cases, questioning whether these are inseparable parts or components of the product, or simply packaging that contains the 'real' product through its period of usefulness.

4. Here I am deliberately glossing over debates, covered in more detail by Hesmondhalgh (2002: 53–4), about whether those working in design, marketing and related professions can accurately be described as cultural intermediaries or whether, instead, this term should be reserved for those professions specified by Bourdieu (1984: 359) in his original formulation. For some authors (such as Nixon 1997; 2003), the term 'cultural intermediaries' is appropriate in the context of advertising and marketing, while Hesmondhalgh would prefer something more like 'symbolic intermediaries'.

5. Debates among national employers about the merits of outsourcing various service functions, such as customer call centres, to foreign countries (see Brignall 2006) must be understood in this context; quantifiable savings in production costs must be weighed against unquantifiable, or at least uncertain, losses in revenue due to customer complaints or negative publicity. It should also be noted, of course, that these in turn often reflect customer xenophobia and its appropriation by a range of interested actors such as commercial competitors, the media and national trade unions. In Britain, for example, some companies now advertise the fact that they use 'UK-only call centres'.

6. The fact that such consumer protection legislation is implemented nationally rather than internationally does, however, have implications in relation to the circulation of brands on a global market – see Chapter Six.

7. Orthodox economic accounts see brands as performing a useful and necessary service for consumers in providing reassurance and reducing risk in a situation of imperfect information. In this respect they have a use-value for which many customers are quite reasonably prepared to pay a premium. See Wheelan (2002: 90–3) for one of the more populist accounts of branding from the perspective of orthodox economics.

CHAPTER 3 BRANDS, CULTURE AND ECONOMY

1. 'Above-the-line' advertising media include press, radio, television, cinema and outdoor and transport media (Ellwood 2000). This can be contrasted with 'below-the-line' media, which refers to 'a group of media including point of purchase, public relations, direct mail, in-store promotions and all other media' (Ellwood 2000: 304).

2. Tango is a British soft drinks brand that was known in the early 1990s for its high-profile and irreverent advertising campaigns.

3. In 1987 HHCL ran a campaign in the trade press showing a couple making love on a sofa while the television played in the background. The slogan was 'according to current audience research, this couple are watching your ad. Who's really getting screwed?' (Armstrong 2006).

4. This is similar to – but also an extension of – Andrew Wernick's (1991)

argument about products that promote themselves, or 'promotional commodities'. The same informant also talked about the Ministry of Sound, a London club, which had built its reputation on its club nights, but which had gone on to launch a successful magazine, a record label, a clothing range and package holidays. In both instances, spatial extension is part of market extension – that is, the extension of the brand into other product/service areas.

5. *The Independent* is a British newspaper.

6. *Birds of a Feather* was a popular British sitcom that ran between 1989 and 1998. It centred around the lives of two sisters and their friend living in Chigwell in Essex, an area described by the programme's makers as 'a real-life Essex millionaire's row populated by footballers, TV stars, pools winners, wide-boys made good'.

7. A number of informants mentioned the work of the Henley Centre, which markets itself on the basis of its up-to-date analyses of social, economic and 'lifestyle' trends. Much of its research uses methods such as ethnography and participant observation more usually associated with academic work. Such research is also increasingly conducted inside branding consultancies. See Pavitt (2000: 106) and www.henleycentre.co.uk.

8. I am grateful to Paul Springer for bringing this to my attention.

9. This is not uncommon in industries and agencies that position themselves as 'creative', and in which employees are therefore often seen as embodying 'cutting-edge' tastes and preferences. Sometimes employees will be obliged to 'perform' such qualities – for example through styles of dress – even if they do not feel a genuine affinity for them (see for example Ross 2003a).

10. See Nixon (2003: 95) for demographic information about those employed in the British advertising industry. A Design Council Survey in 2005 found that 62 per cent of designers were under forty years of age, 61 per cent were male, and only 6 per cent were from ethnic minority backgrounds (see Design Council 2005). The homogeneity of industry personnel, in terms of ethnicity and age in particular, is part of the reason for the more recent emergence of specialist marketing consultancies, including so-called 'ethnic' marketing consultancies such as (in the UK) Media Moguls. These new consultancies market themselves on the basis that they are able to engage with target audiences assumed to be unresponsive to marketing output from agencies dominated by white staff.

CHAPTER 4 BRANDED SPACES

1. Attributed to a fan of Manchester United football club, interviewed by Jonathan Legard as part of 'In Search of the Glazers', broadcast on Radio Five Live, 11 April 2006.

2. Other commentators have noted factors such as the lifting of the wage cap

and the shift to all-seated stadiums, the new volumes of capital necessary to respond to this, the associated rise in ticket prices and the increasing involvement of business consortia motivated by profit-seeking rather than by love of a particular club.

3. The more stringent application and enforcement of intellectual property rights by football clubs would be a case in point here, as would the involvement of private companies in funding anti-racist initiatives in sport. In 2002 Arsenal football club successfully prosecuted fan Matthew Reed for selling unofficial club merchandise outside the club's ground (see Osborn 2002). The club argued that Reed, who had been selling merchandise outside the ground for thirty years, had infringed the club's trademark; Reed argued that the Arsenal shield was not in fact a trademark but rather a 'badge of allegiance', and that he had been using it as such (the club had only registered its badge as a trademark in 1989). The European Court of Justice overturned previous rulings in the British courts that had supported Reed's case, paving the way for greater power for clubs and kit manufacturers over smaller operations. Although sales of unofficial merchandise continue to grow, the case may have important implications for fans' use of their clubs' emblems, in contexts that are sometimes only tangentially commercial. In 2005, Nike initiated its 'Stand Up, Speak Up' campaign against racism in football, selling black and white wristbands and donating the proceeds to anti-racist groups. The move was criticized by some as an attempt by Nike to get free PR by associating itself with ongoing anti-racist efforts within the game (Kelso 2005); others praised the initiative for encouraging displays of solidarity among fans, while Thierry Henry, who spearheaded the campaign, won an award from the Commission for Racial Equality. The case is further complicated by the fact that one of the campaign's major critics, the (white) Manchester United player Gary Neville, appeared to deny that there was a significant problem with racism in English football, while Nike itself (which can undoubtedly build considerable brand equity out of an initiative that costs relatively little) clearly has much greater power and reach than the smaller anti-racist groups it funds from the initiative. This in turn relates to the arguments made above about neo-liberal governance and its 'outsourcing' of social and political responsibilities (see also Gilroy 2004: 163 on the broader political context of market-driven forms of anti-racism).

4. Guy Julier (2005) points out that earlier projects, such as those in Barcelona, were in reality much less programmatic than many commentators have since assumed.

5. Julier (2005: 884) argues that the re-branding of Hull, and its associated design scheme, attempted to provide 'an aspirational narrative for everyday practice and a new vector in the urban habitus'. The city's five key brand values – 'challenging', 'discovering', 'creating', 'innovating' and 'leading' – were widely circulated in the local press (where they were the subject of

heated debate), and even taught to children via their incorporation into the curriculum at primary schools.

CHAPTER 5 INTELLECTUAL AND OTHER FORMS OF PROPERTY

1. This has of course become especially apparent since the rise of digital tech-nologies that allow music to be distributed and shared via the internet.
2. The broader context for such developments is the possibility that there will in the future be less scope for wealthy countries to 'dump' their goods in poorer markets, and a diminution in their ability to protect their own farmers with subsidies. The ability to patent or trademark crops ensures a new and lucrative source of revenue – in the form of license fees for use of particular seed varieties – even as the goods in which a particular company trades may change.
3. Similar examples can also be found in other areas of intellectual property law. In 1993 the British fashion chain Monsoon began a series of legal actions against the copying of its textile designs, which were protected by copyright and various other design rights. A department store and two retail chains were ordered to pay compensation and costs, and to destroy the infringing stock (Johnston 1995). Yet Monsoon's designs are themselves often based on traditional Indian prints; there is nothing illegal about this, but the case illustrates the discrepancies made possible by a system that defines ownership in terms of a 'legal individual' rather than collective or traditional knowledge.
4. The underlying rationale for this appears to have been the recognition that intellectual property laws are often better suited to protecting those economies that are already well established rather than those that are trying to expand; the reluctance of many emerging markets to enforce strict intel-lectual property laws to protect foreign companies reflects a similar aware-ness.
5. Sodipo (2004: 149) for example, notes the large number of complaints received by the Hong Kong Tourist Association following the implementation of new regulations to remove traders of counterfeit goods from public areas.
6. Another interesting example concerns corporate efforts to police fan sites on the internet. Fans tend to dispute that their favourite characters from books, films and television shows are private property and see their (sometimes unorthodox) appropriations as entirely legitimate. Indeed in some cases – Coombe (1998: 125) discusses *Star Trek* fans – fans create their own 'moral economy' around these characters, and see their interventions as 'fulfilling the inherent promise and potential of the series – a potential unrealized or betrayed by those who "own" the intellectual property rights in it' (see Coombe 1998: 105–26).

CHAPTER 6 NATIONAL BRANDS AND GLOBAL BRANDS

1. International drinks group Diageo, for example, describes only eight of its sixty-eight brands as 'global' (source: www.diageobrands.com). It is also worth noting that the majority of North American and European merchandise exports take place inter-regionally, i.e. between nations in the same region (World Trade Organization 2005).

2. Heinz, for example, is often believed by British consumers to be a British brand.

3. The interview with Micky Denehy from Saatchi and Saatchi's London office was conducted by myself and Paul Frosh in August 2005.

4. Saatchi and Saatchi itself has expanded its operations beyond conventional advertising and into areas such as sales promotion and direct marketing. The London office includes a sub-unit, Saatchi and Saatchi X, which specialises in point-of-sale communications. See www.saatchi.co.uk for more details.

5. Ireland was the second largest national market for Guinness at that time; Britain, Nigeria, the United States and Cameroon were the first, third, fourth and fifth largest markets, respectively (source: www.diageo.com).

6. For example, the PR team deliberately sought out 'cool'-looking consumers in the target age range in bars in Dublin and gave them free invitations to special promotional events featuring high-profile British acts prior to the festival, in the hope that these 'opinion formers' would in turn conduct further 'word of mouth' promotion among their friends (Musselbrook 2001).

7. See www.klp.co.uk/agency.php.

8. In fact, the idea that companies should position their brands 'within' media culture, rather than simply using television and press advertisements to persuade customers to buy a particular product, can be traced back to the 1950s (see Lury 2004: 38; Arvidsson 2006: 26).

9. See www.americanapparel.net.

10. See www.waitrose.com/about/thewaitrosefoundation.asp.

11. The only exceptions to this is when a geographical indicator has already been registered as part of a trademark, or where the name has become the generic term for a particular category of goods. It is also important to note that the geographies of recognized areas do not necessarily correspond with existing territorial boundaries (I am grateful to Andy Pike for pointing this out).

12. One important issue here is whether Geographical Indications, or any other form of intellectual property law, are an appropriate tool for promoting rural development and welfare; another is the highly static conception of place, and land-based definitions of 'culture', encoded in current definitions of Geographical Indications (see Parry 2006).

13. Pun's account of women from rural China working in 'special economic

zones' of Shenzhen suggests that the popularity of shopping as a leisure activity for these women relates directly to their desire to *distance* themselves from their rural homes and to capture some of what they perceive to be the 'cosmopolitan' lifestyle of city-dwelling women.

14. The failure in 2006 of Dubai Ports World to take over the running of a number of major US ports, caused by objections within the House of Representatives and a wider political controversy, was characterized by many commentators as a form of economic nationalism, driven by the desire of certain politicians (including many prominent Democrats) to capitalize upon anti-Middle-Eastern sentiment in the United States for political purposes.

CHAPTER 7 CONCLUSION

1. Here I am paraphrasing Paul Gilroy's (2004: 163) observations on the 'market-driven pastiche of multiculture' produced by corporations, which, he suggests, appears compelling primarily because of the absence of more substantive political visions in other spheres.

Bibliography

Aaker, D.A. (1991), *Managing Brand Equity: Capitalizing on the Value of a Brand Name*, London: Jossey Bass Wiley.

Amin, A. and Thrift, N. (2002), *Cities*, Cambridge: Polity.

Anderson, B. (1991 [1983]), *Imagined Communities: Reflections on the Origin and Spread of Nationalism*, revised edition, London and New York: Verso.

Anderson, C. (2000), '*Godna*: Inscribing Indian Convicts in the Nineteenth Century', in Jane Caplan (ed.) *Written on the Body: The Tattoo in European and American History*, London: Reaktion.

Appadurai, A. (1996), *Modernity at Large: Cultural Dimensions of Globalization*, Minneapolis: University of Minnesota Press.

Armstrong, G. (1998), *Football Hooligans: Knowing the Score*, Oxford: Berg.

Armstrong, S. (2006), 'Great Expectations', in *The Guardian*, 31 July.

Arvidsson, A. (2006), *Brands: Meaning and Value in Media Culture*, London and New York: Routledge.

Baker, S. (1989), 'Re-reading "The Corporate Personality"', in *Journal of Design History*, Vol. 2, No. 4.

Barnett, C., Cloke, P., Clarke, N. and Malpass, A. (2004), 'Articulating Ethics and Consumption', Cultures of Consumption Working Paper Series, No. 17, available at www.consume.bbk.ac.uk/publications.html.

Batchelor, A. (1998), 'Brands as Financial Assets', in S. Hart and J. Murphy (eds), *Brands: The New Wealth Creators*, Basingstoke: Macmillan.

Batsleer, J., Cornforth, C. and Paton, R., eds (1992), *Issues in Voluntary and Non-profit Management*, Wokingham: Addison-Wesley.

Ben-Atar, D.S. (2004), *Trade Secrets: Intellectual Piracy and the Origins of American Industrial Power*, New Haven and London: Yale University Press.

Bender, D. (2003), 'A Foreign Method of Working', in D. Bender and R. Greenwald (eds), *Sweatshop USA: The American Sweatshop in Historical and Global Perspective*, New York and London: Routledge.

Bender, D. and Greenwald, R., eds (2003), *Sweatshop USA: The American Sweatshop in Historical and Global Perspective*, New York and London: Routledge.

Bent, R. (2003), 'Face Value', in *The Guardian*, 13 October.

Bhatt, C. (2001), *Hindu Nationalism: Origins, Ideologies and Modern Myths*, Oxford: Berg.

Billig, M. (1995), *Banal Nationalism*, London, Thousand Oaks, New Delhi: Sage.

Blackburn, J. (2001), Interview with Josh Blackburn, Wolff-Olins, London, 19 November.

Blackshaw, T. and Long, J. (2005), 'What's the Big Idea? A Critical Exploration of the Concept of Social Capital and its Incorporation into Leisure Policy Discourse' in *Leisure Studies*, Vol. 24, No. 3: 239–58.

Blanden, J., Gregg, P. and Machin, S. (2005), 'Intergenerational Mobility in Europe and North America', London: Centre for Economic Performance/Sutton Trust, available at www.suttontrust.com/reports/IntergenerationalMobility.pdf.

Blunkett, D. (2004), 'Preface: Striving State, Active Citizens', in Design Council/IPPR, *Touching the State*, London: Design Council.

Bonanich, E. and Applebaum, R. (2003), 'Offshore Production', in D. Bender and R. Greenwald (eds), *Sweatshop USA: The American Sweatshop in Historical and Global Perspective*, New York and London: Routledge.

Bourdieu, P. (1984 [1979]), *Distinction: A Social Critique of the Judgement of Taste*, trans. Richard Nice, London: Routledge.

Bourdieu, P. (2001), 'The Forms of Capital', in N.W. Biggart (ed.), *Readings in Economic Sociology*, Oxford: Blackwell.

Brewer, J. and Staves, S., eds (1995), *Early Modern Conceptions of Property*, London and New York: Routledge.

Brignall, M. (2006), 'Is it Finally Time to Hang-up on Indian Call Centres?', in *The Guardian*, 30 June.

British Design Innovation (2005), *BDI Design Industry Valuation Survey 2004–05*, available at www.britishdesigninnovation.org, accessed 5 April 2006.

Bruce, I. (2005), *Charity Marketing: Meeting Need through Customer Focus*, London: ICSA.

Buckman, G. (2005), *Global Trade: Past Mistakes, Future Choices*, London and New York: Zed Books.

Bull, M., Gilroy, P., Howes, D. and Kahn, D. (2006), 'Introducing Sensory Studies', in *The Senses and Society*, Vol. 1, No. 1: 5–7.

Buskirk, M. (1992), 'Commodities as Censor: Copyrights and Fair Use', in *October* 60.

Callon, M., Méadel, C. and Rabeharisoa, V. (2002), 'The Economy of Qualities', in *Economy and Society*, Vol. 31, No. 2: 194–217.

Carrier, J.G. (1998), 'Introduction', in J.G. Carrier and D. Miller (eds), *Virtualism: A New Political Economy*, Oxford and New York: Berg.

Carrier, J.G. and Miller, D., eds. (1998), *Virtualism: A New Political Economy*, Oxford and New York: Berg.

Castells, M. (1996), *The Rise of the Network Society*, Oxford: Blackwell.

Castells, M. (1998), *End of Millennium*, Oxford: Blackwell.

Clarke, A. (2000), '"Mother Swapping": the Trafficking of Nearly New Children's Wear', in P. Jackson, M. Lowe, D. Miller and F. Mort (eds),

Commercial Cultures: Economies, Practices, Spaces, Oxford: Berg.

Colomina, B. (1994), *Privacy and Publicity: Modern Architecture as Mass Media*, Cambridge, MA: MIT Press.

Conekin, B. (1999), '"Here is the Modern World Itself": The Festival of Britain's Representations of the Future', in B. Conekin, F. Mort and F. Waters (eds), *Moments of Modernity: Reconstructing Britain, 1945–64*, River Orams Press.

Constantine, S. (1986), '"Bringing the Empire Alive": the Empire Marketing Board and Imperial Propaganda, 1926–33', in J. Mackenzie (ed.), *Imperialism and Popular Culture*, Manchester: Manchester University Press.

Coombe, R. (1998), *The Cultural Life of Intellectual Properties: Authorship, Appropriation and the Law*, Durham, NC: Duke University Press.

Coombe, R. (2004), 'Commodity Culture, Private Censorship, Branded Environments and Global Trade Politics: Intellectual Property as a Topic of Law and Society Research', in A. Sarat (ed.), *The Blackwell Companion to Law and Society*, Malden, MA: Basil Blackwell.

Coombe, R. (2005), 'Cultural Rights and Intellectual Property Debates', in *Human Rights Dialogue*, Vol. 2, No. 12: 34–6, available at www.yorku.ca/rcoombe/publications.htm, accessed 6 September 2006.

Coombe, R. and Herman, A. (2000), 'Trademarks, Property, and Propriety: The Moral Economy of Consumer Politics and Corporate Accountability on the World Wide Web', in *DePaul Law Review*, 50: 597–632, Winter 2000.

Coombe, R. and Herman, A. (2002), 'Culture Wars on the Net: Intellectual Property and Corporate Propriety in Digital Environments', in *South Atlantic Quarterly* 100: 4: 919–47.

Cottam, H. and Rogers, B. (2004), 'Introduction: Touching the State', in Design Council/IPPR, *Touching the State*, London: Design Council.

Crewe, L., Gregson, N. and Brooks, K. (2003), 'Alternative Retail Spaces', in A. Leyshon, R. Lee and C.C. Williams (eds), *Alternative Economic Spaces*, London: Sage.

Daunton, M. and Hilton, M. (2001), *The Politics of Consumption: Material Culture and Citizenship in Europe and America*, Oxford: Berg.

Davis, A. (1967), *Package and Print: The Development of Container and Label Design*, London: Faber and Faber.

Dean, J. (2005), 'Dov Charney, Like It or Not', in *Inc.*, September 2005.

Denehy, M. (2005), Interview with Micky Denehy, Saatchi and Saatchi, London, 17 August (with Paul Frosh).

Denny, C. and Elliott, L. (2002), 'Shaping up for Seattle at the beach', in *The Guardian*, 4 September.

Design Council (2004a) 'Lambeth Borough Council – Council Tax Bill', case study available at www.designcouncil.org.uk.

Design Council/IPPR (2004b), *Touching the State*, London: Design Council.

Design Council (2005), *The Business of Design: Design Industry Research 2005*, London: Design Council.

Duchrow, U. and Hinkelammert, F.J. (2004), *Property for People, Not for Profit: Alternatives to the Global Tyranny of Capital*, London, New York and Geneva: World Council of Churches/Zed Books.

Durant, A. (2006), 'Describing the "Distinctive"/"Descriptive" Distinction: Naming and Meaning in Verbal Trade Mark Signs', paper given at Trademarks workshop, Centre for Intellectual Property and Information Law, Cambridge University, 3 July.

Du Gay, P. and Pryke, M., eds. (2002), *Cultural Economy: Cultural Analysis and Commercial Life*, London: Sage.

Ellwood, I. (2000), *The Essential Brand Book*, London: Kogan Page.

Elmer, G. (2004), *Profiling Machines: Mapping the Personal Information Economy*, Boston, MA: MIT Press.

Ennis, A. (2005), *Graphic Design Practice: Impersonation, Invocation and Multiple Audiences*, unpublished MA thesis, Concordia University.

Ewen, S. and Ewen, E. (1982), *Channels of Desire: Mass Images and the Shaping of American Consciousness*, New York: McGraw-Hill.

Ferguson, N. (2005), 'When Does a Celebrity Become Too Famous?', in *The Guardian*, 14 October.

Fletcher, R. (2003), 'Burberry Takes a Brand Check', in *The Telegraph*, 22 June.

Fox, R. (2000), Interview with Rebecca Fox, London, 6 December.

Frank, D. (1999), *Buy American: The Untold Story of Economic Nationalism*, Boston: Beacon Press.

Frow, J. (2003), 'Signature and Brand', in J. Collins (ed.), *High-Pop: Making Culture into Popular Entertainment*, Oxford: Blackwell.

Gaines, J. (1991), *Contested Culture: The Image, the Voice, and the Law*, Chapel Hill and London: University of North Carolina Press.

Gangjee, D. (2006) 'Melton Mowbray and the GI Pie in the Sky: Exploring Cartographies of Protection', paper given at Trademarks workshop, Centre for Intellectual Property and Information Law, Cambridge University, 3 July.

Gereffi, J. and Korzeniewicz, M., eds (1994), *Commodity Chains and Global Capitalism*, Westport, Conn and London: Praeger.

Gilroy, P. (1993), *The Black Atlantic: Modernity and Double Consciousness*, London and New York: Verso.

Gilroy, P. (2000), *Between Camps: Nations, Culture and the Allure of Race*, London: Penguin.

Gilroy, P. (2004), *After Empire: Melancholia or Convivial Culture?* London: Routledge.

Gladwell, M. (2000), *The Tipping Point: How Little Things Can Make a Big Difference*, Boston: Little, Brown.

Goldsmith, R. (2002), *Viral Marketing: Get Your Audience to Do Your Marketing for You*, London: Prentice Hall Business.

Gregson, N., Brooks, K. and Crewe, L. (2000), 'Narratives of Consumption and the Body in the Space of the Charity/Shop', in P. Jackson, M. Lowe, D. Miller and F. Mort (eds), *Commercial Cultures*, Oxford: Berg.

Gregson, N. and Crewe, L. (2003), *Second-Hand Cultures*, Oxford, New York: Berg.

Hall, S. and Jacques, M., eds (1989), *New Times: The Changing Face of Politics in the 1990s*, London: Lawrence and Wishart.

Hankinson, P. (2000), 'Brand Orientation in Charity Organisations: Qualitative Research into Key Charity Sectors', in *International Journal of Nonprofit and Voluntary Sector Marketing*, Vol. 5, No. 3.

Hansen, K.T. (2000), *Salaula: The World of Secondhand Clothing and Zambia*, Chicago and London: University of Chicago Press.

Haraway, D. (1997), *Modest_Witness@Second_Millennium.FemaleMan©_Meets_ OncoMouse™*, London and New York: Routledge.

Harris, J. (2006), 'Be Afraid...', in *The Guardian*, 23 June.

Hart, S. (1998), 'The Future for Brands', Hart, S. and Murphy, J. (1998) *Brands: The New Wealth Creators*, Basingstoke: Macmillan.

Hart, S. and Murphy, J. (1998), *Brands: The New Wealth Creators*, Basingstoke: Macmillan.

Harvey, D. (1989), *The Condition of Postmodernity*, Oxford: Blackwell.

Harvey, D. (2005), *A Brief History of Neoliberalism*, Oxford and New York: Oxford University Press.

Heath, J. and Potter, A. (2006), *The Rebel Sell: How the Counterculture Became Consumer Culture*, Chichester: Capstone.

Hebdige, D. (1988), *Hiding in the Light: On Images and Things*, London and New York: Routledge.

Heffernan, R. (1999), 'Media Management: Labour's Political Communications Strategy', in G.R. Taylor (ed.), *The Impact of New Labour*, Basingstoke: Macmillan.

Henrion, F.H.K. and Parkin, A. (1967), *Design Coordination and Public Image*, London: Studio Vista.

Hesmondhalgh, D. (2002), *The Cultural Industries*, London, Thousand Oaks, CA and New Delhi: Sage.

Hewitt, P. and Baxter, M. (2004), *The Fashion of Football: From Best to Beckham, from Mod to Label Slave*, Edinburgh: Mainstream Publishing.

Hine, T. (1995), *The Total Package: The Evolution and Secret Meanings of Boxes, Bottles, Cans and Tubes*, Boston, London: Little, Brown.

Hochschild, A. (1983), *The Managed Heart: Commercialization of Human Feeling*, Berkeley and London: University of California Press.

Hopkins D., Kontnik, L. and Turnage, M. (2003), *Counterfeiting Exposed: Protecting Your Brand and Customers*, Hoboken, NJ: John Wiley and Sons.

Horne, J. (2006), *Sport in Consumer Culture*, Basingstoke and New York: Macmillan.

Hudson, R. (2005), *Economic Geographies: Circuits, Flows, Spaces*, London, Thousand Oaks, New Delhi: Sage.

Hughes, A. and Reimer, S., eds (2004), *Geographies of Commodity Chains*, London and New York: Routledge.

Hughson, J., Inglis, D. and Free, M. (2005), *The Uses of Sport: A Critical Study*, London and New York: Routledge.

Jackson, D. (2001), Interview with Dan Jackson, Sonic Brand, London, 5 December.

Jankowski, J. (1998), *Shelf Space: Modern Packaging Design, 1945–1965*, San Francisco: Chronicle Books.

Johnston, D. (1995), *Design Protection: A Practical Guide to the Law on Plagiarism for Manufacturers and Designers*, London: Design Council.

Julier, G. (2000), *The Culture of Design*, London: Sage.

Julier, G. (2005), 'Urban Designscapes and the Production of Aesthetic Content', in *Urban Studies*, 42: 689–888.

Kapferer, J.-N. (1992), *Strategic Brand Management*, New York: The Free Press.

Kearns, G. and Philo, C., eds (1993), *Selling Places: The City as Cultural Capital, Past and Present*, Oxford: Pergamon.

Kelso, P. (2005), 'Nike Denies Cashing in on Anti-racism', in *The Guardian*, 11 February.

Klein, N. (2000), *No Logo*, London: Flamingo.

Lamacraft, J. (1998), *Retail Design: New Store Experience*, London: Financial Times Retail and Consumer publishing.

Landry, C., Morley, D., Southwood, R. and Wright, P., eds (1985), *What a Way to Run a Railroad: An Analysis of Radical Failure*, London: Comedia.

Lash, S. (2002), *Critique of Information*, London: Sage.

Lash, S. and Urry, J. (1994) *Economies of Signs and Space*, London: Sage.

Leach, N. (2002), 'Belonging: Towards a Theory of Identification with Space', in J. Hillier and E. Rooksby (eds), *Habitus: A Sense of Place*, Aldershot: Ashgate.

Leiss, W., Kline, S. and Jhally, S. (1986), *Social Communication in Advertising: Persons, Products and Images of Well-being*, Toronto: Methuen.

Leonard, M. (1997), *Britain™: Renewing Our Identity*, London: Demos.

Littler, J. (2008, forthcoming), *Radical Consumption: Shopping for Change in Contemporary Culture*, Buckingham: Open University Press.

Littler, J. and Moor, L. (2008, in press), 'Fourth Worlds and Neo-Fordism: American Apparel and the Cultural Economy of Consumer Anxiety', in *Cultural Studies* Vol. 22 Nos. 5–6.

Lodziak, C. (2002), *The Myth of Consumerism*, London, Sterling, VA: Pluto.

Lovell, J. (2001), Interview with Jessica Lovell, St Lukes advertising agency, London, 14 June.

Lupton, E. and Miller, J.A. (1992), *The Kitchen, the Bathroom and the Aesthetics of Waste*, New York: Princeton Architectural Press.

Lury, A. (2001), Interview with Adam Lury, London, 26 November.

Lury, C. (1993), *Cultural Rights: Technology, Legality and Personality*, London: Routledge.

Lury, C. (2000), 'The United Colors of Diversity: Essential and Inessential

Culture', in S. Franklin, C. Lury and J. Stacey (eds), *Global Nature, Global Culture*, London: Sage.

Lury, C. (2002a), 'Portrait of the Artist as a Brand', in D. McClean and K. Schubert, (eds), *Dear Images: Art, Copyright and Culture*, London: Ridinghouse.

Lury, C. (2002b), 'From diversity to Heterogeneity: A Feminist Analysis of the Making of Kinds', in *Economy and Society* Vol. 31 No. 4: 588–605.

Lury, C. (2004), *Brands: The Logos of the Global Economy*, London and New York: Routledge.

Lury, C. and Warde, A. (1996), 'Investments in the Imaginary Consumer: Conjectures Regarding Power, Knowledge and Advertising', in M. Nava, A. Blake, I. MacRury and B. Richards (eds), *Buy This Book: Studies in Advertising and Consumption*, London: Routledge.

McClintock, A. (1995), *Imperial Leather: Race, Gender and Sexuality in the Colonial Contest*, New York and London: Routledge.

McCracken, G. (1988), *Culture and Consumption*, Bloomington and Indianapolis: Indiana University Press.

McCracken, G. (2005), *Culture and Consumption II: Markets, Meaning and Brand Management*, Bloomington and Indianapolis: Indiana University Press.

McFall, L. (2004), *Advertising: A Cultural Economy*, London: Sage.

MacKenzie, J.M. (1984), *Propaganda and Empire: The Manipulation of British Public Opinion, 1880–1960*, Manchester: Manchester University Press.

Maguire, P.J. (1997), 'Patriotism, Politics and Production', in P. Maguire and J. Woodham (eds), *Design and Cultural Politics in Postwar Britain: The* Britain Can Make It *Exhibition of 1946*, London and Washington: Leicester University Press.

Maguire, P. and Woodham, J., eds (1997), *Design and Cultural Politics in Postwar Britain: The* Britain Can Make It *Exhibition of 1946*, London and Washington: Leicester University Press.

Manovich, L. (2000), *The Language of New Media*, Cambridge, MA: MIT Press.

Manovich, L. (2002), 'The Poetics of Augmented Space', available at www.manovich.net, accessed 19 August 2006.

Manzini, E. (1989), *The Material of Invention*, London: Design Council.

Mathiason, N. (2006), 'High Street, Clone Town, 2015', in *The Guardian*, 12 February.

May, C. (2000), *A Global Political Economy of Intellectual Property Rights: The New Enclosures?* London and New York: Routledge.

Mertha, A. (2005), *The Politics of Piracy: Intellectual Property in Contemporary China*, Ithaca and London: Cornell University Press.

Miller, D. (1997), *Capitalism: An Ethnographic Approach*, Oxford: Berg.

Miller, D. (1998), 'Conclusion: A Theory of Virtualism', in J.G. Carrier and D. Miller (eds), *Virtualism: A New Political Economy*, Oxford and New York: Berg.

Miller, D. (2005), 'Reply to Michel Callon', in *Economic Sociology, European*

Electronic Newsletter, Vol. 6, No. 1, July 2005. Available at http://econsoc. mpifg.de/archive/esjuly05.pdf accessed 31 July 2006.

Milligan, A. (2004), *Brand It Like Beckham*, London: Cyan.

Mollerup, P. (1997), *Marks of Excellence: The History and Taxonomy of Trademarks*, London: Phaidon.

Molotch, H. (2003), *Where Stuff Comes From*, New York and London: Routledge.

Moor, L. (2003), 'Branded Spaces: The Scope of "New Marketing"', in *Journal of Consumer Culture*, Vol. 3, No. 1: 39–60.

Moor, L. (2006), '"The Buzz of Dressing": Commodity Culture, Fraternity, and Football Fandom', in *South Atlantic Quarterly*, 105. 2.

Mukerji, C. (1983), *From Graven Images: Patterns of Modern Materialism*, New York: Columbia University Press.

Murphy, J.M. (1990), *Brand Strategy*, Cambridge: Director Books.

Murphy, J.M. (1998), 'What is Branding?', in S. Hart and J. Murphy (eds), *Brands: The New Wealth Creators*, Basingstoke: Macmillan.

Murray, R. (1989), 'Fordism and Post-Fordism', in S. Hall and M. Jacques (eds), *New Times: The Changing Face of Politics in the 1990s*, London: Lawrence and Wishart.

Musselbrook, C. (2001), Interview with Claire Musselbrook, KLP Euro RSCG, London 27 January.

Nevett, T.R. (1987), *Advertising in Britain: A History*, London: Heinemann.

Nixon, S. (2002), 'Re-imagining the Ad Agency: The Cultural Connotations of Economic Forms', in P. Du Gay and M. Pryke (eds), *Cultural Economy: Cultural Analysis and Commercial Life*. London: Sage.

Nixon, S. (2003), *Advertising Cultures*, London: Sage.

Olins, W. (1978), *The Corporate Personality: An Inquiry into the Nature of Corporate Identity*, London: Design Council.

Osborn, A. (2002), 'Win for Arsenal as Europe Bans Sale of Replica Kit', in *The Guardian*, 13 November.

Palmer, R. (2004), *European Cities and Capitals of Culture: Part I*, Palmer/Rae Associates, available at www.palmer-rae.com/culturalcapitals.htm.

Parry, B. (2006) 'Geographical Indications: Not all "Champagne and Roses"', paper given at Trademarks workshop, Centre for Intellectual Property and Information Law, Cambridge University, 3 July.

Patel, S. (2001), Interview with Shilen Patel, Marketing Manager of Guinness Ireland, London, 31 May 2001.

Paterson, M. (2006), *Consumption and Everyday Life*, London: Routledge.

Patterson, O. (1982), *Slavery and Social Death: A Comparative Study*, New York and London: Harvard University Press.

Pavitt, J., ed. (2000), *Brand.New*, London: V&A Publications.

Pettinger, L. (2004), 'Brand Culture and Branded Workers: Service Work and Aesthetic Labour in Fashion Retail', in *Consumption, Markets and Culture*, Vol. 7, No. 2: 165–84.

Pike, A. (2006), '"Beyond Geography"? Brand Attachments to Place and Territorial Development', unpublished paper.

Pilditch, J. (1961), *The Silent Salesman: How to Develop Packaging that Sells*, London: Business Books.

Pilditch, J. (1970), *Communication by Design: A Study in Corporate Identity*, New York: McGraw-Hill.

Pilditch, J. and Scott, D. (1965), *The Business of Product Design*, London: Business Publications.

Pine, J. and Gilmore, J. (1999), *The Experience Economy*, Boston: Harvard Business School Press.

Posey, D. (2004), 'The "balance sheet" and the "sacred balance": Valuing the knowledge of traditional and indigenous peoples', in K. Plenderleith (ed.), *Indigenous Knowledge and Ethics: A Darrell Posey Reader*, New York and London: Routledge.

Power, M. (1997), *The Audit Society*, Oxford: Oxford University Press.

Pun, N. (2005), *Made in China: Women Factory Workers in a Global Workplace*, Durham and London: Duke University Press.

Raghuram, P. (2004), 'Initiating the Commodity Chain: South Asian Women and Fashion in the Diaspora', in A. Hughes and S. Reimer (eds), *Geographies of Commodity Chains*, London and New York: Routledge.

Rajagopal, A. (2001), *Politics after Television: Religious Nationalism and the Reshaping of the Indian Public*, Cambridge: Cambridge University Press.

Rajagopal, A. (2004), 'The Menace of Hawkers: Property Forms and the Politics of Market Liberalization in Mumbai', in K. Verdery and C. Humphrey (eds), *Property In Question: Value Transformation in the Global Economy*, Oxford and New York: Berg.

Ramamurthy, A. (2003), *Imperial Persuaders: Images of Africa and Asia in British Advertising*, Manchester: Manchester University Press.

Ramesh, R. (2006), 'Indians Get Taste of Western Retail While Foreign Firms Wait in Wings', in *The Guardian*, 5 June.

Rangnekar, D. (2004) 'The Socio-Economics of Geographical Indications: A Review of Empirical Evidence from Europe', UNCTAD-ICTSD Project on IPRs and Sustainable Development, Issue Paper No. 8, Geneva: UNCTAD/ICTSD.

Raymond, K. and Shaw, M. (1996), *Better Government by Design: Improving the Effectiveness of Public Purchasing*, Social Market Foundation Memorandum, No. 21.

Ritzer, G. (1993), *The McDonaldization of Society: An Investigation Into the Changing Character of Contemporary Social life*, Thousand Oaks, London, New Delhi: Pine Forge Press.

Rose, N. (1989), *Governing the Soul: The Shaping of the Private Self*, London and New York: Routledge.

Rose, N. (1999), *Powers of Freedom: Reframing Political Thought*, Cambridge: Cambridge University Press.

Ross, A. (2003a), *No Collar: The Humane Workplace and Its Hidden Costs*, New York: Basic Books.

Ross, A. (2003b), 'The Rise of the Second Antisweatshop Movement', in D. Bender and R. Greenwald, (eds), *Sweatshop USA: The American Sweatshop in Historical and Global Perspective*, New York and London: Routledge.

Sheldon, R. and Arens, E. (1932), *Consumer Engineering: A New Technique for Prosperity*, New York and London: Harper and Bros.

Shove, E., Watson, M. and Ingram, J. (2005), 'The Value of Design and the Design of Value', paper presented to *Joining Forces* international design conference, Helsinki, September 2005.

Silk, M., Andrews, D.L. and Cole, C.L., eds (2005), *Sport and Corporate Nationalisms*, Oxford and New York: Berg.

Simmel, G. (1971), 'The Metropolis and Mental Life', in D. Levine (ed.), *Georg Simmel: On Individuality and Social Forms*, Chicago and London: University of Chicago Press.

Skeggs, B. (1997), *Formations of Class and Gender: Becoming Respectable*, London: Sage.

Slater, D. (1997), *Consumer Culture and Modernity*, Cambridge: Polity.

Slater, D. (2002a), 'Capturing Markets from the Economists', in P. Du Gay and M. Pryke (eds), *Cultural Economy: Cultural Analysis and Commercial Life*, London, Thousand Oaks, New Delhi: Sage

Slater, D. (2002b), 'From Calculation to Alienation: Disentangling Economic Abstractions', in *Economy and Society*, Vol. 31, No. 2: 234–49.

Slater, D. and Tonkiss, F. (2001), *Market Society: Markets and Modern Social Theory*, Cambridge: Polity.

Soar, M. (2002), 'An Insular Profession: Graphic Design and Consumer Culture', in *Journal of Consumer Culture*, Vol. 2, No. 2.

Sodipo, B. (1997), *Piracy and Counterfeiting: GATT, TRIPS and Developing Countries*, International Economic Development Law, Vol. 5. London: Kluwer Law International.

Sparke, P. (1986), *Did Britain Make It? British Design in Context, 1946–1986*, London: Design Council.

Stride, H. (2006), 'An Investigation into the Values Dimension of Branding: Implications for the Charity Sector', in *International Journal of Nonprofit and Voluntary Sector Marketing*, Vol. 11, No. 2: 115–24.

Sudjic, D. (2004), 'The Shape of a Nation', in Design Council/IPPR, *Touching the State*, London: Design Council.

Sutton, M. (2002), Interview with Michelle Sutton, London, 15 February.

Tapp, A. (1996), 'Charity Brands: A Qualitative Study of Current Practice', in *Journal of Nonprofit and Voluntary Sector Marketing*, Vol. 1, No. 4: 327–36.

Taylor, G.R. (1999), 'Power in the Party', in *The Impact of New Labour*, Basingstoke: Macmillan.

Thrift, N. (1997), 'The Rise of Soft Capitalism', in *Cultural Values*, 1: 29–57.

Thrift, N. (1998), 'Virtual Capitalism: The Globalisation of Reflexive Business

Knowledge', in J.G. Carrier and D. Miller (eds), *Virtualism: A New Political Economy*, Oxford and New York: Berg.

Thrift, N. (2002) 'Performing Cultures in the New Economy', in P. Du Gay and M. Pryke (eds), *Cultural Economy: Cultural Analysis and Commercial Life*, London, Thousand Oaks, New Delhi: Sage.

True, J. (2005), 'Country before Money? Economic Globalization and National Identity in New Zealand', in E. Helleiner and A. Pickel (eds), *Economic Nationalism in a Globalizing World*, Ithaca and London: Cornell University Press.

Upshaw, L. (1995), *Building Brand Identity: A Strategy for Success in a Hostile Marketplace*, New York: John Wiley and Sons.

Usunier, J.-C. and Lee, J.A. (2005), *Marketing Across Cultures*, fourth edition, Edinburgh: Pearson Education.

Van Doren, H.L. (1940), *Industrial Design: A Practical Guide*, New York: McGraw-Hill.

Van Gelder, S. (2003), *Global Brand Strategy: Unlocking Branding Potential Across Countries, Cultures and Markets*, London and Sterling, VA: Kogan Page.

Venturi, R., Scott Brown, D. and Izenour, R. (1977), *Learning from Las Vegas: The Forgotten Symbolism of Architectural Form*, Cambridge, MA: MIT Press.

Vidal, J. (2000), 'Biopirates who Seek the Greatest Prizes', in *The Guardian*, 15 November.

Ware, V. (1992), *Beyond the Pale: White Women, Racism and History*, London and New York: Verso.

Watts, J. (2005), 'European Luxury Brands Challenge Chinese Pirates', in *The Guardian*, 4 November.

Wernick, A. (1991), *Promotional Culture*, London: Sage.

Wheelan, C. (2002), *Naked Economics: Undressing the Dismal Science*, New York: W W Norton.

Wicks, P.G., Nairn, A. and Griffin, C. (2006), 'Beckham: Hero, Villain or a Bit of Both? The Children's Viewpoint', University of Bath, available at www.bath.ac.uk/news/pdf/beckham.pdf, accessed 29 August 2006.

Williams, C.C. (2005), *A Commodified World? Mapping the Limits of Capitalism*, London and New York: Zed Books.

Williams, C.L. (2006), *Inside Toyland: Working, Shopping, and Social Inequality*, Berkeley, Los Angeles and London: University of California Press.

Williamson, J. (1978), *Decoding Advertisements: Ideology and Meaning in Advertising*, London: Calder and Boyars.

Wirth, L. (1995 [1938]), 'Urbanism as a Way of Life', in P. Kasinitz (ed.), *Metropolis: Center and Symbol of Our Times*, New York: New York University Press.

Wolff Olins (n.d.), *Hull: Pioneering City*, available at www.wolff-olins.com/files/Hull_0202New815000.pdf, accessed 20 April 2006.

Woodham, J. (1983), *The Industrial Designer and the Public*, London: Pembridge.

Woodham, J. (1997), *Twentieth Century Design*, Oxford: OUP.

World Trade Organization (1994), *Trade-Related Aspects of Intellectual Property Rights*, (Annex 1c of the Marrakesh Agreement Establishing the World Trade Organisation), available at www.wto.org .

World Trade Organization (2005), *International Trade Statistics 2005*, available at www.wto.org, accessed 13 September 2006.

Young, I.M. (2000), *Inclusion and Democracy*, Oxford: Oxford University Press.

Yúdice, G. (2003), *The Expediency of Culture: Uses of Culture in the Global Era*, Durham, NC and London: Duke University Press.

Index

Note: References to illustrations appear in *italics*